Aristophanes

Acharnians
Lysistrata
Clouds

Aristophanes

Acharnians
Lysistrata
Clouds

Translated with Introductions and Notes

Jeffrey Henderson

Focus Classical Library
Focus Publishing/R Pullins Company
Newburyport MA 01950

The Focus Classical Library
Series Editors • James Clauss and Michael Halleran

Hesiod's Theogony • Richard Caldwell • 1987
The Heracles of Euripides • Michael Halleran • 1988
Aristophanes' Lysistrata • Jeff Henderson • 1988
Sophocles' Oedipus at Colonus • Mary Whitlock Blundell • 1990
Euripides' Medea • Anthony Podlecki • 1991
Aristophanes' Acharnians • Jeff Henderson • 1992
Aristophanes' The Clouds • Jeff Henderson • 1992
The Homeric Hymns • Susan Shelmerdine • 1995
Euripides' Bacchae • Steve Esposito • 1997
Aristophanes: Acharnians, Lysistrata, Clouds • Jeff Henderson • 1997

The Focus Philosophical Library
Series Editor • Albert Keith Whitaker

Plato's Sophist • E. Brann, P. Kalkavage, E. Salem • 1996
Plato's Parmenides • Albert Keith Whitaker • 1996
Plato's Symposium • Avi Sharon • 1997

ISBN 0-941051-58-7

10 9 8 7 6 5 4 3 2

Contents

General Introduction

Aristophanes and Old Comedy

Aristophanes of Athens, the earliest comic playwright from whom whole works survive, was judged in antiquity to be the foremost poet of Old Attic Comedy, a theatrical genre of which he was one of the last practitioners and of which his eleven surviving plays are our only complete examples. His plays are valued principally for the exuberance of their wit and fantasy, for the purity and elegance of their language, and for the light they throw on the domestic and political life of Athens in an important era of its history. Legend has it that when the Syracusan tyrant Dionysius wanted to inform himself about 'the republic of the Athenians,' Plato sent him the plays of Aristophanes.

Little is known about Aristophanes' life apart from his theatrical career. He was born *ca.* 447/6, the son of one Philippus of the urban deme Cydathenaeum and the tribe Pandionis, and he died probably between 386 and 380. By his twenties his hair had thinned or receded enough that his rivals could call him bald. He seems to have had land-holdings on, or some other connection with, the island of Aegina, a connection that detractors and enemies exploited early in his career in an attempt to call his Athenian citizenship into question. He was twice prosecuted by a fellow demesman, the popular politician Cleon, for the political impropriety of two of his plays (*Babylonians* and *Knights*), but he was not convicted. Early in the fourth century he represented his tribe in the prestigious government position of Councillor. Four comic poets of the fourth century, Araros, Philetaerus, Philippus and Nicostratus, are reputed in ancient sources to be his sons.

In the dialogue *Symposium* Plato portrays Aristophanes as being at home among the social and intellectual elite of Athens. Although the historical truth of Plato's portrayal is uncertain, Aristophanes' plays do generally espouse the social, moral and political sentiments of contemporary upper-class conservatives: nostalgia for the good old days of the early democracy, which defeated the Persians and built the empire; dismay at the decadence, corruption and political divisiveness of his own day; hostility toward the new breed of popular leaders who emerged after the death of the aristocratic Perikles in 429; impatience with the leadership and slow progress of the Peloponnesian War (431-404); unhappiness about current artistic and intellectual trends. There is no question that Aristophanes' comic expression of such views reflected, and to a degree shaped, community opinion, and that comedy could occasionally have a distinct political impact. But the fact that Aristophanes emerged politically and artistically unscathed from the war, from two oligarchic revolutions (411 and 404), and from two democratic restorations (411 and 403) suggests that on the whole his role in Athenian politics was more satirical, moral(istic) and poetical than practical; and the perennial popularity of his plays would seem to indicate that the sentiments they express were broadly shared among the theatrical public.

The period of Old Comedy at Athens began in 486 BC, when comedy first became part of the festival of the Greater Dionysia; by convention it ended in 388 BC, when Aristophanes produced his last play. During this period some 600 comedies were produced. We know the titles of some fifty comic poets and the titles of some 300 plays. We have eleven complete plays by Aristophanes, the first one dating from 425, and several thousand fragments of other plays by Aristophanes and other poets, most of them only a line or so long and very few deriving from plays written before 440.

The principal occasions for the production of comedies were the Greater Dionysia, held in late March or early April, and (from 440) the Lenaea, held in late January or early February. These were national festivals honoring the wine-god Dionysus, whose cult from very early times had included mimetic features. The theatrical productions that were the highlight of the festivals were competitions in which poets, dancers, actors, producers and musicians competed for prizes that were awarded by judges at the close of the festival. The Greater Dionysia was held in the Theater of Dionysus on the south slope of the Acropolis, which accommodated some 17,000 spectators, including both Athenian and foreign visitors. The Lenaea, which only Athenians attended, was held elsewhere in the city (we do not know where). By the fourth century the Lenaea was held in the Theater of Dionysus also, but it is unclear when the relocation occurred.

At these festivals comedy shared the theater with tragedy and satyr-drama, genres that had been produced at the Greater Dionysia since the sixth century. The first "city" contest in tragedy is dated to 534, when the victorious actor-poet was Thespis, from whose name actors are still called thespians. But it is not certain that Thespis' contest was held at the Greater Dionysia, and in any case this festival seems to have experienced major changes after the overthrow of the tyranny and the establishment of democracy, that is, after the reforms of Cleisthenes in 508. Tragedy dramatized stories from heroic myth, emphasizing dire personal and social events that had befallen hero(in)es and their families in the distant past, and mostly in places other than Athens. By convention, the poetry and music of tragedy were highly stylized and archaic. Satyr-drama, which was composed by the same poets who wrote tragedy, had similar conventions, except that the heroic stories were treated in a humorous fashion and the chorus was composed of satyrs: mischievous followers of Dionysus who were part human and part animal.

Comedy, by contrast, had different conventions of performance (see III, below) and was less restricted by conventions of language, music and subject. That is probably why the composers and performers of tragedy and satyr-drama were never the same ones who composed and performed comedy. The language of comedy was basically colloquial, though it often parodies the conventions of other (particularly tragic) poetry, and was free to include indecent, even obscene material. The music and dancing, too, tended to reflect popular styles. The favorite subjects of comedy were free-form mythological burlesque; domestic situations featuring everyday character types; and political satire portraying people and events of current interest in the public life of the Athenians. Our eleven surviving comedies all fall into this last category. Mythological and domestic comedy continued to flourish after the Old Comic period, but political comedy seems to have died out: a casualty not merely of changing theatrical tastes but also of the social and political changes that followed the Athenians' loss of the Peloponnesian War, and with it their empire, in 404. To understand the significance of political comedy, we must look first at the political system of which it was an organic feature: the phase of radical democracy inaugurated by the reforms of Ephialtes in 462/1 and lasting until the end of the century.

Democracy means 'rule of the demos' (sovereign people). In fifth-century Athens democracy was radical in that the sovereignty of the demos was more absolute than in any other society before or since. The demos consisted of all citizen males at least eighteen years of age. All decisions affecting the governance and welfare of the state were made by the direct and unappealable vote of the demos. The state was managed by members of the demos at least thirty years of age, who were chosen by lot from a list of eligible citizens and who held office in periods ranging from one day to one year. The only exceptions were military commanders, who were elected to one-year terms, and holders of certain ancient priesthoods, who inherited their positions. The demos determined by vote whether or not anyone holding any public position was qualified to do his job, and after completion of his term, whether he had done it satisfactorily. All military commanders, and most holders of powerful allotted offices, came from the wealthy classes, but their success depended on the good will of the demos as a whole.

One of the most important allotted offices in the democracy was that of choregus, sponsor of a chorus. Choregi were allotted from a list of men wealthy enough to hold this office, for they had to recruit and pay for the training, costuming and room and board of the chorus that would perform at one of the festivals. In the case of a comic chorus this involved 24 dancers and the musicians who would accompany them. Being choregus gave a man an opportunity to display his wealth and refinement for the benefit of the demos as a whole and to win a prize that would confer prestige on himself and his dancers. Some wealthy men therefore volunteered to be a choregus instead of waiting for their names to be drawn. On the other hand, a man who put on a cheap or otherwise unsatisfactory chorus could expect to suffer a significant loss of public prestige.

All other festival expenses, including stipends for the poet and his actors and for prizes, were undertaken by vote of the demos and paid for from public funds. A poet got a place in the festival by submitting a draft some six months in advance to the office-holder in charge of the festival. Ancient sources say that at least the choral parts of the proposed play had to be submitted. How much more was submitted we do not know. But revision up to the day of the performance was certainly possible, since many allusions in comedy refer to events occurring very shortly before the festival: most notably the death of Sophocles shortly before the performance of *Frogs* in 405.

If he got on the program, the poet would be given his stipend and assigned his actors. He and the choregus would then set about getting the performance ready for the big day, the poet acting as music master, choreographer and director, the choregus rounding up, and paying the expenses of, the best dancers he could find. While tragic poets produced three tragedies and a satyr-drama, comic poets produced only one comedy.

Thus comedy, as a theatrical spectacle, was an organic feature of Athenian democracy. But its poetic, musical and mimetic traditions were much older, deriving from forms of entertainment developed by cultivated members of the aristocratic families that had governed Attica before the democracy. One such traditional form was the komos (band of revellers), which gave comedy (komoidia: 'song of the komos') its name. A komos was made up of some solidary group (a military, religious or family group, for example), often in masks or costumes, which entertained onlookers on many kinds of festive and religious occasions.

Part of the entertainment was abuse and criticism of individuals or groups standing outside the solidarity of the komos. The victims might be among the onlookers or they might be members of a rival komos. The komos sang and danced as a group, and its leader (who was no doubt also the poet) could speak by himself to his komos, to the onlookers or to a rival komos-leader. No doubt at a very early stage the komos was a competitive entertainment by which a given group could, in artistic ways, make those claims and criticisms against rival groups which at other times they might make in more overtly political ways. The targets of komastic abuse were often the village's most powerful men and groups. Thus the tradition of the komos was useful in allowing the expression of personal and political hostilities which would otherwise have been difficult to express safely: the misbehavior of powerful individuals, disruptive but unactionable gossip, the shortcomings of citizens in groups or as a whole. Here komos served a cathartic function, as a kind of social safety valve, allowing a relatively harmless airing of tensions before they could become dangerous, and also as a means of social communication and social control, upholding generally held norms and calling attention to derelictions.

But in addition to its critical and satiric aspects, komos (like all festive activities) had an idealistic side, helping people to envision the community as it would be if everyone agreed on norms and lived up to them, and a utopian side as well, allowing people to imagine how wonderful life would be if reality were as human beings, especially ordinary human beings, would like it to be. In this function komos provided a time-out from the cares and burdens of everyday life.

Old Comedies were theatrical versions of komos: the band of dancers with their leader was now a comic chorus involved in a story enacted by actors on a stage. The chorus still resembled a komos in two ways: (1) as performers, it competed against rival choruses, and (2) in its dramatic identity it represented, at least initially, a distinct group or groups: in *Clouds*, for example, it initially represents the guiding spirits of Socrates' Thinkery. The comic chorus differs from a komos in that at a certain point in the play it drops its dramatic identity and thereafter represents the festival's traditional comic chorus, which reflects the celebrating community as a whole. At this point, its leader steps forward, on behalf of the poet, to advise and admonish the spectators, and his chorus might sing abusive songs about particular individuals in the audience.

The actors in the stage-area had been amalgamated with the chorus during the sixth century. Their characteristic costumes (III, below) and antics were depicted in vase-paintings of that period in many parts of Greece, suggesting a much older tradition of comic mimesis. As early as the Homeric period (8th and 7th centuries) we find mythological burlesque and such proto-comedy as the Thersites-episode in the second book of the *Iliad*. In this period, too, the iambic poets flourished. Named for the characteristic rhythm of their verses, which also became the characteristic rhythm of actors in Athenian drama, the iambic poets specialized in self-revelation, popular story-telling, earthy gossip, and personal enmities, often creating fictitious first-person identities and perhaps also using masks and disguise. They were credited with pioneering poetic styles invective, obscenity and colloquialism.

The characters on the Old Comic stage preserved many of these traditions, but like the chorus they were an adaptation to the democratic festivals, most notably in political comedy. In Aristophanes' plays, the world depicted by the plot and the characters on stage was the world of the spectators in their civic roles: as heads of families and participants in governing the democratic state. We see the demos in its various capacities; the competitors for public influence; the men who hold or seek offices; the social, intellectual and artistic celebrities. We hear formal debate on current issues, including its characteristic invective. We get a decision, complete with winners and losers, and we see the outcome. This depiction of public life was designed both to arouse laughter and to encourage reflection about people and events in ways not possible in other public contexts. Thus it was at once a distorted and an accurate depiction of public life, somewhat like a modern political cartoon.

Aristophanic comedies typically depict Athens in the grip of a terrible and intractable problem (e.g. the war, bad political leaders, an unjust jury-system, dangerous artistic or intellectual trends), which is solved in a fantastic but essentially plausible way, often by a comic hero. The characters of these heroic plays fall into two main categories, sympathetic and unsympathetic. The sympathetic ones (the hero and his/her supporters), are fictitious creations embodying ideal civic types or representing ordinary Athenians. The unsympathetic ones embody disapproved civic behavior and usually represent specific leaders or categories of leaders. The sympathetic characters advocate positions held by political or social minorities and are therefore 'outsiders.' But they are shown winning out against the unsympathetic ones, who represent the current status quo. Characters or chorus-members representing the demos as a whole are portrayed as initially sceptical or hostile to the sympathetic character(s), but in the end they are persuaded; those responsible for the problem are disgraced or expelled; and Athens is recalled to a sense of her true (traditional) ideals and is thus renewed. In the (thoroughly democratic) comic view, the people are never at fault for their problems, but are merely good people who have been deceived by bad leaders. Thus the comic poets tried to persuade the actual demos (the spectators) to change its mind about issues that had been decided but might be changed (the war, as in *Acharnians* and *Lysistrata*), or to discard dangerous novelties as in *Clouds*). Aristophanes at least once succeeded: after the performance of *Frogs* he was awarded a crown by the city for the advice that was given by the chorus-leader in that play and that was subsequently adopted by the demos.

In this way, the institution of Old Comedy performed functions essential to any democracy: public airing of minority views and criticism of those holding power. In this function, the Old Comic festivals were organized protest by ordinary people against its advisers and leaders. But they were also an opportunity to articulate civic ideals: one identified the shortcomings of the status quo by holding it up against a vision of things as they ought to (or used to) be. The use of satire and criticism within a plot addressing itself to important issues of national scope was thus a democratic adaptation of such pre-democratic traditions as komos and iambic poetry. That the comic festivals were state-run and not privately organized, a partnership between the elite and the masses, is striking evidence of the openness and self-confidence of a full democracy: the demos was completely in charge, so it did not fear attacks on its celebrities or resent admonition by the poets. In particular, the Athenians were much less inclined than we are to treat their political leaders with fear and reverence: since the Athenian people were themselves the government, they tended to see their leaders more as advisors and competitors for public stature that august representatives of the state. And even comic poets enjoyed the traditional role of Greek poets and orators generally: to admonish, criticise and advise on behalf of the people. In Socrates' case, the demos seems to have taken Aristophanes' criticisms to heart, however exaggerated they may have been: as Plato reported in his *Apology*, the *Clouds*' 'nonsensical' portrait of Socrates was a factor in the people's decision, 24 years later, to condemn him to death.

The comic poets did not, however, enjoy a complete license to say anything they pleased: were that the case they could not have expected anyone to take what they had to say seriously. Following each festival there was an assembly in which anyone who had a legal complaint could come forward. Although the Athenians recognized freedom of speech, they did not tolerate any speech whatever. No one who spoke in public, comic poets included, could criticize the democratic constitution and the inherent rightness of the demos' rule, or say anything else that might in some way harm the democracy or compromise the integrity of the state religion. And abuse of individuals could not be slanderous. But the Athenian definition of slander differed from ours. Our slander laws are designed to protect individuals, whereas the Athenian slander laws were designed to protect the institutions of the democracy: they forbade malicious and unfounded abuse of individuals if and only if the abuse might compromise a man's civic standing or eligibility to participate in the democracy, for example, accusations that would, if taken seriously, make a man ineligible to participate in public life. And so, if the criticism and abuse we find in Old Comedy often seems outrageous by our standards, it is because we differ from the fifth-century Athenians in our definition of outrageous, not because comic poets were held to no standards.

Aristophanes, for example, was twice sued by the politician Cleon, once for slandering the demos and its officers in front of visiting foreigners (in *Babylonians* of 426) and once for slandering him (in *Knights* of 424). In the first instance the demos decided not to hear the case. In the second the poet and the politician settled out of court (in his play *Wasps* Aristophanes subsequently boasted that he had not abided by the agreement). The demos could also enact new laws restricting comic freedoms, to protect the integrity of the military or legal systems. One of these laws was enacted in 440, when Athens went to war against her own ally Samos; another, enacted in 415, forbade mention by name in comedy of any of the men who had recently been implicated in the parody of the Eleusinian Mysteries of Demeter. Possibly the demos wanted to protect from public innuendo those who might be suspected, but might not ultimately be convicted, of this crime: as we have seen, such innuendo would fall within the legal definition of slander. And possibly the demos did not want to take the chance that a comic poet might speak sympathetically of the profaners, as they often spoke for other underdogs; it is perhaps relevant that three of the men condemned seem to have been comic poets.

Production

Since fifth-century comic poets put on a play for a particular competition and did not envisage future productions, an original script that later circulated as a text for readers contained only the words, with few if any attributions of lines to speakers and no stage directions. These had to be inferred from the words of the text itself, so that all editions and translations, ancient and modern, differ to some extent in reconstructing the theatricality of the text. This means that anyone reading or performing an ancient comedy has a perfect right to bring the text to life in any way that seems appropriate: we have no information external to the text itself about how lines were originally distributed or performed, or about the original action on-stage and in the orchestra. Thus there can be no 'authentic' productions of ancient comedies, only productions that strive, to a greater or lesser degree, to approximate what little we know of performance conditions at the time of their original production. In any case it is pointless to argue about 'authenticity': in the end only satisfied spectators really count.

In this translation I assign speakers who seem to be the likeliest candidates for given lines; the reader is free to differ. I do not, however, supply stage-directions in the text itself: one of the pleasures of reading or performing an ancient comedy is imagining how it might be realized in action. I hesitate to put my own imagination in the way of a reader's, an actor's or a director's. But I do occasionally draw attention, in the notes, to likely action that is not quite obvious from the words of the text.

We do know some facts about fifth-century comic theater, however, and there is no harm in reviewing them for their historical interest.

Although Aristophanes' comedies are highly sophisticated as poetry and as drama, they nevertheless respected some ancient Dionysiac traditions that we should bear in mind if we want to respond to the characters in historical perspective. The actors wore masks, made of cork or papier-mâche, that covered the entire head. These were generic (young man, old woman, etc.) but might occasionally be special, like a portrait-mask of a prominent citizen (as in the case of Socrates in *Clouds*) or an animal or god. Although the characters' clothing was generically suited to their dramatic identities, mostly contemporary Greeks, there were several features that made them unmistakably comic:

wherever possible, the costumes accommodated the traditional comic features of big stomach and rump and (for male characters) the grotesque costume penis called the phallos, made of leather, either dangling or erect as appropriate, and circumcised in the case of outlandish barbarians. Apparently by comic convention, male characters appearing without a phallos were marked as being in some way unmanly. And, as in every other dramatic genre, all roles were played by men. Even the naked females who often appear on stage, typically in the traditionally festive ending, were men wearing body-stockings to which false breasts and genitalia were attached. But the convention of all-male actors does not mean that Old Comedy was a kind of drag show: the same convention applied to all other kinds of drama as well (as it still did in Shakespeare's time), and nowhere in our comic texts is any female character ever understood to be anything but the character she is supposed to be, never a male playing a female.

The city supplied an equal number of actors to each competing poet, probably three, and these actors played all the speaking roles. In *Birds*, for example, there are 22 speaking roles, but the text's entrances and exits are so arranged that three actors can play them all. Some plays do, however, require a fourth (or even a fifth) actor in small roles. Perhaps in given years the allotment changed, or novices were periodically allowed to take small parts, or the poet or producer could add extra actors at his own expense.

In the orchestra ('dancing space') was a chorus of 24 men who sang and danced to the accompaniment of an aulos, a wind instrument that had two recorder-like pipes played simultaneously by a specially costumed player; and there could be other instruments as well. Like actors, members of the chorus wore masks and costumes appropriate to their dramatic identity. There could be dialogue between the chorus-leader and the actors on-stage, but the chorus as a whole only sings and dances. There was no ancient counterpart to the 'choral speaking' often heard in modern performances of Greek drama. The choral songs of comedy were in music and language usually in a popular style, though serious styles were often parodied, and the dancing was expressive, adding a visual dimension to the words and music.

The stage-area was a slightly raised platform behind the large orchestra. Behind it was a wooden two-story building called the *skene* ('tent', from which our word 'scene'). It had two or three doors at stage-level, windows at the second story, and a roof on which actors could appear. On the roof was a crane called the *mechane* ('machine'), on which actors could fly above the stage (as gods, for example, whence the Latin expression *deus ex machina*, 'god from the machine'). Another piece of permanent equipment was a wheeled platform called the *ekkyklema* ('device for rolling out'), on which actors and scenery could be wheeled on-stage from the skene to reveal 'interior' action. A painted or otherwise decorated plywood facade could be attached to the skene if a play (or scene) required it, and movable props and other scenery were used as needed. Since plays were performed in daylight in a large outdoor amphitheater, all entrances and exits of performers and objects took place in full view of the spectators. All in all, more demand was made on the spectators' imagination than in modern illusionistic theater, so that performers must often tell the spectators what they are supposed to see.

A fifth-century comedy was played through without intermission, the performance probably lasting about two hours. The usual structure of a comedy was a Prologue (actors); the Parodos, or entry, of the chorus into the orchestra (chorus); an Agon, or contest (actors and chorus); the Parabasis, or self-revelation, of the chorus (chorus-leader and chorus); and a series of episodes (actors) articulated by choral songs (chorus). In some plays, like *Clouds*, there can be a second parabasis and/or a second agon. In this translation I have supplied appropriate divisions of the action, but performers should, as always, feel free to arrange their own performance as they see fit.

The Translations

I have translated the plays into contemporary American verse, designed for both readers and performers, and presupposing no knowledge of classical Greece or classical Greek theater. I render the Greek text line by line so as to give a sense of its original scope and pace, using for the dialogue and songs verse-forms that are familiar to modern audiences. Where the original text refers to people, places, things and events whose significance modern audiences cannot reasonably be expected to know or to infer from the text, and which are inessential to its main themes, I have tried to find easily comprehensible alternatives that preserve the import of the original. What may be unfamiliar in the text is discussed in footnotes.

The conventions of Aristophanic comedy included the frank portrayal and discussion of religion, politics and sex (including nudity and obscenity). I have reproduced this feature as accurately as possible within my general guideline of easy intelligibility. To do otherwise would be to falsify the plays. These three areas are of fundamental importance to any society; one of Aristophanes' chief aims was to make humor of them while at the same time encouraging his audience to think about them in ways discouraged, or even forbidden, outside the comic theater. The issue of freedom of speech and thought (especially religious and moral thought) is especially relevant to Aristophanes' plays. For those made uncomfortable by such provocative theater, these plays provide an opportunity to ask themselves why.

Since these translations are designed to be perfectly comprehensible to contemporary readers, the best way to stage them is to make them just as comprehensible to the audience for whom they are to be performed, using whatever human and other resources are available. Balloons, for example, make perfectly good comic phalloi, and music for the songs and moves for the dancers can be as simple or elaborate as one cares to make them. I have translated the songs into standard poetic forms, so that they might be sung to any number of appropriate modern tunes. Adaptations of characters, and insertion of allusions to current events make for liveliness (Aristophanes himself did this), and if the intended audience knows little about classical Athens, a modern producer may insert explanatory material or devise some other topical adaptation without violating any sort of standard of authenticity. The best guide for performance are the texts themselves.

The translations are based on the Greek texts by Alan H. Sommerstein (*Acharnians*, Warminster 1980), Jeffrey Henderson (*Lysistrata*, Oxford 1987), and Sir Kenneth Dover (*Clouds*, Oxford 1968), except where I adopt different readings or line assignments.

General Bibliography

Ancient sources for the production of classical drama are collected and discussed in:

Csapo, E. and Slater, W.J. *The Context of Ancient Drama* (Ann Arbor 1995)

Green, J.R. *Theatre in Ancient Greek Society* (London and New York 1994)

Pickard-Cambridge, A.W. *Dithyramb, Tragedy and Comedy*, rev. by T.B.L. Webster (Oxford 1962)

_______ *The Dramatic Festivals of Athens*, rev. by J. Gould and D.M. Lewis (Oxford 1968, rev. 1988)

Taplin, O. *Comic Angels and Other Approaches to Greek Drama through Vase-Paintings* (Oxford 1993)

Walcot, P. *Greek Drama in its Theatrical and Social Context* (Cardiff 1976)

Webster, T.B.L. *Greek Theatre Production* (London 1970)

Good general treatments of Aristophanic comedy are:

Arnott, P. *Greek Scenic Conventions in the Fifth Century B.C.* (Oxford 1962)

Bowie, A.M. *Aristophanes. Myth, Ritual and Comedy* (Cambridge 1993)

Cartledge, P. *Aristophanes and his Theatre of the Absurd* (London 1990)

Dover, K.J. *Aristophanic Comedy* (California 1972)

Harriott, R.M. *Aristophanes, Poet and Dramatist* (Baltimore 1986)

Hubbard, T.K. *The Mask of Comedy. Aristophanes and the Intertextual Parabasis* (Ithaca 1991)

MacDowell, D.M. *Aristophanes and Athens* (Oxford 1995)

McLeish, K. *The Theatre of Aristophanes* (New York 1980)

Moulton, C. *Aristophanic Poetry* (Hypomnemata 68: Göttingen 1981)

Reckford, K.J. *Aristophanes' Old-and-New Poetry* (Chapel Hill 1987)

Russo, C.F. *Aristophanes, an Author for the Stage* (London 1994)

Sifakis, G. *Parabasis and Animal Choruses* (London 1971)
Sommerstein, A.H. et al., eds. *Tragedy, Comedy and the Polis* (Bari 1993)
Stone, L.M. *Costume in Aristophanic Comedy* (New York 1981)
Whitman, C.H. *Aristophanes and the Comic Hero* (Cambridge MA 1964)
Winkler, J.J. and Zeitlin, F.I., eds. *Nothing to Do With Dionysos? Athenian Drama in its Social Context* (Princeton 1990)

Aristophanes' Acharnians

Acharnians: Comic Hero, Comic Poet and Society

Acharnians is a comedy about the ordinary farmer Dicaeopolis, evacuated from his land and pressed into service in the Peloponnesian War. Failing to interest his fellow Athenians in seeking peace, he arranges a magical private peace for himself. On the way back to the good life in the countryside, he is confronted by a crowd of patriotic charcoal-burners from Acharnae who want to stone him as a traitor. But by restaging himself as a tragic hero, Dicaeopolis convinces the Acharnians of the justice of his actions and proceeds to expose the corruption of the politicians and generals, especially General Lamachus. After establishing his own free-trade zone and collecting food for a sumptuous banquet, Dicaeopolis wins the national drinking contest, while General Lamachus suffers from ignominious wounds.

Acharnians was Aristophanes' third (and first extant) play, produced at the Lenaea festival in 425, and it won the first prize for comedy. Its plot is characteristic of Aristophanes' heroic plays (the others are *Peace*, *Birds*, *Lysistrata*, and *Assemblywomen*). By means of a fantastic scheme a hero(ine), who represents a class of citizens who feel frustrated or victimized by the operations of contemporary society, manages to evade or alter the situation of which (s)he initially complains and proceeds to effect a triumph of wish-fulfillment over reality. Those powers human, natural or divine which would obstruct the scheme are either converted by argument or overcome by guile, magic or force. At the end there is a restoration of normality (typically portrayed in terms of an idealized civic past) and a celebration (typically portrayed in terms of food, wine and sex). The celebration is reserved for the hero(ine) and the hero(ine)'s supporters, for the initial obstructors and those who would undeservedly benefit by the hero(ine)'s success have been expelled or disgraced.

Although the hero(ine) typically represents the views of a social or political minority, and the scheme bypasses or undermines the powers currently enforcing the status quo, the hero(ine)'s goal is one likely to be shared by most spectators when in an idealistic mood, and the arguments (s)he uses to defend it are designed to appeal to their interests and sense of justice. The powers are portrayed entirely without sympathy as self-interested, corrupt and misguided, and the status quo as unnecessarily burdensome for ordinary, decent people. The status quo is shown to be as it is because ordinary people have been deceived by their leaders. Once the leaders are exposed, the hero(ine) can resume the comfortable and just life that (in comic myth) had existed before troublemakers disrupted it.

In this utopian scenario, the harsh and intractable realities of life, politics and international aggression are comically transformed so that an ordinary farmer can arrange a separate peace, discredit powerful politicians and generals, and alone enjoy the blessings of peace. The transformation seems quite plausible because Aristophanes appeals to the wishes of the spectators for a better world, the world as it presumably was before the war, where all would be happy and prosperous and where there would be no more violence. He also appeals to the feeling of the average citizens that their wishes would be more likely to come true were there no authorities in the way, constantly reminding them of unpleasant duties. After all, the god Dionysos, patron of the theatrical festivals, was emblematic of peace and freedom. This combination of regressive wish-fulfillment and oedipal rebellion allowed a communal release of tensions. Insofar as their release was motivated by acceptable civic ideals (peace and fairness) and achieved in humorous fantasy, it was safe: cohesive not disruptive. But insofar as it was a valid expression of people's real war-weariness, an expression of social discontent running beneath the surface of official public discourse, it was also fair warning to the people's leaders that public patience might not last indefinitely.

Like Aristophanes' preceding two plays, *Acharnians* was produced not by the poet himself, but by his friend Callistratus; not until the following year was the young poet (then in his early 20's) confident enough to produce plays on his own. But that does not mean that Callistratus was thought to be the author: entrusting production to others, as is the rule today, was not unusual in Aristophanes' day either, and Aristophanes would for various reasons occasionally do so throughout his career; moreover, in *Knights* 512-13 Aristophanes says that many people had for a long time been asking him why he had not yet produced one of his own plays. The issue of authorship is important in the case of *Acharnians* because of the play's unusual identification of its hero with the poet himself. In order to understand this identification, we must review the contemporary Athenian situation and Aristophanes' stance toward it, which had become a public issue.

Since 431 Athens and Sparta had been fighting what is now called the Peloponnesian War, a war that involved nearly all Greeks and even the Persian

Empire. The principal issue was the Athenians' growing imperial power. The alliance of Aegean states that had begun fifty years earlier as the Delian League, a panhellenic defensive alliance against future Persian invasions, had gradually been changed into a collection of tribute-paying allies subject to Athens. As a result Athens had become dominant at sea, very wealthy and aggressively expansionist. In addition, Athens used her empire to spread democracy at the expense of traditional ruling elites, sometimes by force. Sparta and her allies (the "Peloponnesians") considered democracy to be a dangerous idea and the Athenians to be imperial tyrants (a label that the Athenians did not wholly reject); Athenian strength, if unchecked, dangerously threatened the balance of power in the Greek world.

In 431 Pericles, Athens' leading general and statesman, convinced his countrymen to resist Peloponnesian demands that Athens abandon such aggressive policies as the economic blockade of Megara. He predicted that, if war was the result, Athenian wealth and naval power would quickly force the Peloponnesians to abandon their resistance and acquiesce to Athenian dominance. But his plan required that the Athenians not oppose the Spartans on land, where they were superior, so that the Attic countryside would have to be evacuated and its residents moved into fortified Athens for the duration. That meant extremely uncomfortable quarters for those without relatives or friends in the city. Thucydides (2.16) describes the reaction of the rural population of whom this sacrifice was asked:

> For the better part of their history the Athenians had lived in independent country settlements. Even after the political unification of Attica, most Athenians, both in earlier generations and down to the time of this present war being born and raised in the country, retained their traditional rural character. So it was not easy for them to have to move with their entire households, especially since they had only recently re-established themselves after the Persian invasions. They felt oppressed and resentful at having to abandon their homes and their temples, venerable symbols of a patriotic past, and at having to change their whole way of life, each leaving behind what he regarded as his own polis.

In spite of these hardships, however, the rural Athenians supported the war: like all Athenians, they benefitted from the empire and would do their part to resist Spartan interference.

But by 425 it was clear that Pericles had overestimated Athenian superiority and underestimated the determination of the Peloponnesians; and there had been additional unforeseen difficulties. Most serious was the terrible plague that decimated the Athenians in 429 and would continue to break out, on and off, for the next five years; Pericles was one of its victims. By 428 the war-fund had run out, requiring the Athenians to levy emergency taxes and to raise the tribute quotas. Some members of the empire had begun to revolt or to contemplate revolt, thus requiring the Athenians to divert valuable energy policing their own allies. After six years of fighting, the Athenians had won important victories, but so had the enemy. No one could say when victory could be expected, or even how it was to be defined. These conditions produced political unrest. In particular, the devastation of the Attic countryside and the suffering of the evacuees was very demoralizing. Many had begun to question the rationale for continued fighting and to consider whether a negotiated settlement might not be preferable.

But such views were still opposed by the majority, including the majority of evacuees, whose initial support of the war had indeed been fortified by a determination to get revenge on the Peloponnesians whatever the cost. The policy of continued war was championed and guided by Cleon, who had replaced Pericles as the leading politician of Athens. Cleon, a forceful orator and the first great populist (enemies said "demagogue"), strove to maintain unity and morale behind the war effort, to assure adequate finances and to enforce efficient civic, imperial and military administration. He ruthlessly attacked as unpatriotic, even treasonous, anyone he thought was undermining these goals: Athenian or allied rebels, dissidents, malingerers, hoarders, black-marketeers, Spartan sympathizers, advocates of negotiated peace.

Aristophanes himself was one of those attacked. After *Babylonians* (produced in 426), in which Aristophanes had criticized Athenian imperial rule and perhaps also the war, Cleon denounced him before the Council for having slandered the magistrates, Councillors and Athenian people before an audience that included foreign allies. He also seems to have called Aristophanes's Athenian birth (and therefore his citizenship) into question by citing the poet's ties to Aegina. Evidently the Council did not refer the charges to the Assembly or to a court for trial, but dismissed them. Nevertheless, Aristophanes thought that Cleon's attack had to be answered. In *Acharnians*, Aristophanes frontally challenges the rationale for the war and the motives of its political and military advocates, and defends both his own patriotism and the value to democracy of free comic expression.

The hero, Dicaeopolis ("Just City"), represents the displaced countrymen, who have sacrificed most for the war, and the common soldiers, who do the actual fighting. Tired of combat and the discomforts of urban life, he longs to return to his rural deme (local community) to resume the happy peacetime life that has been disrupted by the war. He has repeatedly gone to the Assembly to raise the issue of negotiations, but his effort is wasted. Dicaeopolis's fellow Athenians want only to gape at the politicians, ambassadors and their barbarian allies and mercenaries; no one has the least interest in talking about peace. Dicaeopolis himself is ruled out of order and roughed up by barbarians, while his fellow citizens turn a deaf ear to his cries.

At this point Dicaeopolis decides on a radical solution. With the help of a magical friend, he acquires a 30-year peace for himself and his family, which takes the form of bottle of 30-year-old wine. This peace enables Dicaeopolis to return to the country, where he will be able to live on his own produce, trade with whomever he likes (even enemy states), drink his own wine at the local festivals and resume a life of ease and sexual gratification. He and his family celebrate by holding the festival of the Rural Dionysia.

But Dicaeopolis is soon confronted by a Chorus of outraged old men: veterans of the glorious Athenian struggle against the Persians, builders of the empire and supporters of the war. They are charcoal-burners from the deme Acharnae, the largest rural deme and one that had from the beginning of the war been especially hard-hit by Spartan incursions. The Acharnians as a result were perhaps the most fiercely pro-war and anti-Spartan of all Athenians, and they intend to stone Dicaeopolis to death as a traitor even before they hear what he has to say in his own defense. But by taking a coal-scuttle hostage, Dicaeopolis secures a hearing and bets his life on his ability to convince the Acharnians (and beyond them, the spectators) of the justice of his separate peace.

At this critical juncture the forward motion of the plot suddenly stops and the action onstage becomes invisible to the chorus. Dicaeopolis announces that, before he makes his speech, he must first go to the house of the tragic poet, Euripides, to borrow pitiful garb and persuasive eloquence. The audience, he says, will know him for who he truly is, while the Acharnians will be deceived. The scene with Euripides, where Dicaeopolis rummages through the tragedian's stock of costumes and props and reconstitutes himself as the tragic hero, Telephus, is a splendid example of metatheater (dramatist and performers calling attention to their own theatrical artifices), by which Aristophanes locates his play within comedy's wider theatrical and political contexts.

The myth of Telephus had most recently been dramatized by Euripides in 438. Although only fragments of the play survive, its main outlines are clear. Although he was the son of the great Greek hero Heracles and Auge, daughter of King Aleus of Arcadia, Telephus had become king of barbarian Mysia, a kingdom south of Troy. When the Greek expedition against Troy mistakenly attacked Mysia, Telephus was wounded by Achilles. When an oracle told him that his wound could be healed only by its inflictor, Telephus went to Argos, disguised as a Mysian beggar, to look for Achilles. In a speech, he defended himself and the Mysians by arguing that the Greeks would have acted the same way if they had suffered an unprovoked attack. He probably also questioned the Greeks' motive for the Trojan War (the abduction of Helen) and urged the Greeks to look at matters from a Trojan perspective. When Telephus' disguise was exposed and he was threatened with death, he took refuge at an altar, with the baby Orestes as hostage, and convinced the Greeks that he, too, was in fact a Greek. Achilles then agreed to provide a cure for his wound, and as the result of another oracle Telephus agreed to guide the Greeks to Troy.

Dicaeopolis adopts Telephus' strategems of hostage-taking and disguise and adapts elements of Telephus' speech of self-defence to his own situation.

He tells the Acharnians that he has just as much reason to hate the Spartans as they do, but that they are wrong to blame everything on the Spartans, for it was certain Athenians who actually started the trouble. First, base-born informers profited by denouncing Megarian goods; then drunken young gamblers stole a Megarian whore. When the Megarians retaliated by stealing two whores from Pericles' mistress, Aspasia, Pericles turned all Greece upside-down in his wrath. Thus the Spartans had good reason to fight and the Athenians ought to re-examine their own reasons for continuing the war.

It is to be noted that, while Dicaeopolis offers reasons for his decision to make a separate peace, he does not defend the separate peace itself, nor does he ever suggest that anyone else follow his lead. Indeed, he refuses to share his peace with any of those who ask, with the sole exception of a bride (since women had no part in bringing on the war). Dicaeopolis's exposure of the war's inadequate motivation, its self-interested military and political leaders and its lack of rewards for everybody else—at best these arguments make his separate peace seem more understandable and more palatable; most people would agree that there was some truth to them. But however plausible Dicaeopolis's motivation may be, and however enviable his subsequent happiness, Aristophanes evidently had no wish directly to advocate desertion in time of war.

While the embattled Dicaeopolis impersonates Telephus in addressing the Chorus, he simultaneously represents the embattled Aristophanes in addressing the spectators: like Telephus, Aristophanes has been slandered and attacked because of a successful and justified previous attack on his countrymen (the criticisms he had made in Babylonians):

> Do not be angry, you men who watch the play,
> if, though a beggar, I speak before Athenians
> of state affairs while making comedy.
> For comedy too concerns itself with justice,
> and what I will say will shock you but be just.
> And this time Cleon won't make allegations
> that I slander the polis in front of foreigners;
> for we are alone, it's a Lenaean competition,
> the foreigners aren't yet here, nor tribute-money
> nor allied troops from the cities of our empire,
> but now we are by ourselves. (497-507)

Later, in the play's Parabasis (629 n.), Aristophanes further adapts the Telephean defense. He claims that he deserves no anger but praise from the Athenians for having opened their eyes to the flatteries, deceptions, self-interest and general mismanagement of the empire (and also the war?) by Cleon and the other leading politicians. Now the allies gladly come with their tribute, eager to see the poet who alone had the courage to tell the truth, and the King of Persia has told the Spartans that they cannot prevail over a city that has such a poet for its adviser. That is why the Spartans are eager for peace, and as for their demand for Aegina, they want it not for strategic reasons but to get this poet for themselves. For he alone talks justice and truth, and so selflessly and courageously champions the best interests of his people. Like Telephus, Aristophanes is discovered to be a true compatriot, his criticisms are justified, and he will lead his countrymen on to a just victory.

In so adapting Euripides' hero to his own purposes, Aristophanes used a technique, which he himself pioneered, called paratragedy: the usurpation of tragic style and elevation as vehicles to express comic ideas. (Paratragedy may thus be distinguished from parody of tragedy, which merely reproduces tragic style in order to deflate it.) By means of paratragedy Aristophanes could exploit the strengths of each genre. Tragedy could examine social and political problems with great pathos and intensity, but only through the veil of heroic myth, to whose distant world it restricted itself. Comedy was free to deal with such problems topically and directly, with unmediated reference to the spectators and their world, but only in a humorous fashion, since pathos and intensity were alien to the comic mode. As the Assembly scene that opens the play seems to suggest, comedy by itself, like Dicaeopolis by himself, was unable to muster the pathos and intensity needed to persuade the Athenians. Some way had to be found to intensify the comic appeal. Paratragedy was the answer: if the Athenians took Telephus so seriously, would they not listen more seriously to his paratragic counterpart?

Through the paratragic "borrowing" of Telephus from Euripides, Aristophanes creates a play within a play and a complex layering of dramatic disguises. He also, metatheatrically, calls attention to what he is doing as poet and playwright, thus educating the spectators about the role of theatrical illusion and persuasion. Dicaeopolis manages to deceive, and thus to persuade, the Chorus by means of his beggar's disguise, like Telephus before the Greeks. But the spectators have already been shown, in the dressing-scene with Euripides, what to expect and are thus taught to see through the disguise. Behind the beggar is the comic-as-tragic hero, just as behind him is the comic-as-tragic poet: as Dicaeopolis is comically threatened in the play for his courageous nonconformity, so is Aristophanes seriously threatened in the polis for his plays. Those who see through the disguise, who can understand the playful seriousness of comedy, are the clever ones; those who do not (the Chorus and the Cleons in the audience) are the fools.

In these ways Aristophanes, as dramatist and as citizen, challenges the audience to examine and engage with the theatrical event in which they are participants, so that by becoming more reflective and critical as a theatrical audience they might also become more reflective and critical about their role in assemblies, where they must judge the arguments of a Cleon.

Dicaeopolis's defense-speech convinces half of the Chorus but not the other half, who are worsted in a scuffle and invoke the aid of the military commander, Lamachus. In real life a competent soldier (after his death Aristophanes would praise him without irony as a hero), Lamachus represents the high command generally and is caricatured as the Braggart Soldier. From the safety of his separate peace, Dicaeopolis voices the contempt and the complaints dear to the hearts of common soldiers in any era: we do all the fighting for meager pay and bad rations, while the officers live it up on embassies and high pay. More seriously, Dicaeopolis suggests that such profits, not a just cause, are the real reason for Lamachus' support of the war. In this regard, Lamachus was a good choice for Aristophanes' Braggart Soldier: his name aside (it means "Very Warlike"), Lamachus was the poorest of contemporary commanders and so most vulnerable to Dicaeopolis's accusations of featherbedding.

Dicaeopolis goes off to establish his market, where all traders are welcome—except Lamachus. The rest of the Chorus, now convinced that Dicaeopolis is no traitor, rejoin their fellow Choristers to perform the Parabasis. As is typical in Old Comedy, the episodes following the Parabasis illustrate the success of the hero's plan, leaving behind the conflicts and arguments by which it was achieved. Pointed debate gives way to slapstick. The Chorus henceforth plays the role of commentator, mediating between stage and audience and performing, between episodes, songs that mock individuals among the spectators and that are relatively detached from the plot.

Free to deal with Athens' enemies, Dicaeopolis demonstrates his shrewdness as a trader and his good fortune in being able freely to enjoy what was forbidden to other Athenians because of the war. A starving Megarian is willing to part with his two young daughters for a bunch of garlic and a quart of salt. From a Theban he gets a Copaic eel (a delicacy) in return for an informer, a type much feared by wartime Athenians but whom Dicaeopolis packs up like a piece of pottery. When the Pitcher Feast with its drinking-contest is announced, Dicaeopolis prepares a festive dinner that includes the sort of delicacies that would make most spectators' mouths water. To a farmer who has lost his oxen and a bridegroom who offers to trade a piece of meat Dicaeopolis refuses to share any of his peace, but he does send some to a bride, since women are not responsible for the war.

This exception helps us to understand and to sympathize with Dicaeopolis's refusal to share his peace, which some commentators regard as indefensible selfishness. As we saw in the prologue, Dicaeopolis decided to get his private treaty only after none of his fellow-citizens would heed his call for discussions about peace or come to his aid when he was roughed up by barbarians. They favored the war then; why should they now enjoy the hard-won blessings of Dicaeopolis's peace? Aristophanes seems to be saying to the spectators, "If you want to enjoy what Dicaeopolis has (and who would not?), then you had better stop ignoring or silencing people like him (and like me) and make peace for yourselves." As was argued above, Aristophanes does not want to hold Dicaeopolis's own method up as a model in real life.

The play ends with a memorable confrontation between Dicaeopolis, the man at peace, and Lamachus, the man at war. As Lamachus prepares arms and field-rations to defend the border passes from Boeotian bandits in the dead of winter, Dicaeopolis prepares a sumptuous banquet for the pitcher feast, to which he has been invited by the Priest of Dionysus. Lamachus subsequently returns on a stretcher, wounded by a vine-prop as he leapt over a ditch—a symbolically apt wound for one who opposes Dionysus by rejecting peace and bringing war to the countryside. Lamachus' cries of woe are counterpointed by Dicaeopolis's cries of joy: he enters drunk, supported by a pair of amorous girls, to celebrate his victory in the drinking-contest.

Aristophanes invites the spectators to identify in fantasy with Dicaeopolis and thus indulge in some vicarious wish-fulfillment. For a while an escapist vision lets them forget the hardships of the war. But Aristophanes surely hoped that the urgings of the first part of the play—that the spectators re-examine the rationale for continued war and be more critical of their leaders—would not be forgotten when the spectators left the theater.

Suggestions for Further Reading

Readers interested in the Greek text are referred to the editions with commentary by W.J.M. Starkie (London 1909, repr. Amsterdam 1968); W. Rennie (London 1909); R.T. Elliott (Oxford 1914); A.H. Sommerstein (Warminster 1980), which has an excellent literal translation.

Good treatments of *Acharnians* are:

De Ste. Croix, G.G.M. *The Origins of the Peloponnesian War* (London/Ithaca 1972), see index and Appendix XXIX.

Edmunds, L. "Aristophanes's Acharnians," in *Yale Classical Studies* 26 (1980)

Foley, H.P. "Tragedy and Politics in Aristophanes's Acharnians," in the *Journal of Hellenic Studies* 108 (1988)

Harriott, R.M. "Aristophanes and the Plays of Euripides," in the *Bulletin of the Institute for Classical Studies* 9 (1962)

————. "The Function of the Euripides-Scene in Aristophanes's *Acharnians*," in *Greece and Rome* 29 (1982)

MacDowell, D.M. "The Nature of Aristophanes's Acharnians," in *Greece and Rome* 30 (1983)

Newiger, H.-J. "War and Peace in the Comedy of Aristophanes," in *Yale Classical Studies* 26 (1980)

Taplin, O. "Tragedy and Trugedy," in the *Classical Quarterly* 33 (1983)

Aristophanes' Acharnians

CHARACTERS

SPEAKING CHARACTERS

Dicaeopolis of Cholleidae, a rustic
Herald
Godson, son of Lycinus, an immortal
Ambassador returned from the King of Persia
Pseudo-Artabas, the Persian King's "Eye"
Theorus, a politician
Daughter of Dicaeopolis
Slave of Euripides
Euripides, the tragic poet
Lamachus, a general
Megarian
Girls (two), daughters of the Megarian
Informer
Theban
Nicarchus, another informer
Slave of Lamachus
Dercetes of Phyle, a farmer
Best Man
Messenger I (from the generals)
Messenger II (from the priest of Dionysus)
Messenger III (from the battlefield)

MUTE CHARACTERS

Officers of the Athenian Assembly
Citizens attending the Assembly
Policemen policing the Assembly
Eunuchs, two
Thracian Mercenaries
Xanthias, slave of Dicaeopolis
Slaves of Dicaeopolis
Ambassadors returned from the King of Persia
Wife of Dicaeopolis
Children of Dicaeopolis
Soldiers under Lamachus
Ismenias, slave of the Theban
Pipers from Thebes
Maid of Honor
Dancing-Girls, two

CHORUS

Old Men of Acharnae, twenty-four

PROLOGUE

(Dicaeopolis, Herald, Godson, Ambassador, Pseudo-Artabas, Theorus; Officers, Citizens, Policemen, Ambassadors, Eunuchs, Thracian Mercenaries)

Dicaeopolis

How often have I chewed my heart with rage!
My pleasures? Very few; in fact just four.
My pains? The grains in a million heaps of sand.
Let's try to recall a case of real euphoria.
I know! It's something my heart rejoiced to see:
that million-dollar fine coughed up by Cleon°
That really gave me joy! I love the Knights
for that indictment: a banner day for Greece!
But then I had another pain, quite tragic:
I was waiting for a play by Aeschylus,°
then heard, "Theognis, bring your chorus on."°

---

6 What had pleased Aristophanes, a personal enemy of Cleon (see Introduction), also pleases his hero. But the precise nature of the incident referred to in these lines is obscure. Ancient commentaries explain that some island allies had bribed the demagogue Cleon to argue for a reduction of their property taxes or tribute and that the Knights, motivated by an old grudge, had made him "cough up" the money. If so, the case cannot have gone to trial: conviction for bribery would have resulted in a more severe penalty and at least some interruption of Cleon's political career. Cleon probably made restitution to avoid trial by the procedure known as *probole*. Some scholars think that the incident is not historical at all but took place in a comedy, perhaps Aristophanes's *Babylonians* (see lines 377 ff.), but that is very unlikely, since the Knights do not seem to have played a role in any comedy before *Knights*: see 299 ff., *Knights* 507 ff..

10 The great tragic poet, who had died thirty years before, was a favorite of older men like Dicaeopolis, nostalgic for the empire-building years after the Persian wars. The patriotic and inspirational qualities of Aeschylus' plays are dramatized in Aristophanes's *Frogs*.

11 The comic poets nicknamed this "frigid" tragic poet "Snow".

Imagine how that shook up my poor heart!
Another joy was after Moschus played:
Dexitheus did some Theban country-tunes.°
But recently I died and went to hell,
when Chaeris played the Anthem on his pipes.°
But never since I first began to wash
with soap have I cried such tears as I cry now,
whenever the Assembly holds a meeting
and all the seats are empty, just like now,
while everybody's gossiping in the market
and trying to avoid the summoner.
The Magistrates aren't even here; they're late,
and when they come you can't imagine how
they'll fight each other for the front-row seats,
like a river in spate. But as for talk of peace,
not a single moment's thought. My poor, poor Polis!
And I'm the one who always gets here first.
I come and sit, and in my solitude
I sigh, I yawn, I stretch myself, I fart,
I fiddle, draw, pick boogers, figure sums;
I watch the countryside and yearn for peace,
I hate the city and want to see my farm,
my village where you never hear "Buy coal,
buy vinegar, buy oil, buy this, buy that."
I grow my own and need no Mister Buy.
So now I'm here, all ready to make some noise,
to shout and interrupt and give 'em hell
if anyone speaks of anything but peace!
Hey look, the Magistrates! They're hours late.°
What did I tell you? And just as I predicted,
each one is pushing for a front-row seat.

Herald

Move on, move on!
Inside the sacred precinct, all of you!

---

14 Two noted *kithara* (lyre) players; Dicaeopolis's preference was determined by Dexitheus' choice of song.

16 The comic poets considered Chaeris a bad piper and lyre-player.

40 The Herald, Officers, Policemen and Citizens enter, followed by Godson, in the Greek "Amphitheus," which means "divine on both sides of the family," so that this character's name may simply be a comic invention suitable to his fantastic plot-function. But there was a man by that name (its only attestation in Attica), a demesman of Aristophanes who is known to have belonged to a club whose members included one of Aristophanes's producers and the knight Simon, who is represented by one of the choristers in the following year's play, *Knights*.

Godson

Has anybody spoken?

Herald

Who wants to speak?

Godson

Me.

Herald

Who are you?

Godson

I'm Godson.

Herald

Mortal?

Godson

No,
immortal. Godson was Demeter's child°
with Triptolemus, the father of Celeus,
the husband of Phaenarete my grandma,
of whom was born Lycinus. Being his son,
I'm immortal. And to me the gods entrust
the making of a treaty with the Spartans.
But though immortal, I've got no travel-money;
the Magistrates won't provide it.

Herald

Officers!

Godson

Triptolemus and Celeus, see my plight!

Dicaeopolis

Oh Magistrates, gentlemen, this is out of line,
arresting the man who wanted to help us get
a treaty of peace, a chance for an armistice!

Herald

Sit down, shut up!

Dicaeopolis

I certainly will *not*,
unless you start a discussion about peace.

---

47 A genealogy derived from the Mysteries at Eleusis, the most august Attic cult, but so comically mangled as to suggest lunatic pretension.

Herald

Ambassadors from the King!°

Dicaeopolis

You and the King! I'm sick of ambassadors
and all their fancy peacocks and their bragging.

Herald

Be quiet!

Dicaeopolis

Eldorado, what a get-up!°

Ambassador

You sent us to the King of Persia's palace,
with a salary of a thousand bucks a day,
eleven years ago today—

Dicaeopolis

The waste!

Ambassador

We're tired out from riding on the plains,
meandering about beneath umbrellas,
reclining softly in our carriages.
What hell!

Dicaeopolis

I must have been in heaven, then,
reclining in the garbage by the ramparts.°

Ambassador

And when we dined they forced us to drink wine
from crystal flutes inlaid with solid gold,
a vintage pure and fine.

Dicaeopolis

Ancestral polis!
You see how these ambassadors laugh at you?

Ambassador

Barbarians, you see, define a man
by how much food and wine he can consume.

---

61 The fabulously wealthy King of Persia. Both Athens and Sparta sought money for the war from the King, but old soldiers like Dicaeopolis hated and despised him as a barbarian and as their one-time enemy.

64 A group of sumptuously dressed Ambassadors enters; "Eldorado" translates "Ecbatana," the wealthy middle-eastern capital of Media.

72 Dicaeopolis represents either one of the common soldiers who stood watch at the walls (Thuc. 2.13) or one of the many refugees from the countryside who "took up quarters in the towers along the walls or indeed wherever they could find space to live in" (2.17), or both.

Dicaeopolis
For us it's sucking cocks and bending over.°

Ambassador
So three years later we got to the Great King's palace,
but he'd gone off with his army to take a dump.
He shat for eight whole months in the Golden Hills.

Dicaeopolis
How long did he take to close his royal asshole?
From moon to moon?

Ambassador
And then the King came home,
and feasted us with whole oxen, baked
in giant ovens.

Dicaeopolis
And who has ever seen
an oven-baked ox? What absolute baloney!

Ambassador
And then, I swear, he gave us birds three times
the size of Cleonymus; he called them cons.°

Dicaeopolis
That figures, since you're conning all of us.

Ambassador
And now we're back, with Pseudo-Artabas,°
the Great King's Eye.

Dicaeopolis
May a crow peck it out with his beak,
and your eye too, you great Ambassador!

Herald
The Great King's Eye!°

Dicaeopolis
O holy Heracles!
Ye gods, what's this? You look just like a warship.

---

79 Comic poets routinely assumed that successful politicians had prostituted themselves to higher-ranked men for advancement.

89 A political crony of Cleon's, ridiculed by comic poets as a glutton and a coward.

91 The comic "Pseudo-" suggests fraud; Aristophanes's caricature of such Persian officials was calculated to arouse both derisive laughter and indignation at the policy of seeking Persian help in the war.

94 Enter Pseudo-Artabas, accompanied by two eunuchs. He represents the Persian official who held the title, "King's Eye," here taken literally by having a great eye painted on his mask; Dicaeopolis is reminded of a warship's oarports (called "eyes").

You're rounding the point and looking for a berth?
Is that a porthole-flap there under your eye?

Ambassador

So tell us what the King sent you to tell
the Athenians, Oh my Pseudo-Artabas.

Pseudo-Artabas

Iartaman exarxas apisona satra.°

Ambassador

You all hear what he says?

Dicaeopolis

I surely didn't.

Ambassador

He says the King is going to send you gold!
Speak louder and more plainly about the gold.

Pseudo-Artabas

No gettum goldum, gapey arse Atheni-o.°

Dicaeopolis

Good Grief, that's pretty plain!

Ambassador

Why? What's he saying?

Dicaeopolis

Say what? He says we've all got gaping assholes
if we really expect to get the barbarian gold.

Ambassador

No no! He says, you'll get the gold, no hassle.

Dicaeopolis

What do you mean, no hassle? You're a liar!
Get lost! I'll do the questioning myself.
So come clean, Persian, in front of this witness here,
or else I'll dye you Middle Eastern purple:
does the King intend to send us any gold?
So we're being deceived by our ambassadors?
It's very Greek, the way these Persians nod.
I wonder if they're not a couple of homeboys.
One of these eunuchs, this one, looks familiar.
I know him! Cleisthànes son of Sibyrtius!°

---

100 Mock-Persian of doubtful meaning.

104 A "gaping asshole" indicated both unmanly submission and prostitution.

118 Comic poets mocked Cleisthenes as a beardless effeminate, and Strato is elsewhere mentioned as his lover. Sibyrtius, who ran a wrestling-school, may really have been Cleisthenes' father, but more likely Aristophanes mentions him as a joke. If so its

Oh you who shave thy hot and horny asshole,
do you, oh monkey, with a beard like yours,
show up at assembly decked out like a eunuch?
And who might this other be? It can't be Strato!

Herald

Be quiet! And sit down!
The council's pleased to ask the Great King's Eye
to dine at City Hall.°

Dicaeopolis

I'm ready to puke!
I guess I'm just supposed to hang around
while these guys get the royal welcome mat.
No, I'm going to do a great and awesome deed!
Where'd that Godson get to ?

Godson

Over here.

Dicaeopolis

Look, here's a hundred bucks for you to arrange
a peace with the Spartans for me and me alone,
for my kiddies too, of course, and the little woman.
You jerks can keep on gaping at Ambassadors.

Herald

Theorus, lately come from Poohbah!°

Theorus

Present!

Dicaeopolis

And yet another phony is announced.

Theorus

We wouldn't have stayed in Thrace so very long—

---

meaning is unclear: perhaps the manly sport of wrestling was absurd in connection with the pansy Cleisthenes, or perhaps Aristophanes suggests that Sibyrtius had enjoyed Cleisthenes sexually: wrestling-schools were prime venues for homosexual relationships, and wrestling is a common Greek metaphor for sex.

125 The Prytaneum, in the Agora, which was used to entertain, at public expense, foreign ambassadors and Athenians returning from embassies. Individuals could be rewarded for especially great services to the state with meals there for life. Within a year Cleon was to be so rewarded for the great Athenian victory at Pylos, a victory Aristophanes disgustedly claimed (in *Knights*) should rightfully have been credited to Cleon's colleague, Demosthenes.

134 "from the court of Sitalces," the King of the Odrysae in Thrace, who had aided the Athenians in an abortive invasion of Macedonia four years earlier. Theorus is mentioned elsewhere as a crony of Cleon.

Dicaeopolis

If you hadn't drawn some pretty hefty paychecks.

Theorus

but the whole of Thrace was shoulder-deep in snow,
and all the rivers froze at the very same time,
when Theognis' play was leaving you all cold.°
I stayed on duty, drinking with the Poohbah,
and I must say he's very pro-Athenian.
He actually has the hots for you. His walls
are plastered over with Men of Athens pinups.
His son, the one we'd made a citizen,
kept pining to be a genuine Greek by blood,°
and begged his dad to send us aid and succor.
Poohbah agreed, and swore he'd send an army
so big that all Athenians would have to say,
"What a giant swarm of locusts heads our way!"

Dicaeopolis

May lightning strike me if I believe a word
of what you've said here, except the locust part.

Theorus

May I present his gift: some mercenaries,
the nastiest tribe in Thrace.

Dicaeopolis

That's plain enough.

Theorus

Come forward, Thracians that the Poohbah sent.

Dicaeopolis

The hell is this?

Theorus

The army of Odomanti.

Dicaeopolis

Odomanti my ass. What's this supposed to be?
Who chopped the Odomantians' foreskins off?°

Theorus

A hundred bucks a day for each of them,°

140 See 11 n.

146 "yearned to eat blood-pudding at the Apaturia," a festival at which children and new citizens became members of Athenian kinship-groups.

158 The Greeks considered circumcision barbaric; these Odomanti were evidently equipped with the kind of large, red-tipped phalloi that Aristophanes in *Clouds* mentions in a list of trite ways to get a laugh.

159 "two drachmas": absurdly high pay for such mercenaries.

and they'll rape the whole of Boeotia with their spears.°

Dicaeopolis

A hundred a day for guys without a foreskin?
The men who row our ships and guard our polis°
would yell about that! Hey, dammit! Now I'm done for:
the Odomantians have swiped my lunch!
Hey, drop that sandwich!

Theorus

Wait, you idiot,
don't rush them when they're in a feeding frenzy!°

Dicaeopolis

Oh Magistrates, do you let me suffer this
in my own polis, at the hands of barbarians?
I move that the Assembly be adjourned
and the subject of Thracian pay be tabled. I say
I felt a drop of rain, a sign from Zeus.°

Herald

Depart, you Thracians, return in two days' time.
The Magistrates say this Assembly is adjourned.

Dicaeopolis

Alas, alas, what a tasty lunch I've lost!
But look, here's Godson coming back from Sparta.
Hey Godson, slow down.

Godson

Not til it's safe to stop.
The Acharnians are after me, gotta run!°

Dicaeopolis

Say what?

Godson

I was on my way back with some treaties,
but they got wind of them, some tough old men,
Acharnians, as tough as hardwood, veterans

---

160 For Boeotia, a major enemy of Athens, see 624 n.

162 Rowers on an Athenian warship got one drachma per day.

166 "when they're garlic-primed," like fighting-cocks.

171 Although official business could be suspended by storms, earthquakes or other signs of divine displeasure, such a motion would have to be approved by religious authorities. Here Aristophanes motivates the exit of the assemblymen by making them only too willing to use such a flimsy excuse to adjourn.

177 For the Acharnians, represented in this play by the chorus, see Introduction.

of Marathon. They all started yelling, "Traitor,°
do you bring treaties when our vines are slashed?"
They began to fill their pockets up with stones.
I ran away from there; they chased me, shouting.

Dicaeopolis

Well, let them shout. You've got the treaties with you?°

Godson

I do indeed. Three samples for you to taste.
This here's a five-year treaty. Have a sip.

Dicaeopolis

Yuk.

Godson

What's the matter?

Dicaeopolis

I can't stomach this.
It smells of pitch and battleship construction.°

Godson

OK then, here's a ten-year treaty. Try it.

Dicaeopolis

But this one smells like embassies to the allies,°
a sour smell, like someone being bullied.

Godson

Well, this one's a treaty lasting thirty years°
by land and sea.

Dicaeopolis

Sweet feast of Dionysus!

---

182 The battle of Marathon was fought in 490, which would make our Acharnians at least 82 years old. But we are not to calculate their claim literally: "Marathon-fighters" was a conventional comic way to refer to the oldest living generation—the generation that repulsed the Persians, established the democracy and acquired the empire—by way of contrasting it with the present generation, always portrayed in comedy as inferior and less successful.

186 The Greek for "treaty" is *spondai*, literally "libations" of wine, part of the ceremony by which a treaty was ratified. Here Aristophanes equates the wines themselves with the potential treaties, so that their vintage and character refer also to the length and provisions of the treaties.

190 Pitch was used to caulk ships and to flavor inferior wines; the pitchy *retsina* is still a common table-wine in Greece.

192 An official delegation from Athens would warn allies tempted to revolt from the empire of severe punishment, like that meted out to the people of Mytilene in 428 (Thucydides 3.1-50).

194 Athens and Sparta had agreed to a thirty-year treaty twenty years earlier; the fifty-year treaty agreed to in 421 actually lasted barely six years.

This treaty smells of nectar and ambrosia,
and never hearing "get your three days' rations."
It says to my palate "go wherever you like"!
I accept it; I pour it in libation; I drink it off.
I tell the Acharnians to go to hell.
For me it's no more hardships, no more war:
it's home to the farm and a feast for Dionysus!°

Godson

For me it's getting clear of the Acharnians!

PARODOS I°

Chorus Leader

This way, everybody, chase him,
  question every passerby,
find out where the man has run to,
  take him into custody!
Do our fatherland a favor.
  Anybody out there know
where on earth this man is heading,
  carrying the peace treaty?

Chorus (1[1])

He's gone, he's away,
  his trail is cold.
It's our misfortune
  to be so old!

When young we could tote
  our coal by the ton
and still pace the lead°
  in a marathon.

---

202 The Country Dionysia, celebrated each winter by the demes (local communities) both urban and rural; because of the war, Dicaeopolis (like many spectators) has been unable to celebrate this festival in his own deme for six years.

204 "Parodos" was technically the word for the path taken by an entering chorus into the orchestra ("dancing-space"), but it came to be used also of the section of a play when this takes place. In *Acharnians*, the parodos is split into two parts by Dicaeaopolis' hymn to Dionysus.
The songs and dances performed by a Greek dramatic chorus were normally strophic: composed in two or more strophes (stanzas) that had the same rhythmical structure. In this translation, each chorus is numbered consecutively, and each strophe comprising a chorus is numbered by superscript: this is the first strophe of the first chorus (the parodos).

214 "we could have kept up with Phayllus in a race," referring to the famous runner and pentathelete who commanded a ship in the battle of Salamis in 480.

Were we in pursuit
  when we were young men,
we'd never have lost
  the treaty-man then.

Chorus Leader

Now it's different: now because my
  shin's arthritic, now because
old man Lacratides' legs are
  heavy with antiquity,°
off he runs. But let's pursue him!
  Never let him laugh to think
slipping us Acharnians is
  easy, though we're very old.

Chorus (1^2)

Not he, father Zeus
  and gods on high,
who's made his peace
  with our enemy.

For him and his like
  our hatred demands
implacable war
  because of our lands.

We'll never give up
  until like a reed
we pierce them deep
  and painfully,

right up to the hilt,
  in vengeance so fine
that never again
  will they trample our vines.

Chorus Leader

Now we've got to find this fellow.
  Look for him in Stonington,°
chase him up and down the country,
  don't give up until he's caught.
I for one could never have my
  fill of pelting him with stones.

---

220 One of the choristers, possibly the archon who had held office in the previous century and who was remembered for a record snowfall during his year in office.

234 A pun on Pallene, an Attic deme (202 n.), and *ballein*, "to hit" (here with stones).

Dicaeopolis
Silence, holy silence please!

Chorus Leader
Silence, silence, don't you hear the
call for holy silence, friends?
Here's the very man we're seeking.
Move aside and let him through.
Look, it seems the man intends to
hold a sacrificial rite.

LYRIC SCENE I

(Dicaeopolis, Dicaeopolis' Daughter, Xanthias, Dicaeopolis' Slaves, Wife and Children)

Dicaeopolis
Silence, holy silence please!
Please, basket-bearer, move ahead a bit.°
Come, Xanthias, hold the phallos nice and straight.°
Put down the basket, dear, and I'll begin.

Daughter
Oh mommy, hand me the ladle here,
so I can pour some soup on the sacred cake.

Dicaeopolis
You did that very well. Lord Dionysus,
please smile on this parade and sacrifice
that I and my household celebrate for you.
Good fortune attend our Rural Dionysia
and my release from battles. May my thirty
years' peace turn out to be a blessing.
Come, daughter, bear your basket prettily
but make a vinegar face. Ah, lucky the man°
who marries you and begets a litter of pups
as good as you at farting in the morning!°

---

242 Basket-bearers in festive processions were typically marriageable young girls; here Dicaeopolis's daughter. Being a basket-bearer was a great distinction and conferred honor on the whole family, so that Dicaeopolis already benefits from his sole possession of peace.

243 A large model of the penis (phallos) was a symbol of fertility and therefore appropriately carried in the procession of a country festival honoring Dionysus.

254 The daughter is told to look solemn in the procession, as if the crowd that would normally watch were present; actually, the watching crowd here are the spectators.

256 "farting" is a surprise substitution for "fucking," implying that the husband will not actually be so "lucky": farting in bed exemplified laziness. Dicaeopolis's jests at his daughter's expense may sound insulting, but jocular cynicism at the expense of brides and bridegrooms is normal in festive contexts.

Set forth, and in the crowd hold on to your jewels,
so no one tries to finger you for a snatch.°
And Xanthias, you and your partner have to hold
the phallos erect, behind the basket-bearer.
I'll follow along and sing the phallic hymn.
Dear wife, you watch us from the roof. Let's go!

Phales, friend of good old Bacchus,°
  party-mate when evening nears,
lover of lads and lover of lasses,
  greetings after six long years!

Glad am I to see my village,
  glad at last to have my peace,
free at last from war and pillage,
  from General Lamachus released!°

It's far, far nicer, Phales, Phales,
  to catch a slave-girl stealing coal,
that Thracian girl of Strymodorus,°
  to throw her down and give her a roll
and put her berry on my pole!

Phales, Phales,
  if you drink with us and happen to get hung over,
in the morning you'll get a cup of peace to drink,
  and over the fireplace I'll hang my shield.

PARODOS II

(Dicaeopolis, Chorus Leader, Chorus)

Chorus

It's him! It's him!°
  Pelt him, pelt him, pelt him, pelt him!
Hit him, hit the dirty bastard!
  Can't you hit him with your stones?

---

258 Girls in a procession wore jewelry and so might be targets for thieves; Greek *khrysia* (jewelry) puns on *kysos* (vulva).

263 Phales is the personification of the processional phallos (243 n.) and this is the sort of song, called *phallikon*, that was typically sung in such a procession. Its uninhibited ribaldry was a traditional form of Dionysiac merriment.

270 "Lamachus" means "great warrior" and thus is emblematic of all warriors here. But Lamachus was also a real general who will later appear in this play (see 566).

273 Many Athenian slaves were Thracian; the name Strymodorus seems to be generic in comedy for old men. Although the activity described here may be mere bravado on the part of Dicaeopolis, in reality pretty young slave-girls may well have been at risk of being molested or raped by their owners and/or their owners' friends during a rowdy wine-festival, especially if caught stealing.

Dicaeopolis (2[1])°
Holy Heracles, what's up?
Watch it, want to smash my cup?

Chorus Leader
No, you dirty scoundrel you!
You're the one we want to stone!

Dicaeopolis
Honored old Acharnians,
what's the cause of all this rage?

Chorus
What's the reason?
Shameless man!
Wretch who betrayed the
fatherland!
You alone have
made a peace;
now you flaunt it
in my face!

Dicaeopolis
Want to hear my reasoning?
want to know why I made peace?

Chorus Leader
Listen hell! You're dead, my man
buried under heaps of stones!

Dicaeopolis
Not until you hear my reasons!
Wait a bit, dear gentlemen!

Chorus
Nothing doing!
Save your breath!
Even Cleon
we hate less,
Cleon whom we
plan to slice
into shoeleather
for the Knights!°

---

280 The Chorus rushes the procession, sending all but Dicaeopolis into the house.

284 This whole lyric interchange between Dicaeopolis and the Chorus Leader (284-302) responds rhythmically and structurally with its counterpart below (335-46).

302 Here the Chorus suddenly steps out of character (the Acharnians have no reason to hate Cleon) to speak as Aristophanes's own chorus, voicing his hatred of Cleon and advertising next year's play, *Knights*: for Aristophanes's hatred of Cleon, see Introduc-

Chorus Leader

I refuse to listen to you!
  I won't hear you speechify!
You're the one who treats with Spartans.
  Now we're going to punish you!

Dicaeopolis

Gentlemen, forget the Spartans.
  Put that issue to the side.
Think about the treaty question,
  whether what I did was right.

Chorus Leader

How can what you did be righteous,
  dealing first of all with *them*,
Spartans who have no respect for
  gods or oaths or covenants?

Dicaeopolis

I'm convinced that even Spartans,
  whom we treat with too much spite,
can't be held responsible for
  all the troubles that we have.

Chorus Leader

Not responsible? You scoundrel!
  Dare you say that openly,
right to our face, and after that you
  think that we would let you off?

Dicaeopolis

Not for all our troubles, not for
  all, I said, and in a speech
I could show you how in some ways
  we're the party in the wrong.

Chorus Leader

Dreadful are the words you utter!
  How they shake me to the heart!
Do you really dare defend our
  enemies in a speech to us?

Dicaeopolis

What is more, if I speak wrongly,
  and the people think I'm wrong,

---

tion. "Shoeleather" is a jibe at Cleon's connection with the tanning business, considered a low, even an immoral trade. Similarly, Dicaeopolis later steps out of character to speak as actor (416) or on behalf of Aristophanes (377 ff., 499).

I'm prepared to put my head
upon a butcher's block and speak.°

Chorus Leader

Fellow villagers, please tell me
why we're hoarding up these stones,
why we don't unravel him
until he's red as a Spartan's coat?

Dicaeopolis

Black the embers of your anger,
how they're flaring up anew!
Won't you listen? Won't you really
listen, dear Acharnians?

Chorus Leader

No we won't, we'll never listen.

Dicaeopolis

Then you do me grievous wrong.

Chorus Leader

I would die before I'd listen.

Dicaeopolis

Don't say that, Acharnians!

Chorus Leader

Rest assured that you're a dead man.

Dicaeopolis

Then I'll have to bite you back,
killing in return the loved one
who's the dearest of all to you.
Some of yours I'm holding hostage;
I intend to cut their throats!°

Chorus Leader

Tell me, fellow villagers, the
meaning of that speech of his,
threatening us Acharnians? He

---

318 For the parody of Euripides' Telephus see Introduction. Here Dicaeopolis literalizes a metaphor from the play: in fragment 706 Telephus tells Agememnon that he will not withhold a just reply "even if a man with an axe were about to strike my neck."
Aristophanes's play *Thesmophoriazusae*, produced in 411, similarly parodies the plot of Telephus. The fact that Aristophanes could parody a play performed thirteen years earlier (twenty-seven in the case of *Thesmophoriazusae*) shows that it had been very memorable. But Aristophanes parodies the tragedy in such a way that even spectators who had not seen or read it could appreciate the humor; of course, those who did know the original would better understand the subtleties of Aristophanes's adaptation.

327 Dicaeopolis goes into the house to get his "hostage"; for the parody see Introduction.

hasn't got somebody's child,
one of ours, inside there, has he?
If he hasn't, why so bold?

Dicaeopolis
Stone me, if you've got a mind to!
If you do, I'll slaughter this!
Soon we'll know if any of you
feels compassion for his coals!

Chorus Leader
Now we're really done for! That's a
charcoal-bucket from my village!°
Please don't do what you're intending,
please, oh please, oh please, oh please!

Dicaeopolis (2^2)
I will kill it. Scream away.
I won't hear a word you say.

Chorus Leader
You'd destroy my friend, a mere
innocent philanthracist?

Dicaeopolis
You refused to hear what I
had to say a while ago.

Chorus
Very well, then,
say your say.
Tell us clearly
right away
why you hold the
Spartans dear.
Little bucket,
we're right here!

Dicaeopolis
First of all, then, please disgorge
all your stones upon the ground.

Chorus Leader
There they are, they're on the ground.
Now put down that sword of yours.

Dicaeopolis
Maybe there's a stone or two

333 Burning wood for charcoal was a significant industry in the Acharnians' deme.

lurking somewhere in your cloaks.

Chorus

Look, we've shaken
out our hoard.
No excuses:
now your sword.
Everything is
on the ground,
shaken out as I
dance around.

LYRIC SCENE II

(Dicaeopolis, Chorus Leader, Chorus, Euripides' Slave, Euripides)

Dicaeopolis

I knew that in the end you'd stop your shouting.
But some coals from Parnes very nearly died,°
and all because their friends are acting manic.
And this bucket, out of fear, has squirted me
with a stream of coal-dust, like a cuttlefish!
A dreadful thing, that passions should become
so vinegary that men throw stones and shout
and are unwilling to listen to all sides,
when I'm prepared to say, upon a block,
in defence of the Spartans what I have to say.

Chorus (3[1])

Then get a block and bring it out
and say what this is all about,
what's so important as to be
the grounds for your audacity.
We'd dearly love to understand
the thought that lies behind your plan.

Chorus Leader

OK, since you're presiding at this trial,
set up the block and then begin your speech.°

Dicaeopolis

All right, then, look: the butcher's block is here,
and here is little me who's going to speak.
Don't worry, I won't hide behind a shield,
but make my case in favor of the Spartans.

---

348 A spur of Parnes, a heavily forested mountain in northern Attica, extended into Acharnae and furnished the wood burned to make Acharnian charcoal.

365 Dicaeopolis goes into the house for a butcher's block.

And yet I'm very scared: I know the ways
of farmers, how delightedly they listen
to any phony speaker with eulogies
of them and of the polis, true or false.
They're unaware of being bought and sold.
I know the minds of the elderly jurors, too:
their only goal is biting with their ballots.°
And I know myself, what Cleon did to me
because of the comedy I staged last year.°
He dragged me in before the Councilors
and slandered me, tongue-lashing me with lies,
a roaring rapids soaking me with abuse;°
I nearly drowned in a sewer of litigation.
So first allow me, before I make my speech,
to dress myself in a guise most piteous.

Chorus (3^2)

Why twist and turn and scheme this way,
  why this contrivance of delay?
Go ask that pansy sitting there°
  if he would lend a shock of hair,
a fright-wig shaggy, dark, unclean,
  and wear it so you can't be seen.°

Chorus Leader

And they expose your trickster's machinations;°
for in *this* contest no one cops a plea.

Dicaeopolis

It's now the time to have a steadfast heart,
and I must go to see Euripides.°
Boy, boy!

---

376 In democratic Athens, full popular sovereignty was rooted in the jury-system, where individuals brought lawsuits or prosecutions personally (there were no official prosecutors or advocates). Cases were heard by large juries that represented the whole people and whose verdict was unappealable. Any citizen 30 or older could be a juror and would be paid three obols a day. But this was much less than could be earned by work, so that jury-service attracted men unable to work and juries came to be composed largely of old men and the urban poor. This arrangement produced friction between the generations and social classes: many litigants were wealthy and powerful men who resented being at the mercy of a "mob", and jurors might indeed use their power vindictively against those they resented, especially when encouraged by demagogues like Cleon. Here Dicaeopolis is concerned with the jurors' support of the war. In *Wasps*, produced in 422, Aristophanes satirizes these and other problems of the Athenian jury-system.

378 For Cleon's attack on Aristophanes before the Council see Introduction.

381 "roared like the Cycloborus," an Attic stream known for its loudness in spate.

Slave

Who's there?

Dicaeopolis

Euripides at home?

Slave

He is and isn't, if you take my point.°

Dicaeopolis

He is and isn't home?

Slave

That's right, old man.
His mind is out collecting choice conceits,
while he himself is home, upon the couch,
composing tragedy.

Dicaeopolis

Lucky Euripides,
whose very slave thinks up such clever bits!
Go get him.

Slave

Can't.

Dicaeopolis

Go get him anyway.°
I won't go away, I'll knock on the door myself.
Euripides, dear Euripides, answer me,
if ever thou didst answer any mortal!
It's Dicaeopolis from Cholleidae here.°

Euripides

I'm busy.

---

386 They refer to the tragic and dithyrambic poet, Hieronymus, whose long hair opened him to abuse as a pathic homosexual. Ancient commentaries note his fondness for using frightening masks in his plays.

390 The "cap of Hades" (the lord of the underworld whose name means "unseen") made its wearer invisible, just as Hieronymus' hair covers his face.

391 "your Sisyphean strategems": Sisyphus, a mythical king of Corinth, was legendary for his craftiness and reportedly had even cheated Death itself.

394 The central stage-door now represents Euripides' house, where Dicaeopolis hopes to get the costume and props necessary for his "performance." In Old Comedy, a fantastic rather than a naturalistic kind of drama, such miraculous changes of place and suspensions of action are common.

396 Among tragic poets, Euripides is especially fond of such paradoxical phrases, here comically aped by his slave.

Dicaeopolis

Please, have yourself wheeled out.°

Euripides

No way.

Dicaeopolis

Please do.

Euripides

Oh, very well. Too busy to leave the couch.

Dicaeopolis

Euripides—

Euripides

Why criest thou?

Dicaeopolis

You compose
feet up, not down? No wonder you're fond of cripples!°
And why are you dressed in all those tragic rags,
a raiment piteous? No wonder you like beggars!
Euripides, I beg on bended knee,
please give me a bit of rag from that old play.°
I've got to make a long speech to the Chorus,
and if I fail, it means my certain death.

Euripides

Which ragged garb? Not that wherein this Oeneus,
the star-crossed ancient, trod upon the boards?°

---

402 The slave shuts the door in Dicaeopolis's face.

406 Here the audience first learns the hero's name. The deme Cholleidae was not far from Acharnae; why Dicaeopolis is associated with Cholleidae is unclear. It may simply pun on cholos ("lame"), though the idea of lameness has yet to be introduced (411).

408 The *ekkyklema* was a platform that could be wheeled on stage to reveal indoor action; here Euripides' house is envisioned as having the same apparatus as a stage-house. The following action shows that Euripides was revealed reclining on a couch; near to hand were raggedy costumes and props, perhaps hanging on a plywood panel behind the couch.

411 Aristophanes often exploits the popular idea that what is true of an artist's creations must also be true of the artist himself. In his plays, Euripides often confounded conventional notions about the connection between outward status and inward virtue; one of his methods was to portray noble personages crippled or in rags; examples follow.

415 Dicaeopolis's inability to recall the name of Telephus, the hero he has in mind, allows Aristophanes both to create suspense (at least some spectators would not yet have recognized the parody) and to have fun with six other pitiable Euripidean characters.

419 Oeneus, aged king of Calydon, was deposed by his brother Agrius after the death of his only surviving son, Tydeus, and became an impoverished exile. Euripides' play told how Tydeus' son, Diomedes, expelled Agrius and restored Oeneus.

Dicaeopolis
No, not from Oeneus; someone still more wretched.

Euripides
From Phoenix, that was blind?°

Dicaeopolis
Not Phoenix, no,
from someone even wretcheder than that.

Euripides
What tattered raggedness doth the fellow seek?
Then meanest thou the cripple Philoctetes?°

Dicaeopolis
No, no, it's someone much, much cripplier.

Euripides
Then does thou wish the foul accoutrement
that this Bellerophon, the cripple, wore?°

Dicaeopolis
No, not Bellerophon, though my man too
was lame, a beggar, glib, a forceful speaker.

Euripides
I know, 'twas Mysian Telephus.°

Dicaeopolis
It was!
Ah, give me, I beg you, Telephus' swaddlings.

Euripides
Boy, give him the tattered rags of Telephus.
They're closeted above Thyestes' rags,°
twixt them and Ino's.

---

421 Phoenix, prince of Hellas, was falsely accused by his father's concubine of trying to seduce her; his defense-speech was unconvincing, and he was blinded and exiled.

424 Philoctetes, who accompanied the Greeks to Troy, was cast ashore on the island of Lemnos because of a wound in his foot that stank and would not heal. Euripides had portrayed him as living for ten years on the charity of the Lemnians until he was recalled to Troy as the result of a prophecy. In Sophocles' extant play *Philoctetes*, by contrast, the island is deserted and the hero lives on what he can shoot with his bow.

427 The hero Bellerophon, who rode the winged horse Pegasus, tried to fly to heaven but was unhorsed by a gadfly sent by Zeus and ended his days as a cripple. Bellerophon's ride is parodied in Aristophanes's play *Peace*.

430 See 318 n.

433 Euripides' *Thyestes* evidently dramatized the hero's life as an exile after his brother Atreus had expelled him from Mycenae.

Slave

Here they are, they're yours.°

Dicaeopolis

O Lord that seest through and under all—
[may I dress myself in guise most piteous.]°
Euripides, since you've been so kind to me,
I'd also like what goes along with these,
the little Mysian beanie for my head.°
The crippled beggar must I play today:
be what I am, yet seem to be another.
The audience will know me for who I am,
while the Chorus stands there like a bunch of fools:
with my pointed phrases I'll be giving them the finger.°

Euripides

Then take, for thy gross mind doth finely plan.

Dicaeopolis

God bless you, and my best to Telephus, too.
That's good: I'm filling up with wit already!
But I can't go on without a cripple's cane.

Euripides

Then take, and hie thee from these marble halls.

Dicaeopolis

My soul, thou seest how I'm driven from the halls
while I still need lots of props, so now be whiny
and wheedly and beggarly. Euripides,
I need a basket burnt through by a lamp.

Euripides

What need, poor wretch, to have such wickerwork?

Dicaeopolis

No need to have it, I want it anyway.

Euripides

Know thou art irksome, and depart my halls.

---

434 Athamas, a Thessalian king, believing that his wife Ino (daughter of the Theban king, Cadmus) had died, remarried. When he found out that Ino was alive, he had her seized and imprisoned; Euripides had evidently staged her in ragged prison-clothes.

436 = 384, which however makes less sense in this context and must therefore have been mistakenly inserted by a scribe.

439 "Mysian": During Dicaeopolis's speech in disguise, this prop will keep the issues of identity and foreignness in the spectators' minds.

444 For Dicaeopolis's distinction between the Chorus, who will be fooled, and the spectators, who will not be, see Introduction.

Dicaeopolis

Ah!
Be fortunate, as once your mother was.°

Euripides

And now begone!

Dicaeopolis

I need just one thing more,
a tiny goblet with a broken lip.

Euripides

Take it to blazes, thou troubler of my halls!

Dicaeopolis

You don't yet know how troublesome you are.
Please, sweetest Euripides, give me one thing more,
this little bottle cappered with a sponge.

Euripides

You'd rob me, creature, of all my tragedy!
Take this and then depart.

Dicaeopolis

I'm on my way.
But wait! There's one thing more that, if I fail
to get, I'm lost. My sweetest Euripides,
if this I get I'm gone and won't be back:
I want some withered lettuce for my basket.

Euripides

Thou killest me! Here you are! My plays are gone!

Dicaeopolis

No more; I'm off. Indeed I've been a bother,
though little knew I the kings mislike me so.
Good heavens me, I'm ruined! I forgot
the crucial thing on which my fate depends.
My sweetest darling, dear Euripides,
may lightening strike me if I ask again,
save this one thing and this one thing alone:
give me some chervil from thy mother's stall.°

Euripides

The man's insulting. Shoot the gated bolts!°

---

457 In reality, Euripides' mother was high-born, but Aristophanes often portrays her as an impoverished street-vendor of wild herbs (and therefore as conventionally disreputable). Whether this portrayal has any connection with reality is unknown.

478 See 457 n.

479 Euripides is wheeled inside on the ekkyklema (408 n.).

Dicaeopolis

My soul, sans chervil must we hit the road.°
Knowest what a contest you must soon contest,
by speaking in defence of Spartan foes?
Forward, my soul, get on the mark. Right here.
You're standing still? Move out: you've had a shot
of Euripides! That's it! Come, foolish heart,
go over there and offer them your head
when you've told them how you think the matter stands.
Be bold. Go on. Move out. I applaud my heart!

LYRIC SCENE III

(Chorus, Dicaeopolis, Chorus Leaders, Lamachus, Lamachus' Soldiers)

Chorus (4^{1})

What will you do? What will you say?
You are a shameless, you are an iron man,

you who offer your own neck to the city
and plan to speak alone against us all.

Steady he stays, facing his task.
As you have chosen, so must you speak out now.

Dicaeopolis

Do not be angry, you men who watch the play,
if, though a beggar, I speak before Athenians°
of state affairs while making comedy.°
For comedy too concerns itself with justice,
and what I say will shock you but be just.
And this time Cleon won't make allegations
that I slander the polis in front of foreigners;
for we're alone, it's a Lenaean competition,
the foreigners aren't yet here, nor tribute-money
nor allied troops from the cities of our empire,°

---

480 Epic and tragic heroes address their hearts or souls but never get a recalcitrant response!

498 The original lines from *Telephus* (fragment 703) are

> Do not be angry, leaders of the Greeks,
> if, though a beggar, I speak before nobility.

499 The opening, and much of the rest, of this speech is modelled on the speech of Telephus to the Greeks, in which he had claimed that the Mysians were justified in defending themselves and so could not be called traitors. Dicaeopolis similarly defends himself against the Acharnians' charge of treason, as, behind him, the poet defends himself against Cleon's charges. See further Introduction.

506 Since the sea was dangerous in winter, few non-resident foreigners or allied troops would attend the Lenaea, as they did the City Dionysia (see Introduction), where tribute payments from Athens' subject allies were officially witnessed by the Athenians and when allied troops would be mustered for the campaign-season.

but now we're by ourselves, like grain that's hulled:
I count the immigrants as civic bran.°
Myself, I hate the Spartans with all my heart,
and hope the god Poseidon once again
will send a quake that shakes their houses down.°
I too have vines the Spartans have cut down.
But friends—for there are only friends here listening—
why blame these things entirely on the Spartans?
It was men of ours—I do not say our polis;
remember that, I do not say our polis—
but some badly-minded troublemaking creeps,
some worthless counterfeit foreign currency,°
who started denouncing shirts from Megara°
and if they spotted a cucumber or a bunny
or piglets, cloves of garlic, lumps of salt,
it was Megarian, grabbed, sold off that very day.
Now that was merely local; small potatoes.
But then some young crapshooters got to drinking°
and went to Megara and stole the whore Simaetha.°
And then the Megarians, garlic-stung with passion,
got even by stealing two whores from Aspasia.°

---

508 The citizens are compared to unsifted flour, in which some bran (immigrant non-citizens) would remain after the milling.

511 In 464 Sparta had been devastated by a great earthquake that many attributed to the anger of the god Poseidon following the Spartans' execution of some of their subject populace (helots), who had taken refuge in his temple at Cape Taenarum.

518 The metaphor from counterfeit coin amounts to an accusation that the men in question are not Athenian by birth and are therefore not entitled to citizen rights, such as prosecuting black-marketeers (next n.).

519 Goods from Megara were contraband in Athens by the provisions of a decree that the Spartans, on the eve of the war, had demanded the Athenians rescind as being provocative; the Athenians, on the urging of Pericles, had refused. Informers who prosecuted men in possession of contraband are denounced here as acting not from the acceptable motives of personal enmity or the public interest but as extortionists and blackmailers. Such an informer is portrayed later in the play (818 ff.).

524 In the party-game *kottabos*, drinkers would try to hit targets with wine-lees thrown from their cups.

525 Ancient commentators say that this prostitute counted among her lovers Alcibiades (716 n.), whose mother's cousin was Pericles, in whose house he was raised. At this time he was prominent among the ambitious young prosecutors later criticized by the Chorus (676 ff.). By tracing the origins of the present war to woman-stealing, Dicaeopolis parodies a mythological motif found in the *Iliad*, in tragedy and in Herodotus' *Histories*. In his speech (499 n.), Telephus may well have questioned the justice of the Trojan War, fought to recover Menelaus' wife Helen, who had absconded to Troy with Paris as his reward for judging in the goddess Aphrodite's favor in a beauty-contest.

527 Aspasia was a well-educated and free-born immigrant from Miletus who for many years lived with Pericles as his lover. Comic poets insinuated that she procured women for Pericles or even (as here) that she was a trainer of courtesans.

From this the origin of the war broke forth
on all the Greeks: from three girls good at blow-jobs.
And then in wrath Olympian Pericles°
did lighten and thunder and turn Greece upside-down,
establishing laws that read like drinking-songs:
"Megarians shall be banned from land and markets
and banned from sea and also banned from shore."°
Whereupon the Megarians, starving inch by inch,°
appealed to Sparta to help make us repeal
the decree we passed in the matter of the whores.
But we refused although they repeatedly asked.
And then it came to a clashing of the shields.
You say they shouldn't have; but what instead?
Come, what if a Spartan spotted a puppy imported
from Seriphus, then denounced it and sold it off,°
would you have calmly sat at home? Far from it!
Why, you'd have instantaneously despatched
three hundred ships; the city would be filled
with shouting soldiers, clamor for the skippers,
with pay disbursed, with figureheads being gilded,
with noisy markets, rations being rationed,
with wallets, oarloops, people buying jars,
with garlic, olives, onions packed in nets,
with crowns, anchovies, dancing-girls, black eyes,
with the dockyard full of oarspars being planed
and dowelpins hammered, oarports being drilled,
with pipes and bosuns, whistles and tootle-oo.
I know that's what you'd do: and do we think
that Telephus would not? Then we lack sense!°

Leader of First Semichorus

Is that right, you damnable scurvy villain you?
Do you, a beggar, dare say this of us,
and, if there be the odd informer, blame us?

---

530 Because of Pericles' long career as the leading statesman of Athens, comic poets like to portray him as a Zeus-like ruler (or tyrant); here the war is attributed to personal (and sordid) motives.

534 For this decree see 519 n. Dicaeopolis's version of the decree is modelled on an actual drinking song (by Timocreon of Rhodes.).

535 A starving Megarian will later appear (730 ff.).

542 This small Cycladic island was one of the least important Athenian allies.

556 Dicaeopolis lays his head on the block; half the Chorus move toward him, the other half intervene.

Leader of Second Semichorus
He does, by god, and everything he says
is just; in no particular does he lie.

Leader of First Semichorus
Well, even so, had he any right to say it?
He won't be glad that he dared to say such things!

Leader of Second Semichorus
Hey you, where are you running? Stop! Don't hit
this man, for if you do you'll soon get yours!

First Semichorus (4^2)
Yo, Lamachus, o lightning of eye,°
come to our aid, o thou of the fearsome crest!
Yo, Lamachus, thou friend and fellow tribesman,
or any other officer, general or
stormer of walls, come to our aid,
anyone, quickly: we're in a strangle hold!

Lamachus
Whence came this martial din upon mine ear?
Where must I help? Where throw the hurly-burly?
Who's roused my Gorgon from her carrying-case?°

Dicaeopolis
Heroic Lamachus! What crests, what ambushes!

Leader of First Semichorus
O Lamachus, has this man not for hours
been spewing slander on our entire polis?

Lamachus
How dare you, you mere beggar, say such things?

Dicaeopolis
Heroic Lamachus, please be merciful
if I, a beggar, spoke and prattled some.

Lamachus
What did you say of me? Well?

Dicaeopolis
Can't recall:

---

566 In addition to having a warlike name (270 n.), Lamachus was a good choice to exemplify the military establishment because he was the least wealthy of the contemporary commanders and thus best suited Aristophanes's argument that the military leadership, like the politicians, favored the war not out of concern for the people's interest and safety but rather to line their own pockets.

574 Lamachus' shield, which he says he has just now uncased, bore the blazon of a Gorgon, a mythical female monster whose face literally petrified anyone who saw it.

your terrifying armor makes me dizzy.
I beg you, take away that bogyman!

Lamachus

There.

Dicaeopolis

Lay it upside-down in front of me.

Lamachus

OK.

Dicaeopolis

Now from your helmet take a feather.

Lamachus

So here's a feather.

Dicaeopolis

Now please hold my head,
so I can puke. Your crests are sickening!

Lamachus

Hey, what're you doing? Use my feather to puke?

Dicaeopolis

What feather is this? Tell me from what bird
this feather comes: perhaps the roaring boastard?

Lamachus

Oh! Now you die!

Dicaeopolis

Oh no no, Lamachus,
I don't doubt that you're strong. Though if you are,
why don't you skin my cock? You're well equipped.°

Lamachus

Do you, a beggar, say this to a general?

Dicaeopolis

What, me a beggar?

Lamachus

Well, what are you then?

Dicaeopolis

What am I? A solid citizen, no placehunter,
and ever since the war began, a soldier;

---

592 An insulting double-meaning. In one sense "skin my cock" refers to circumcision, regarded by the Greeks as a barbaric mutilation, which Dicaeopolis invites Lamachus to perform with his sword. In the other it refers to retraction of the foreskin by stimulating an erection, and "well equipped" refers to Lamachus' stage-phallos, which Dicaeopolis (in double-meaning) professes to find arousing.

while you've become Lord Lofty Salary.

Lamachus

They elected me—

Dicaeopolis

A bunch of cuckoos did!
That sickened me and drove me to make peace,
the sight of greybeards fighting in the ranks
and strapping men like you avoiding battle:
those drawing mega-pay on the Thracian coast,
those General Puffers and slippery Sgt. Bilkos,
those guys with Chares, those in Suckerville,°
those Captain Bullshots, Colonel Racketeers,
those way out west in Scamtown or in Jokeville.

Lamachus

They were elected.

Dicaeopolis

But what's the reason, then,
that you guys always get paid missions somewhere,
but these folks never do? Say, Mr. Coaldust,°
you're pretty old: did you ever get a mission?
He hasn't, though he's solid and works hard.
And what of Coalson, Porter, or Oakwood there:
has any of you seen Ecbatana or Chaonia?°
They haven't. Lamachus and the bluebloods go,°
though yesterday their friends were warning them,
because they owe back-taxes and old debts,
to get out of the way, like people dumping slops.°

---

604 Chares is otherwise unknown. "Suckerville" translates "Chaonians," a fierce people of Epirus with whom Athens was apparently negotiating. Their name is intended to remind us of the verb *khaskein*, "to gape" (be gullible).

606 "in Camarina and Gela and Catagela": the first two are actual towns in Sicily, Camerina being presently among the towns allied with Athens against Syracuse and her allies (including Gela). Gela reminds us of *gelos* ("laughter"), and Catagela (literally "lower Gela") is an invented name modelled on *katagelos* ("derision").

609 The Acharnians, here addressed by Dicaeopolis, are given invented names appropriate to their chief local industry (333 n.).

613 For Ecbatana see 64 n.; for Chaonia 604.

614 "L. and the son of Coisyra": Megacles, like Pericles a member of the wealthy aristocratic family of the Alcmaeonidae, is identified this way to emphasize his non-Athenian ancestry on his mother's side: Coisyra was of Eretrian origin, having probably come to Athens as a small child in 490, when Eretria was occupied by the Persian invaders.

617 Lamachus' debts will have resulted from his poverty (566 n.), Megacles' from his extravagance.

Lamachus

Democracy, can such talk be endured?

Dicaeopolis

Hell no, unless our Lamachus draws his pay!

Lamachus

Well, I for one on all the Peloponnesians
will wage the war and harry them everywhere
with ships and troops to the utmost of my power.

Dicaeopolis

And I proclaim to all the Peloponnasians,
to the Megarians and to the Boeotians too,°
that they can trade with me, but not with Lamachus.

PARABASIS°

(Chorus Leader, Chorus)

Chorus Leader

The man has triumphed with his logic;
he's convinced the populace
about the treaty. Let's strip down, then,
let's essay the anapests.°

In all the time since our producer's
been staging comic choruses,
he's never faced the audience
to claim superior cleverness.°

624 Since both Megara and Boeotia were enemies of Athens, none of their goods could be imported or traded. But now that Dicaeopolis is at peace he will be free to trade with whomever he likes, and we will presently see him trading with a Megarian and a Boeotian.

626 Lamachus exits with his men, Dicaeopolis goes into his house. The Chorus then performs their parabasis (self-relevation), a traditional structural feature of Old Comedy that typically occurs when the initial plot-conflict is settled. It was the Chorus' big production-number; thereafter they no longer play an important role in the action, but merely sing songs to articulate episodes.

627 The Chorus removed items of clothing before dancing or other vigorous movement, such as was required in a parabasis.

629 This play, like Aristophanes's first two plays, was produced by Callistratus, but the Chorus Leader speaks of poet and producer interchangeably. *Knights* 512-13, where Aristophanes says that "many people" had long been asking him why he had not yet produced plays on his own, is evidence that he was known to be the author of the plays produced by Callistratus.

A parabasis usually (as here) consisted of a prelude (626-7) and a speech by the Chorus Leader typically written in (and thus referred to simply as the) anapests (628-64); and an epirrhematic syzygy: a strophe (204 n.) by the Chorus followed by an epirrhema (speech) by the Chorus Leader, then a responding antistrophe and antepirrhema ("syzygy" designates the ABAB structure). In the "anapests" the Chorus

But now his enemies have denounced him
  before Athenians quick to judge,
as one who ridicules our city
  and insults its citizens.°
So now he asks to plead his case to
  Athenians with open minds.
Our poet says that he deserves your
  thanks for many benefits:
he's stopped you being taken in too
  easily by foreigners
and taking joy in flatterey and
  being sucker-citizens.
When ambassadors from allied cities
  used to come to hoodwink you,
they'd start by calling you "violet-crowned,"°
  and every time they called you that
at once that little word would get you
  sitting on your buttock-tips.
And if in buttering you up some
  speaker said that Athens "gleams,"
you'd give him anything he asked, for
  honoring you like mere sardines.
For doing that our poet merits
  thanks for many benefits,
for showing what democracy meant for
  peoples of the allied states.°
And that's why people from the allies
  bearing tribute for you all
will come to Athens: just to see the
  poet who's the best of all,
who took the risk of speaking to the
  Athenians what is right and just.
So far, so wide has news of his great
  courage spread already that
the Persian King himself, when testing

Leader typically speaks on behalf of the poet: praising his skill, denigrating his rivals and often offering the spectators good advice. In the syzygy the Chorus, in character, address their own complaints and advice to the spectators.

632 Referring to Cleon's denunciation (see Introduction).

637-9 These two terms of praise for Athens came from a poem by Pindar and had evidently become patriotic cliches.

642 Since we do not have *Babylonians*, in which Aristophanes had treated this subject, we cannot know whether he refers to poor democratic self-government in the allied states or to poor Athenian administration of them, or both.

out the Spartan embassy,°
first asked them which combatant was the
stronger in her naval force,
then asked them which combatant was the
target of this poet's abuse;
"for these," he said, "are people who've been
turned into much better men,
and they will be decisive victors,
having him to give advice."
And that's the reason why the Spartans
want you now to treat for peace
and ask that you return Aegina:°
not to get the island back,
they're not concerned with that, they only
want this poet for themselves.°
But don't you ever let him go,
for in his plays he'll say what's right.
He says he'll give you good instruction,
bringing you true happiness,
and never flatter, never tempt you,
never diddle you around,
deceive or soften you with praise, but
always say what's best for you.
That said, let Cleon hatch his plots
against me, let him do his worst;
for what is right and just shall be
my ally, nor will I be found
to be a citizen like him,
a coward and a punk-ass.°

Chorus (5^1)

This way come, blazing Muse,
wield the force of fire,
vehement, Acharnian!

---

647 The Spartans had in recent years sent embassies to Persia for financial help against Athens.

653 Early in the war Athens had expelled the people of this island (near Attica) and replaced them with Athenian colonists; the Spartans had given the exiles refuge and demanded their restoration.

654 Evidently Aristophanes had some connection with Aegina (family or property), but its nature is unknown. These lines strongly suggest that in his attack on Aristophanes (see Introduction) Cleon had questioned his Athenian citizenship.

664 Greek *katapygon*, designating a man who allows another man to penetrate him anally, need not be taken in its strict sense (though comic poets routinely assume that popular politicians had sold their bodies to get ahead, cf. 79 and 716 nn.), since it was conventionally applied to weak, shameless or meretricious behavior generally.

Like a spark that leaps aloft
from oaken coals when roused
by the bellows' favoring wind,
and meat for the grill lies by,
and cooks stir up fine relish
agleam with pickle-jewels
and knead the dough:

this way come, sing a song
rousing, ardent, rustic,
to us your deme compatriots!

Chorus Leader

We ancient geezers have a gripe to
  lodge against the city.
Unworthily of all the naval
  battles we have fought in,
we get no care as aged men but
  suffer dire treatment.
Although we're elderly you throw us
  into courtroom trials,
allowing us to be the sport of
  stripling prosecutors,
old men who're nothing now, as mute as
  broken worn-out trumpets,
whose rod and staff that comfort us is
  just the cane we lean on,
so old that when we stand in court we
  mutter only mumbles
and see before us nothing but the
  foggy gloom of justice.
The stripling, who has cut a deal to
  make the case against him,
attacks him quickly, pelting him with
  hard and rounded phrases;
and then he drags him up for questions,
  setting verbal pitfalls,
assaulting, pounding, shaking up a
  ghostly old Tithonus.°
The victim mumbles his reply and
  totters off convicted.

688 Tithonus, mortal husband of the goddess Dawn, asked Zeus for immortality but forgot to include agelessness, so that eventually he withered away to a mere squeaking voice.

And then he groans and then he weeps, and
says to his companions,
"The fine I owe must come from money
saved to buy my coffin."

Chorus (5^2)

How is this fair or right,
ruining a greybeard
in court beside the water-clock?°

He has borne his share of toil,
he has wiped off manly sweat
by the bucket when he fought
for the city at Marathon.°
In our prime, at Marathon,
we pursued the enemy.
But nowadays

evil men eagerly
sue and pursue us.
What can the shysters say to this?°

Chorus Leader

Yes, where's the fairness when a stooping
old Thucydides is
destroyed by being grappled by this
wilderness of Asia,
I mean Cephisodemus' son, that
smooth-tongued prosecutor?°
I felt great pity, wiped away a
tear as I beheld the
old gentleman so hard beset by

693 In the lawcourts, the length of each litigant's speech was timed by allowing the same amount of water to run out of a container specially designed for that purpose.

697 See 182 n.

702 They mention Marpsias, ridiculed elsewhere in comedy as a troublesome orator and parasite. The name, otherwise unattested, means "Grappler" and so is probably a nickname.

705 Thucydides, son of Milesias, now nearly eighty years old, had twenty years earlier been the most important of Pericles' political rivals but was exiled in 443 for ten years. When he returned he tried to make a comeback by prosecuting Pericles' friend, Anaxagoras the philosopher. But his career came to an end in the trial mentioned here, when for some reason he became tongue-tied and was unable to make his defence speech. The son of Cephisodemus was Euathlus, mentioned elsewhere in comedy for his zeal for prosecution; another of his victims was the sophist Protagoras. The references here to Asian archers play upon gossip or accusations that Cephisodemus (and therefore his son) had Scythian blood. Scythians were barbarians and noted for their skill at archery; many Scythian slaves were used by the city of Athens as policemen.

nothing but an archer.
But when that old Thucydides was
younger, by Demeter,
he'd not have been as easy mark for
any adversary.
No, first he'd wrestle to the canvas
ten such prosecutors,°
and then he'd lift his voice and bellow
down three thousand archers,
and then outshoot the kinsmen of the
prosecutor's father.
But since you won't allow the old a
peaceful night of sleeping,
at least you ought to change the law to
make indictments separate:
for old defendants, prosecutors
just as old and toothless,
for youths an Alcibiades, the
glib-tongued little pansy.°
In future, if there's banishment or
someone owes the city,
let oldsters charge the oldsters, let the
youngsters charge the youngsters.

EPISODE I

(Dicaeopolis, Megarian, Girls, Informer)

Dicaeopolis

These stones will mark the boundary of my market.
It's open for trade to all the Peloponnesians,
to all Megarians and Boeotians too,°
provided they trade with me, not Lamachus.
As trade commissioners I appoint these three
duly elected straps from Whippington.°
And let no squealers try to enter here,

710 A metaphor appropriate to this family: Melesias (705 n.) had been a distinguished trainer of wrestlers, and Thucydides' own sons were the leading Athenian wrestlers of their time.

716 See 525 n. "Pansy" translates *euryproktos* ("having a wide ass-hole"), an insult often enough applied to popular politicians (79 and 664 nn.) but here especially appropriate for Alcibiades, who was notorious for both homosexual and heterosexual excess.

721 see 624 n.

724 "from Leproi," a fictitious place-name chosen for its connection with *lepein*, "peel," Athenian slang for "flog." Since Dicaeopolis's market is private he will have to enforce its laws himself rather than, as he would in reality, by appealing to the market-commissioners.

nor any other species of canary°
I'll fetch the pillar with my treaty inscribed
and display it clearly in my market-place.°

Megarian°
Hello, Athenian market, dear to Megara!
I need you—holy friendship!—like a mommy.
You dirty little brats, go get some chow
for your poor dad, if you can turn some up.
And listen! Give me your undivided bellies:
you wanna be sold or friggin starve to death?

Girls
Sold, sold!

Megarian
I'd say the same. But who'd be dumb enough
to pay a cent for merchandise like you?
So I've cooked up a real Megarian scam:°
I'll pass you off as pussycats for sale.°
Put on these collars with the little bells,
and look like kitties from a purebred cat.
'Cause, by the God of Traders, you get home
unsold, I'll starve you both to death myself!
Now put these whisker-patches on your mugs,
and then climb up here into this here sack,
and do a little yowling and meowing.
Make just like kitties at the kitty-show.°
I'll yell around for Dicaeopolis.
Hey Dicaeopolis, wanna buy some kittens?

---

726 For informers see 519 n. "Canary" (modern slang for informer) translates *phasianos*, "pheasant" or "man from Phasia" with a play on phasis, "denunciation."

728 Dicaeopolis goes inside; a shabbily dressed Megarian enters with his two young daughters.

729 For the decree that has impoverished Megara see 519 n. This Megarian speaks in his local dialect, a member of the Doric family of dialects that included Spartan Laconian. Since the Athenians considered Megarians stupid and crude ("Megarian jokes" occupying the same category as modern "Polish jokes"), I have given this Megarian a coarse sound.

738 The Megarians had a reputation for low trickery.

739 Throughout this scene Aristophanes plays on the double sense of Greek *khoiros* "pig" (a staple meat and sacrificial animal) and "female genitals" (specifically the hairless genitals of young girls). Unfortunately, the American slang usages "pork" and "meat" are unavailable for translation, since they refer to the penis. I have therefore decided to use "pussy" even though the jokes about hairiness and about cooking and eating pork do not quite fit it (the Greeks did not eat cats).

747 "at the Mysteries": initiates at the Eleusinian Mysteries (47 n.) brought pigs with them to sacrifice at the preliminary ceremonies.

Dicaeopolis
What's this? A Megarian?

Megarian
Yeah, I've come to trade.

Dicaeopolis
How goes it there?

Megarian
We sit in the bar and shrink.°

Dicaeopolis
That's nice, by god, if there's a live band there.
What else is new in Megara?

Megarian
Same old stuff.
When I hit the road to make the trip up here,
the government was doin' all they could
to see that we get totally destroyed.

Dicaeopolis
You'll soon be out of trouble, then!

Megarian
That's right.

Dicaeopolis
What else at Megara? How's the price of grain?

Megarian
As high as it can get, just like the gods.

Dicaeopolis
So what've you got, some salt?

Megarian
Don't you control it?

Dicaeopolis
Some garlic?

Megarian
Garlic? Every time you guys
invade our country, you're like a horde of mice,
you dig up all the garlic bulbs with hoes.

Dicaeopolis
What have you got?

751-2 The Megarian makes a grim joke about his country's miserable poverty; Dicaeopolis hears (or feigns to have heard) "drink" so that his pleasantry is inappropriate.

Megarian

I got some grade-A pussies.

Dicaeopolis

All right! Let's see them.

Megarian

You're gonna like this fine.
Go on and cop a feel. They're nice and soft.

Dicaeopolis

What's this supposed to be?

Megarian

I told you: pussies.

Dicaeopolis

Explain your meaning. Where's this from?

Megarian

From Megara.
You say it ain't no pussy?

Dicaeopolis

Doesn't look it.

Megarian

Well I'll be damned. Look, this guy don't trust nothin'.
He says this ain't no pussy. I tell you what.
You want, I'll bet you a pound of seasoned salt
that this here's pussy in the broad sense of the word.

Dicaeopolis

All right, but it's a human being's!

Megarian

Sure,
belongs to me. Whose else you think it is?
You wanna hear it squeal?

Dicaeopolis

Why certainly
I would.

Megarian

OK now, pussy, make a sound.
You won't? You're clamming up, you goddamned girl?
I swear to God I'll take you home again!

Girl

Meow meow!

Megarian
That ain't no pussy?

Dicaeopolis
Looks like pussy now,
but all grown up it's a beaver.

Megarian
In five years,
I tell you, it'll be just like its momma.

Dicaeopolis
But I can't even cook and eat it.

Megarian
No?
What's to stop you?

Dicaeopolis
Hasn't got the meat.

Megarian
Too young. But when it fleshes out a bit
it'll get the meat that's pink and long and hard.
And if you wanna rear one, here's another.

Dicaeopolis
Its pussy looks just like the other one's!

Megarian
Why sure: it's got the selfsame mom and dad.
And when it fattens up and grows some hair,
it'll be a nice pussy to offer up to Venus.

Dicaeopolis
But pussies don't get offered up to Venus.°

Megarian
So pussy ain't for Venus? Who else then?
And look, the flesh of these here pussies is
delicious when it's skewered on a spit.

Dicaeopolis
So tell me, can they suck without their mother?

Megarian
Hell yes. They'll suck without their father, too.

Dicaeopolis
And what do they like to suck on?

---

793 At Athens Aphrodite (Roman Venus), the goddess of sexual enjoyment, did not receive pigs in sacrifice, reputedly because her lover Adonis had been killed by a boar.

Megarian

Anything.

Ask 'em yourself.

Dicaeopolis

Here pussy.

Girl A

Meow meow!

Dicaeopolis

Would you like to gnaw this hambone?°

Girl A

Meow meow.

Dicaeopolis

Then how about a lollipop?°

Girl A

Meow meow!

Dicaeopolis

And how about you? Want one?

Girl B

Meow meow!

Dicaeopolis

They mew so loud when I say lollipops!
Go inside, someone, get some lollipops
for the pussies. Will they eat them? Oh my god,
just look at them get down! Dear Heracles!
Where are these pussies from? From Hungary?°

Megarian

They didn't gobble all the lollipops.
I managed to snag this lolly for myself.

Dicaeopolis

By god, a real delightful pair of pets.
How much will the pussies cost me? Name your price.

Megarian

I'll give you this one here for a bunch of garlic;
the other one, you want her, a pound of salt.

Dicaeopolis

I'll take them. Just a moment, please.

---

801 "Hambone" translates "chickpeas," Athenian slang for penis.
802 "dried Phibalian figs," a favorite childrens' sweet.
808 "from Tragasae," a city in Asia Minor, punning on *tragein*, "eat."

Megarian

All right!
O God of Traders, may I sell my wife
at such a price, and my dear mother, too!

Informer

Your identity, sir.

Megarian

Megarian pussy-seller.

Informer°

Then I denounce these cats as contraband
and you as well!

Megarian

Ah, here we go again!
We're back to where our troubles first began.

Informer

No Megarian backtalk! Let me have the sack!

Megarian

Dicaeopolis! Dicaeopolis! I'm denounced!

Dicaeopolis

By whom? Denounced by whom? Commissioners,°
aren't you supposed to keep informers out?
And you: you're pecking around without a pecker.°

Informer

I'm not to denounce the enemy?

Dicaeopolis

You'll regret it,
unless you do your informing somewhere else.

Megarian

What a plague they are in Athens, these informers!

Dicaeopolis

Don't fret, Megarian. Here's the price you asked
for the pussies. Take the garlic and the salt,
and best of luck.

Megarian

Luck's alien to my land.

---

818 For informers see 519 n.

824 He refers to his straps (723-4).

826 "Why do you suppose you can shed light on anything without a lamp-wick?" The joke is best explained on the assumption that "wick" here means "penis": perhaps the Informer does not wear a phallos, which would mark him as unmanly.

Dicaeopolis

Is luck forbidden? If so I'll take the blame.

Megarian

Farewell, my pussies. Even without me try
to get jelly with the roll a man may give you.°

Chorus

Chorus (6)°

This man at least is truly blest!
  You've seen his plan mature.
Just sitting in his market-place
  he'll rake it in for sure.

And should some Ctesias appear°
  or other stoolie clown,
he'll scream and cry in agony
  whenever he sits down.

No man will aggravate you here
  and cut into the queue,
no fag will bring his cooties here
  and rub them off on you.°

You'll jostle no Cleonymus°
  and have to wash your shirt;
you'll never bump Hyperbolus°
  and touch his legal dirt.

Cratinus won't walk up to you,°
  old fart with blow-dried curls,
as if that makes him look to be
  a hand with married girls.

This Model T of poetry
  composes in first gear,

---

835 The Megarian departs and Dicaeopolis takes the girls inside.

836 After the parabasis (626 n.) it was normal for the Chorus, between episodes, to abuse individual spectators.

839 Ctesias is otherwise unknown, but the name ('Grasper') is appropriate.

843 They mention Prepis, perhaps the man who a few years later served as Council Secretary.

844 See 89 n.

846 Hyperbolus, whose wealth was associated with lamp-making, was at this time a notorious prosecutor and an ambitious popular politician in the mold of Cleon, whose position as leading "demagogue" he in fact assumed after Cleon's death in 422.

848 Cratinus had been the leading comic poet in the generation before Aristophanes and a pioneer in the creation of political comedy. At this time he was elderly (he died some three years later), but he was still composing and therefore a rival; indeed he was to win his last victory in 423, over Aristophanes's *Clouds*.

and his exhaust-pipe smells so bad
  you'd think a skunk's in there.

Nor yet will vile Pauson come°
  to mock you to your face,
nor yet again Lysistratus,°
  the same of all his race,

a man so deep in misery,
  so hungry and so bleak,
he goes without a decent meal
  eight days in every week.

EPISODE II

(Theban, Dicaeopolis, Nicarchus, Theban's Slave, Pipers, Dicaeopolis' Slaves and Children)

Theban°
By Heracles, my hump is really tired!
Now very carefully, slave, put down the lettuce.
You pipers that have made the trek from Thebes,
pick up your pipes and play "The Dog's Asshole."°

Dicaeopolis
Stop, damn you! Go away, you bumblebees!
From where did all these cursed buzzers come,
these sons of Chaeris, flying to my door?°

Theban
By Heracles' nephew, friend, I owe you one.
They've followed me blowing all the way from Thebes;
they've blown the leaves right off my lettuces.
But maybe you'd like to buy some goods from me?
I've got some game with two wings, some with four.°

Dicaeopolis
My greetings, dear Boeotian, eater of spam.°
What have you?

---

853 Pauson was an impoverished painter known for caricatures, jokes and riddles.

854 There were several men named Lysistratus in this period; this one seems to be the man ridiculed in Aristophanes's *Wasps* as a practical joker.

860 Like the Megarian earlier, this Theban speaks in his local dialect. Boeotia (often bracketed with Sparta as Athens' chief enemy) was, unlike Megara, a rich and fertile region.

863 The song in question, otherwise unknown, suggests rusticity and/or vulgarity.

866 See 16 n.

871 "four-winged" (a surprise for "four-footed") refers to locusts (a poor food).

872 "spam" translates *kollix*, a kind of rough barley bread.

Theban

All the goods Boeotia boasts.
Got marjoram, pennyroyal, rush-mats, wicks for lamps,
got ducks and jackdaws, francolins and coots,
got wrens and grebes—

Dicaeopolis

You've hit my market-place
just like an autumn storm with its fowl winds.

Theban

Got geese, got rabbits, got some foxes too,
got moles and hedgehogs, kitty-cats and badgers,
got martens, otters, eels from Lake Copais—°

Dicaeopolis

The most delectable morsel known to man?
If you've got eels, please introduce me to them!

Theban

Most venerable leader of these Copaic nymphs,
step forth from your sack and greet the gentleman.

Dicaeopolis

O dearest one and long my heart's desire,
you've come, the fondest of wish of comic dancers
and dear to Morychus! Attendants, bring me out°
a barbecue grill and something to fan it with.
Behold, my children, this noblest eel just come
in answer to our prayers of six long years.
Address her nicely, kids, and in her honor
I'll give you a gift of nice charcoal briquets.°
But take her hence, for never death itself
shall part me from her or her sauce tartare!

Theban

There's still the little matter of my payment.

Dicaeopolis

I thought you'd give me that as market-tax.
What else did you say you want to sell to me?

Theban

It's all for sale.

---

880 Copaic eels were a Boeotian delicacy much prized at Athens and used by Aristophanes elsewhere to exemplify the war's deprivations. Suitably to the moment, lines 881-94 parody tragic scenes of reunion.

887 Morychus was a noted lover of fine food.

892 Dicaeopolis apparently teases his children: instead of a real gift, they will get to set up the grill.

Dicaeopolis

Well, how much for the lot?
Or take some goods from here back home?

Theban

A swap?
Hmm, something from Athens that's not found in Boeotia.

Dicaeopolis

Your smartest buy would be Phalerian sprats,
or pottery.

Theban

Sprats or pots? We've got 'em there.
No, something you've got lots of but we've got none.

Dicaeopolis

I've got it. Why not take back an informer?
I'll pack him like a pot.

Theban

By the Twain Gods,
I'd make a handsome sum importing one,
one like a little monkey full of tricks.

Dicaeopolis

And look! Nicharchus on his way to snitch!°

Theban

He's very small.

Dicaeopolis

But not an ounce of quality.

Nicarchus

Whose packages are these?

Theban

Belong to me,
by god, from Thebes.

Nicarchus

In that case I, in person,
denounce them as contraband.

Theban

What's wrong with you,
declaring war and battle on my birdies?

Nicarchus

And I denounce you, too.

---

908 Otherwise unknown.

Theban

For doing what?

Nicarchus

I'll tell you, for the audience's benefit.
From enemy territory you've imported lamp-wicks.

Dicaeopolis

You mean you'd turn him in because of wicks?

Nicarchus

A man could torch the dockyard with this wick.

Dicaeopolis

The dockyard with a wick?

Nicarchus

That's right.

Dicaeopolis

And how?

Nicarchus

A Theban ties the wick to a beetle's back,
then lights it up and sends it to the docks
in a drain as soon as the north wind starts to blow.
The fire, once it started among the ships,
would quickly blaze.

Dicaeopolis

You wretched idiot!
A blaze begun by a beetle and a wick.

Nicarchus

A witness!

Dicaeopolis

Grab him, stuff something in his mouth.
Give me some sawdust, so I can pack him up
like a pot, so he won't be damaged during shipment.

LYRIC SCENE IV

Chorus Leader

Dear fellow, please take care
as you get the parcel packed;
we want our foreign friend
to bring it home intact.

Dicaeopolis

Don't worry! For, you know,
it makes a special sound,
a babble, fire-cracked,
for loathesomeness renowned.

Chorus Leader
Whatever use could it be to him?

Dicaeopolis
A vessel for every use!
A mixing-bowl for evil,
a mortar for lawsuits,
a lamp to expose officials,
a shaker to stir up trouble.

Chorus Leader
But wouldn't you be scared
  to put among your toys
a vessel such as this,
  that's always making noise?

Dicaeopolis
It's very strong, dear sir,
so even if I chose,
I'd never break it, though
I hang it by the toes.

Chorus Leader
You're set now, Theban!

Theban
Can't wait to use it!

Chorus Leader
Now then, dear Theban, use
this man as you see fit;
take him and sic him on
whatever foe you like:
an informer for every use!

Dicaeopolis
It wasn't easy packing the bastard up.
You may load your pot now, Theban, and take it home.

Theban
You there, my slaveling, put your shoulder to it.

Dicaeopolis
Make sure you're very careful carrying it,
although it's pretty rotten merchandise.
If you make a handsome profit on this shipment,
you won't run out of informers to import.°

---

958 The Thebans leave, and Dicaeopolis is on his way inside with their goods when Lamachus' slave approaches on the run.

EPISODE III

(Dicaeopolis, Lamachus' Slave)

Slave

Dicaeopolis!

Dicaeopolis

Why all this yelling?

Slave

Why?
Lamachus gave me a drachma to pay you
to buy some thrushes for the Pitcher Feast,°
and three more drachmas for a Copaic eel.°

Dicaeopolis

Which Lamachus is this who seeks the eel?

Slave

The awesome, strong-armed Gorgon-brandisher
who shakes a triple shadow-casting crest!

Dicaeopolis

No deal, by god, not even for his shield!
He can shake his triple crest at the hotdog stand.
He makes a fuss, I'll call the commissioners.°
I'll take this load of goodies for myself,
and fly inside on thrush and blackbird wings.°

Chorus

Chorus (7[1])

O city, do you see how smart
 this man is, and how wise,
how making peace enables him
 to sell fine merchandise?
His store includes not only things
 for use around the home,
but also things most fittingly

---

961 The Pitcher Feast (*Khoes*) was celebrated on the second day (of three) of the Anthesteria, a great mid-winter festival (around February) honoring Dionysus. The pitcher in question (the *khous*) held about three quarts. Among the many religious and carnivalesque activities that took place on this day (and are reproduced by Dicaeopolis) were drinking contests and a state banquet to which guests were invited by the Priest of Dionysus. Also relevant to our play, with its hymeneal ending, was the Sacred Marriage between the wife of the King Archon, the official in charge of the state religion, and Dionysus (perhaps on this occasion impersonated by the King Archon himself).

962 See 880 n.

968 See 824 n.

970 The phrase parodies a lyric poem otherwise unattested. Dicaeopolis goes inside.

consumed when they're well-done.

Chorus Leader

With ease does he acquire whatever's fine and good.
We'll never ask the War-god to visit our neighborhood,
nor in his presence sing a patriotic tune,°
for when the War-god drinks he acts the perfect goon.
When we were very prosperous he burst upon the scene,
committed crimes, upended and wasted everything.
He'd fight and when we said, "sit down and have a sip;
let's drink a friendly toast to our good fellowship,"
instead he'd turn more violent, set fire to our vines,
and tramp them till he'd squeezed out every drop of wine.

Chorus (7^2)

To dinner he's prepared to fly,
  his pride is very great;
to flaunt his feasting he has tossed
  these feathers from his gate.

Of lovely Aphrodite and
  the Graces her relations
we call upon the foster-child
  sweet Reconciliation.°

Chorus Leader

How fair a face you had I never understood!
I wish that Cupid might unite us two for good,
that Cupid in the painting with flowers in his hat,
unless perchance you think me too antique for that.
But should we grapple I'd still put you down three times.°
I'd first shove in a long hard row of tender vines,°
and then alongside that I'd lay some fresh fig-shoots
and finally some grapes—would I, the ancient coot!—
and all around the plot a stand of olive-trees,
so we could oil ourselves for every New Moon Feast.°

---

980 The "Harmodius Song," a traditional patriotic drinking song that celebrated Harmodius and his friend Aristogeiton, who in 514 assassinated Hipparchus, brother of the last Athenian tyrant, Hippias. Several versions of the song are preserved.

989 The same personification is actually brought on stage, in the form of a naked girl, in Aristophanes's peace-play *Lysistrata*, produced in 411.

994 The ability to copulate three times in succession was a proverbial proof of virility.

995 In these lines, which celebrate the farmer's return to his fields and vineyards as a result of "reconciliation," the agricultural language is, by metaphor, simultaneously understood as sexual activity with "Reconciliation," personified as a young girl.

999 Each month at the new moon people had festive dinners, to which participants would come bathed and anointed with fragrant oil.

LYRIC SCENE V

(Herald, Dicaeopolis, Chorus, Dercetes, Best Man, Maid of Honor)

Herald

Hear this! As custom has it, drink your pitchers
at the trumpet call. The man who drinks up first
will win a wine-skin the size of Ctesiphon's!°

Dicaeopolis

You slaves, you women, aren't you listening?
What are you doing? Don't you hear the Herald?
Now braise and roast and turn and then unskewer
the rabbits, quickly; string the garlands, too.
Bring me the spits, so I can fix the thrushes.

Chorus (8[1])

I envy you your plan so shrewd,
or rather this delicious food,
sir, here before us now.

Dicaeopolis

Just wait until you have a look
at the thrushes being cooked!

Chorus

I think you're quite correct again.

Dicaeopolis

Start poking up the flame.

Chorus

You hear how master chef-ily,
how subtly, how gourmettily
he does the job himself?

Dercetes

Oh dear, what sadness!

Dicaeopolis

Heracles! who's this?

Dercetes

A man with sorrows.

Dicaeopolis

Keep them to yourself.

1002 Evidently Ctesiphon (otherwise unknown) had a "beer belly" of impressive size. The *ekkyklema* (408 n.) is rolled out; on it are Dicaeopolis, some slaves, food, cooking utensils and a lighted brazier.

Dercetes
Dear sir, since you alone possess a treaty,
give me some peace, if only five years' worth.

Dicaeopolis
What's wrong?

Dercetes
I've lost my oxen; now I'm ruined!

Dicaeopolis
Lost where?

Dercetes
Boeotians plundered them at Phyle.°

Dicaeopolis
Thrice wretched man! And you're still wearing white?

Dercetes
And that, my god, when those oxen had kept
me rolling in manure!

Dicaeopolis
So what do you want?

Dercetes
I've ruined my eyes with weeping for my oxen.
If you care at all about Dercetes of Phyle,
put some of your peace in both my eyes right now.

Dicaeopolis
But, foolish man, I'm not a public doctor.

Dercetes
Go on, I beg you, so I can find my oxen!

Dicaeopolis
No way. Go take your tears to Medicare.°

Dercetes
Oh please, just drip me one small drop of peace
into this fennel-stalk I've got with me.

Dicaeopolis
Not even a teeny drop. Cry somewhere else!

Dercetes
Poor me, poor little beasts of burden lost!°

1023 An Attic deme on Mt. Parnes (348 n.) near the Boeotian frontier.
1032 "to Pittalus' clinic;" a public doctor mentioned again in this play (1222) and elsewhere.
1036 Dercetes goes away wailing.

Chorus (8^2)
The man's discovered something rare
in his treaty, but he wants to share
with no one, it would seem.

Dicaeopolis
Pour honey on the sausages,
and brown the cuttlefish!

Chorus
You hear his loud commanding peals?

Dicaeopolis
It's time to broil the eels!

Chorus
I'll die of hunger from the smell
and from your words, my friends as well,
if you keep shouting thus.

Dicaeopolis
Now roast these till they're delicately browned.

Best Man
Dicaeopolis!

Dicaeopolis
Who's this that's calling me?

Best Man
A bridegroom sends this piece of meat to you
from the wedding-feast.

Dicaeopolis
He's nice, whoever he is.

Best Man
And he asks you, in return for the piece of meat,
to pour a cup of peace into this flask,
so instead of fighting he can stay home fucking.

Dicaeopolis
Away with the meat, away, don't give it to me!
I wouldn't pour you any for a million bucks.
But who's this girl?

Best Man
The maid of honor, with
a secret message for you from the bride.

Dicaeopolis
Come, what have you got to say? My god, how funny
this request is from he bride! She asks me, please

arrange for her husband's cock to stay at home.°
Bring me the treaty; with her alone I'll share:
as a woman she's not responsible for the war.
Now hold the flask up here, this way, my girl.
You know how this is used? You tell the bride:
whenever they call up troops, take some of this
and rub it on your husband's cock at night.°
Now take away the treaty. Where's my ladle?
I want to decant my wine for the Pitcher Feast.

EPISODE IV

(Chorus Leader, Messengers I and II, Lamachus, Dicaeopolis, Dicaeopolis' Slave, Lamachus' Slave)

Chorus Leader
But look, here comes a man with furrowed brows,
in a hurry, as if he brings some dire news.

Messenger I
Dear me! Oh hardships, battles, Lamachuses!°

Lamachus
Who makes such racket round my bronze-bossed halls?

Messenger I
The generals command you leave today
and quickly, with your crests and your platoons,
to guard the winter passes in the snow.
They're informed that, on the Pot and Pitcher Feasts,
Boeotian bandits plan a plunder-raid.

Lamachus
Oh generals more numerous than smart!
How awful that I can't attend the Feast.

Dicaeopolis
Hooray for the Lamachean expedition!

Lamachus
Alas and damn, would you now mock at me?

Dicaeopolis
You want to fight, you four-feathered Godzilla?°

1060 In actual life a maid of honor would probably not have used the obscene word Dicaeopolis reports her as using.
1066 The best man and maid of honor leave.
1071 The Messenger runs up to Lamachus' door.
1082 Comparing Lamachus to the hideous monster Geryon, who was robbed and killed by (the Boeotian native) Heracles, and giving him an epithet suggesting insects (traditionally Geryon was triple-bodied).

Lamachus
Ah me!
What an order this messenger messages to me!

Dicaeopolis
Ah me! What's my message from this second runner?

Messenger II
Dicaeopolis!

Dicaeopolis
Yes?

Messenger II
To dinner on the double;
march. Bring your picnic basket and your Pitcher.
The Priest of Dionysus summons you.°
But hurry: you've held up dinner far too long.
Except for you, all's set and ready to go:
the couches, tables, pillows, rugs and blankets,
the garlands, perfume, hors-d'oeuvres, prostitutes,
the cakes, the pastries, sesame-crackers, rolls,
the dancing-girls who'll pipe the anthem—cute!
Come on and hurry up!

Lamachus
Oh woe is me!
[Can flesh endure such grievous deprivation?]°

Dicaeopolis
Well, blame your patron, that big Gorgon there.°
Lock up the house and pack my dinner, boy.

Lamachus
Boy, fetch my mess-kit and bring it here to me.

Dicaeopolis
Boy, fetch my basket and bring it here to me.

Lamachus
My K-ration, boy, my flavored salt and onions.

Dicaeopolis
The salmon-steaks, no onion: I'm tired of that.°

Lamachus
Bring me some hard salt-fish, boy, wrapped in leaves.

1087 See 961 n.

1094 Alan Sommerstein's suggestion for the lost line that must (because of the wording of line 1096) have originally stood here.

1095 Perhaps a cue to withdraw the *ekkyklema* (1002 n.; compare 479).

1100 Onions were staple field-rations.

Dicaeopolis
Bring me a juicy steak; I'll cook it there.

Lamachus
Bring me here the twin plumes from my helmet.

Dicaeopolis
Bring me here the pigeons and the thrushes.

Lamachus
So fair and gleaming is the ostrich-plume!

Dicaeopolis
So fair and lovely brown the pigeon-meat!

Lamachus
Old fellow, cease your laughter at my equipment.

Dicaeopolis
Old fellow, cease your leering at my thrushes.

Lamachus
Bring out my crest-case and my triple crests.

Dicaeopolis
Bring out my casserole and my rabbit stew.

Lamachus
What's this? Have moths been eating up my crests?

Dicaeopolis
What's this? Must I eat the rabbit before dinner?

Lamachus
Old fellow, please refrain from addressing me.

Dicaeopolis
Not you; you see, my slave and I are arguing.
You want to bet, boy, with Lamachus as judge,
which makes the better eating, locust or thrush?

Lamachus
Oh! What impudence!

Dicaeopolis
He's strongly for the locusts.

Lamachus
Boy, boy, take down my spear and bring it hither.

Dicaeopolis
Boy, boy, take off the sausage and bring it here.

Lamachus
Come, let me draw the spear-case off my weapon.

Here, hold on, boy.

Dicaeopolis

Boy, hold the skewer firmly.

Lamachus

Hand me the staves, boy, that support my shield.

Dicaeopolis

Hand me the loaves, boy, that support my belly.

Lamachus

Hand hither my buckler round and Gorgon-faced.°

Dicaeopolis

Give me a pizza round and cheesy-faced.°

Lamachus

Is not this insolence plain in the eyes of men?

Dicaeopolis

Isn't this great pizza in the eyes of men?

Lamachus

Pour on the oil, boy, for in this bronze
I see an old man indictable for cowardice.

Dicaeopolis

Pour honey; for in the cake an old man appears
telling Lamachus, son of Gorgon, to go to hell.

Lamachus

Hand hither, boy, my warlike coat of mail.

Dicaeopolis

Hand over, boy, my drinklike party-suit.

Lamachus

In this I bolster me to meet the foe.

Dicaeopolis

In this I bolster me to meet the drinkers.

Lamachus

My sleeping-bag fasten, boy, upon the shield.

Dicaeopolis

My dinner fasten, boy, upon the basket.

Lamachus

And I shall porter the mess-kit by myself.

1124 see 574 n.
1125 The *plakous* (flat-cake), when topped with cheese, was indeed pizza-like.

Dicaeopolis

And I will take my coat and be running off.

Lamachus

Enclasp and raise the shield, boy, and be off.
It snows, brr brr, we're in for serious weather.

Dicaeopolis

Pick up the dinner, we're off to serious drinking.°

Chorus Leader

Fare well on your expeditions!
How different your conditions!
He'll wear a crown and drink at ease;
you'll stand your lonely watch and freeze,
while he has a whirl
with a fresh young girl
and gets his weenie squeezed.

Chorus (9[1])

Antimachus the bureaucrat,
  composer of bad verse,
who spits while talking, may the Lord
  destroy, as he deserves.
For as sponsor of a comedy
  in this Lenaean show,°
at banquet-time he told us all
  to pack our things and go!
I want to live to see the day
  when squid is what he craves,
and there it is, well cooked and hot,
  come safely through the waves
and making port at tableside,
  and as he fills his tray,
I pray a dog will snap it up
  and carry it away!

Chorus (9[2])

That's one misfortune on his head;
  and here's another curse:
one night, as he walks home alone
  from riding on his horse,
encountering some drunken lout

1142 Lamachus exits to one side of the stage, Dicaeopolis to the other.

1154 Producers were expected to hold a banquet for the troupe after the competition was over (see Introduction); Antimachus' behavior on the occasion recalled here, otherwise undocumented, was perhaps motivated by the failure of his troupe to win.

who wants to break his bones
(the lunatic Orestes!), may°
he fumble for a stone,
but in the darkness may he put
within his groping mitt
a piece of hot manure that
somebody freshly shit,
and may he rush upon his foe
with missile held aloft,
and may he miss his shot and hit
Cratinus in the chops!°

EXODOS

(Messenger III, Lamachus, Dicaeopolis, Dancing Girls)

Messenger III

Ye vassals of the House of Lamachus,
heat water, heat some water in a basin,
prepare lint padding, ready liniments,
some greasy wool, a bandage for his ankle!
He's been wounded, jumping o'er a ditch, by a stake,
his ankle's twisted back and out of joint,
and, falling on a stone, he's cracked his head
and waked the sleeping gorgon from her shield!
When he saw his valiant boastard-feather fall
upon the rocks, he howled this awful cry,
"O brilliant visage, ne'er I'll see you more;
I leave thee, light of mine; I am undone!"
Thus having spoken, and falling in the ditch,
he rose and faced his men in panic flight
and chased and routed bandits with his spear.
And here he is himself! Open the gates!

Lamachus

Ah me! Ah me!
Hateful as hell
my bloody pains, oh woe!
I am no more,
by foeman's spear struck down!
But that would truly be an agony
if Dicaeopolis laughed at my bad luck!

1168 Orestes (a nickname recalling the mythic son of Agememnon, who wandered insane to Athens after killing his own mother) is mentioned elsewhere in comedy as a notorious mugger.

Dicaeopolis
Ah me! Ah me!
What gorgeous tits,
as firm as little quinces!
Tenderly kiss me,
my little golden jewels!
One suck my lips, the other plunge your tongue,
for I'm the first to drain my pitcher dry!

Lamachus
O direful conjunction of my woes!
Oh, oh, the agony of my injuries!

Dicaeopolis
Hey, hey, hello there, Lamachus m'lord!

Lamachus
Hateful am I, cursed am I!

Dicaeopolis
Kissing again? Biting again?

Lamachus
Wretched me! Grievous cost!

Dicaeopolis
You mean they made you pay for the Pitcher Feast?°

Lamachus
Apollo Healer, Healer!

Dicaeopolis
But we're not feasting for Apollo now.

Lamachus
Take hold of my leg, take hold. Ouch ouch!
Hold tightly, comrades mine!

Dicaeopolis
Take hold of my cock, both hold the middle!°
Hold tightly, darlings mine!

Lamachus
I'm dizzy, I feel that rock on my head,
I swoon as night comes on!

1173 See 848 n. Might Antimachus' chorus have been performers in a play by Cratinus?

1211 Probably the usual custom that guests equally share the cost of a banquet was not observed at the Pitcher Feast; likely another dig at Lamachus' poverty as well.

1216 They grab his phallos (see Introduction).

Dicaeopolis
I'm sleepy, I feel a rock in my pants,
I'll fuck as night comes on!

Lamachus
Take me away to the hospital,°
with gentle healing hands!

Dicaeopolis
Take me away to the judges and King;°
I want my wine-skin prize!

Lamachus
A lance most woeful's pierced me to the bone!

Dicaeopolis
My pitcher's empty: hail the champion!

Chorus Leader
As you like, old man, we hail the champion!

Dicaeopolis
What's more, my wine was neat and gulped straight down.

Chorus Leader
Hooray then, noble hero, and take your wine-skin!

Dicaeopolis
Then follow me and sing "All Hail the Champion"!

Chorus (10)
We will follow
  for your sake,
singing 'All Hail'
  in your wake,
for you and for
  your wine-skin!

1222 See 1032 n.
1224 The King Archon (961 n.).

Aristophanes' Lysistrata

Lysistrata, and the Events of 411

The plot of *Lysistrata* is characteristic of Aristophanes' heroic plays (the others are *Acharnians*, *Peace*, *Birds* and *Assemblywomen*) as described in the introduction to *Acharnians*. An Athenian woman named Lysistrata ('Disbander of Armies') organizes and successfully prosecutes a panhellenic conspiracy of citizen wives that forces the chief combatants (Athens and Sparta) and their allies to negotiate a peaceful settlement of the war and promise never again to fight one another. Her conspiracy consists of two plots. One is a conjugal strike staged by young wives from the warring cities and designed to force their warrior-husbands to lay down their arms and come home. The other is the occupation of the Athenian citadel (Acropolis) and its treasuries by the older wives of Athens, so that the politicians will no longer be able to finance the war. The strike-plot (described in the prologue and illustrated at 706-13) succeeds virtually unopposed. The occupation-plot (254-705) contains the agonistic component of the play: strife between choruses of old men and old women, and a contest between Lysistrata and an old Magistrate. When the occupation-plot has eliminated official opposition, and the strike-plot has made the husbands capitulate to their wives, Athenian and Spartan Ambassadors negotiate their differences and promise eternal friendship.

The Peloponnesian War between Athens and her island empire and Sparta and her allies had begun in 431 after several decades of tension. Sparta and Athens had emerged from the Persian Wars fifty years earlier as the two superpowers of Greece. Relying on her navy, Athens had turned a defensive island alliance against Persia into a tribute-paying empire composed of small subject states with democratic governments controlled by the Athenian demos. Sparta, the chief city of the Peloponnesus (lower half of mainland Greece) and the greatest land power in Greece, feared the growing power of this empire and also the spread of 'tyrannical' democracy.

From the outset a significant minority at Athens resisted the war. These were the inhabitants of the Attic countryside: farmers who had little to gain from the war and many of whom were of the landed aristocracy. The war-plan, which granted Sparta supremacy on land, required that these citizens abandon their ancestral estates to the invaders and move into the city for the duration of the war. Athens initially expected a quick victory, but only after ten years of indecisive warfare was the peace of Nicias arranged in 421. The peace proved to be only a time-out, lasting only until 418, when Athens accused Sparta of violating its terms.

The war had begun to go decisively against Athens in 413, when their great expedition to Sicily, launched in 415, was wiped out at Syracuse, with crippling losses of men, material and wealth. By the end of 412, Athens had somehow managed to stave off defeat by winning back some strategic territory and rebuilding an effective navy. The political and fiscal discipline required to do this was facilitated by the appointment of an extraordinary board of ten elderly statesmen who could expedite the war-effort by bypassing the demos assembly. One of these magistrates is the heroine's antagonist in *Lysistrata*. Nevertheless, at the time of *Lysistrata* (January or February 411), the city of Athens was still surrounded by a Spartan army of occupation; many of her subject allies had revolted; all her remaining wealth had been used to rebuild the navy; her leadership was dangerously divided; and anti-democratic groups were busy undermining popular faith in the leadership and even in the democratic constitution. It was clear that getting acceptable terms in negotiation with the Peloponnesians was out of the question unless significant victories were forthcoming.

The audience that watched *Lysistrata* did not yet know that the officers of the main Athenian naval base at Samos had suspended the democratic constitution, entered into secret negotiations with Persia for financial aid, and were negotiating with the exiled aristocrat Alcibiades, who wanted to return to Athens on condition that the constitution were changed in such a way that his democratic enemies would lose power. The general, Pisander, whom Lysistrata calls a thief, had recently returned from Samos to engineer these changes. The following months saw a right-wing terror campaign at Athens, using assassination and intimidation, and by summer the democracy had been replaced by an oligarchic government.

Aristophanes has always opposed the war: conflict between Athens and Sparta weakened Greece and conflict between Athenians weakened the democracy. In his plays he argued for peaceful relations among Greeks and for civic solidarity at home, and he attacked the motives of the pro-war urban majority. In the 420's his anti-war heroes had been relocated Athenian countrymen. In 411 the hero was female. As far as we know, this was a novel idea in political comedy. Tragedy, which dealt with heroic families, had long had heroines, but political comedy portrayed public life, where citizen women were invisible. To understand Aristophanes' surprising choice we must look at *Lysistrata's* real-life counterparts.

In democratic Athens the roles of women and men were mutually exclusive and mutually defining, with no overlap. Women managed the private world of the household and its finances, while men managed the public world of the city. Thus women had no opportunity to voice an opinion publicly on any matter and were in fact, as far as practicable, secluded from public view. The primary reason for this division of roles and seclusion of citizen women was that citizenship depended upon being unquestionably the child of a citizen father and mother, so that one's bride had to be demonstrably virginal and one's wife had to be demonstrably faithful. Not surprisingly, wives were stereotypically frivolous, naive, weak and untrustworthy: creatures who required protective seclusion.

In *Lysistrata* Aristophanes reverses these roles. The world of the household and its female managers becomes dominant over the men's public world. Wives use their traditional domestic weapons (complaint, dereliction of duties and passive resistance) in a corporate conspiracy designed to influence the men's public sphere: they exclude men from the domestic sphere just as men had excluded them from the public sphere. The older women, who had greater freedom of movement owing to their being past childbearing age, forcibly seize and occupy the state treasuries, which are assimilated to the family coffers of an individual household. The women argue that, as mothers, they have a stake in the war equal to the men's, and as household managers they have just as much skill, and more prudence, than do male political managers. Since the men have failed to win the war, it is time for the women to offer advice about how to end it. In the showdown, the husbands choose the security and happiness of wife and household over the danger and hardships of war. The world returns to normality.

The idea of women as saviors appealed to Aristophanes not only because of its brilliant novelty but also because it solved some difficult problems confronting a poet with an anti-war message in early 411. The volatile political atmosphere discouraged the usual finger-pointing, and an appeal for solidarity ruled out any portrayal of embattled political factions, such as the farmer-versus-urbanite scenario of the 420's. Somehow Aristophanes had to find respectable citizens who could make plausible arguments for reconciliation at home and abroad while at the same time standing outside and above the prevailing political turmoil and the military uncertainty. Women were his solution. They had a vested interest in the war and had sacrificed much; they represented every age-group and social class; they were integral to the city and yet stood outside its politics; and they had had nothing to do with bringing on the war in the first place. Through his women, Aristophanes could rebuke and advise the Athenians without appearing to be partisan, and in case the spectators should be offended they would have to admit that it was only women talking.

The heroine is nevertheless extraordinary. She is identified neither as a housewife nor as elderly. In the strike and in the seizure of the citadel she is the strategist and spokesman, while the other women are her agents. She understands and uses her helpers' talents but does not herself share in them, pointedly differentiating herself especially from the young wives. Moreover, she represents not only her own sex and city but advocates traditional values for all Greeks male and female. She is endowed with an intelligence and will that would be extraordinary in a citizen of either sex and that triumphs on all fronts. In her possession of the most admired attributes, in her dual role as defender of home and of city, in her acquaintance with both domestic and martial arts, in her panhellenic outlook, in her advocacy of internal solidarity, in her cool discipline and immunity to sexual temptation, in her appeal to young and old and in her close connection to the citadel, Lysistrata finds her closest analogue in the Athenian city-goddess Athena herself, whose temples were on the Acropolis and symbolized every individual household.

This analogy was facilitated by Lysistrata's resemblance to the most prominent woman in Athens, the priestess of Athena Polias, who in 411 was a woman who bore the virtually identical name Lysimache. Like all Polias priestesses, Lysimache came from the ancient family of the Eteobútadae, for this priesthood was immemorially older than the democracy and represented the most venerable traditions of Athens. Lysimache held office for sixty-four years and appears to have been publicly known, or thought, to be opposed to the war. By assimilating his heroine to such an august person, Aristophanes invested her with the maximum possible respectability. As always, Aristophanes uses the language of democracy to criticize the democracy's policies. Anyone who attacks majority views is wise to wrap himself in the flag.

Aristophanes was also careful in his choice of Lysistrata's opponents, who must represent the majority view and also be portrayed unsympathetically. Here Aristophanes makes different choices than in earlier plays, avoiding active politicians and military commanders. The unnamed Magistrate was a bureaucrat and functionary recently drawn out of retirement, a member of an emergency board that had usurped some of the demos' functions. His comic mistreatment was unlikely to arouse much spectator indignation. The old men of the chorus are irascible bores who earn a miserable living at the city's expense by serving on jury-courts, but who nevertheless behave arrogantly. The young Athenian warriors and ambassadors are caricatured gently, their only weakness being sexual desperation for their wives. Their Spartan counterparts are unmistakably weaker and more eager for peace, and they are easily outbargained in the negotiations.

Thus Aristophanes managed to carry out the aims of political comedy—humorous and reassuring fantasy that made a serious appeal—even on the subject of a war that might well be disastrously lost, and even in the explosive atmosphere of early 411.

Suggestions for Further Reading

Readers interested in the Greek text are referred to the editions with commentary of B. B. Rogers (London 1911), J. J. Henderson (Oxford 1987) and A. H. Sommerstein (Warminster 1990).

Recent studies on *Lysistrata* include:

Dillon, M. "The *Lysistrata* as a Post-Decelean Peace Play," *Transactions of the American Philological Association* 117 (1987)97-104

Foley, H. P. "The 'Female Intruder' Reconsidered: Women in Aristophanes' *Lysistrata* and *Ecclesiazasue,*" *Classical Philology* 77 (1982) 1-21

Harriot, R. M. *"Lysistrata:* Action and Theme," in J. Redmond, ed. *Themes in Drama VII: Drama, Sex and Politics (Cambridge* 1985) 11-22

Henderson, J. "Older Women in Attic Old Comedy," *Transactions of the American Philological Association* 117 (1987) 105-29

Vaio, J. "The Manipulation of Theme and Action in Aristophanes' *Lysistrata,"* *Greek Roman and Byzantine Studies* 14 (1973) 369-80

Westlake, H. D. "The *Lysistrata* and the War," *Phoenix* 34 (1980) 38-54

Aristophanes' Lysistrata

CHARACTERS

SPEAKING CHARACTERS

Lysistrata, an Athenian woman
Calonice, an Athenian wife
Myrrhine, an Athenian wife
Lampito, a Spartan woman
Magistrate, an Athenian bureaucrat
Old Women, three helpers of Lysistrata
Rod, Myrrhine's husband
Spartan Herald
Spartan Ambassador
Athenian Ambassador
Athenian, friend of the Ambassador

MUTE CHARACTERS

Athenian Wives
Foreign Wives
Policewoman with Wives
Slaves with Magistrate
Police with Magistrate
Athenian Old Women
Nurse with Rod
Baby with Rod
Reconciliation, a naked girl
Spartan Husbands
Athenian Husbands
Doorkeeper

CHORUS

Old War-Veterans, twelve
Old Wives, twelve

SCENE I

Lysistrata

If I'd invited them to drink some wine[o]
or talk about the kids or go out dancing,
you'd hear the sound of high heels everywhere.
But now there's not a single wife in sight.

1 Comic wives are conventionally portrayed as very fond of drinking, dancing and noise-making. In reality, wives' everyday access to wine and opportunities for revelry were severely restricted by husbands. But at some festivals (those honoring the wine-god Dionysus, for example) these restrictions were relaxed, and at others (those exclusive to

Well, here's my next-door neighbor, anyway.
Hi, Calonice.°

Calonice

Hi to you, Lysistrata.
Hey, why the dirty looks? Cheer up, kiddo.
Don't frown, you'll wrinkle up your pretty face.

Lysistrata

I'm angry, Calonice, deeply hurt,
in fact offended by the wives, by *us*,
because, according to our husbands we're
the best at clever schemes—

Calonice

And that's the truth.

Lysistrata

—but when I tell them all to meet me here,
to scheme about the most important things,
they're sleeping in and don't show up.

Calonice

They'll show.
It's not so easy getting out this early.
We've got to do our husbands little favors,
we've got to get the servants out of bed,
we've got to wash and feed and burp the kids.

Lysistrata

But they've got more important things to do
than those!

Calonice

OK, Lysistrata, suppose
you tell me why we're meeting here. The deal.
Is it a big one?

Lysistrata

Very big.

Calonice

Not hard as well?

---

women) they were unenforceable. Women could also meet together informally at a shrine: here Lysistrata mentions shrines of Dionysus, Pan and Aphrodite. Comedians, who catered to male audiences, portrayed wives' religious activities as mere excuses for drinking and revelry. Aristophanes exploits this stereotype extensively in his portrayal of the wives in this play, but from the start he is careful to exempt the heroine.

6 In Greek the name Calonice means 'Fair Victory' ('Victoria' would be a modern equivalent), but it is an untypical form of the name and so may have been specially chosen: to suggest an upper-class background, or perhaps even to allude to an actual person.

Lysistrata
It's very hard.

Calonice
Then why aren't we all here?°

Lysistrata
No, no, not that: if it were that, they'd come.
It's something I've been thinking hard *about*:
on sleepless nights I've tossed it back and forth.

Calonice
I guess it must be pretty limp by now.

Lysistrata
It's limp all right! So limp that the salvation
of all of Greece lies in the women's hands!

Calonice
In women's hands? We're goners then for sure!

Lysistrata
The nation's fate is in our hands alone!
The very existence of the Spartan people—

Calonice
It's best they *don't* exist, in my opinion.

Lysistrata
and all of Thebes completely obliterated—

Calonice
Not all of Thebes: please save the caviar!°

Lysistrata
and I don't even want to mention Athens:
You know what I could say: you fill it in.
But all the women, if they'd only come,
the Theban women and the Spartan women
and us, together we could rescue Greece!

Calonice
But what can women do that's sensible,
or grand? We're good at putting make-up on,

24 In addition to fondness for drink (1 n.) ungovernable sexual appetite was another stereotype of wives that Aristophanes fully exploits. By contrast, men were conventionally supposed to be able to discipline their appetites. A main source of humor in this play was the reversal of these gender roles: the women resist sexual temptation while the men succumb.

36 Thebes was the main city of Boeotia, which exported fine eels, a luxury item now contraband in Athens because Thebes was a major enemy. Aristophanes reminds the audience of such war-time deprivations (see 700 ff.).

designer clothes and wigs and necklaces,
imported gowns and fancy lingerie!

Lysistrata

And that's exactly what will save us all:
the little gowns, the perfumes, and the slippers,
the make-up and the see-through lingerie!

Calonice

And how do you figure that?

Lysistrata

No man alive
will want to lift his spear against another—

Calonice

I guess I better go and buy some clothes!

Lysistrata

or lift his shield—

Calonice

I'll put my best dress on!

Lysistrata

or draw his sword.

Calonice

I've got to buy some slippers.

Lysistrata

So don't you think the women should have come?

Calonice

Have come? They should have taken wings and flown!

Lysistrata

But look around, our fellow Athenians
are late as always, chronically delayed.
But I'd have thought the women from the beach towns
and the islands—

Calonice

Lighten up, I know they're coming:
the island girls are good at riding topside.

Lysistrata

But what about the women from that town°
that's always being burnt? I thought that they
would be the first.

---

61 The residents of Acharnae, whose land was especially hard hit during the war and who were therefore especially eager to punish the Spartans. They were the chorus of Aristophanes' peace-play *Acharnians*, produced in 425.

Calonice

That shipping magnate's wife,
at any rate, is coming: she packed her schooner.°
But look, I see some women coming now!

Lysistrata

And there's another bunch!

Calonice

But what's that smell?
What's *their* town?

Lysistrata

Garlicville.

Calonice

I might have guessed:
they must have walked right through it on their way.

Myrrhine°

I hope we're not too late, Lysistrata.
Well. What's the matter?

Lysistrata

I'm upset, Myrrhine,
when a woman's late for such important meetings.

Myrrhine

I couldn't find my girdle: it was dark.
But now we're here: so tell us what's important!

Lysistrata

Let's cool our heels a little while longer,
until the Thebans and the Spartans have a chance
to get here.

Myrrhine

Sure, let's wait, you're running things.
Hey, hold it, here's the Spartan Lampito!°

---

65 schooner (boat and large drinking glass) makes fun of women's fondness for alcohol and teases Theogenes, who apparently had lost a merchant ship the previous year.

69 Myrrhine (meaning 'myrtle') was a very common woman's name, but was chosen in this play because it also was a Greek slang term for the female genitals: 'Pussy' is a good modern equivalent. Myrrhine represents the typical young wife, a category that, in Athenian terms, primarily signified sexuality.

77 The name Lampito is typically Spartan. In this play all the Spartans speak a thick, caricatured version of their local dialect, Laconian from Laconia, the region in southern (Peloponnesian) Greece where Sparta is located; Athenians spoke the Attic dialect of their own region, Attica. Although Attic and Laconian are both dialects of Greek, they differed substantially. Athenians and Spartans were not only different in culture and government but also considered themselves racially different, Athenians being Ionian and Spartans Dorian. Translators and performers are free to choose an appropriate modern dialect.

Lysistrata
Lampito, darling, greetings from us all.
What a gorgeous specimen, you lovely thing!
What healthy skin, what firmness of physique!
You could take on a bull!

Lampito
Is not impossible.
I go to gym, I make my buttocks hard.

Calonice
I've never seen a pair of boobs like that!

Lampito
You feel them: like blue-ribbon ox, you think!

Lysistrata
And this young lady here, where's she come from?

Lampito
Distinguished comrade from collective farm
of Thebes.

Myrrhine
I knew she had to be from Thebes:
she looks so natural and organic.

Calonice
Yes,
her organs have a cultivated look.

Lysistrata
And who is this one?

Lampito
Representative
from Gulf.°

Calonice
She's got some pretty gulfs herself.
Here's one in front, and here's another one.

Lampito
Well: who convenes this revolutionary cell
of women?

Lysistrata
I did.

Lampito
Please to tell us then
agenda of the meeting.

---

91 Corinth, on the Gulf dividing northern (Athens) from southern (Sparta) Greece.

Calonice

Yes, my dear,
we all would like to know what's so important.

Lysistrata

I'll tell you in a sec. But first I'll ask
you all a little question.

Calonice

Go ahead.

Lysistrata

The fathers of your kids: they're off at war.
You miss them, right? I know that each of you
has got a husband fighting in the war.

Calonice

My husband's been away for five whole months.
The northern front. He's guarding his lieutenant.

Myrrhine

Mine's in the south, been gone for *seven* months.

Lampito

And mine, no sooner he come home from war,
he take his shield and mobilize again.

Lysistrata

And how about our lovers? They're gone too.
And since we don't get imports any more,
we can't even buy a decent twelve-inch dildo.
Well, it's not the real thing, but at least it's something.
So, are you ready, if I had a plan in mind,
to help me end the war?

Calonice

By God, I'm ready!
I'd even pawn my best designer jeans
and use the proceeds only to celebrate!

Myrrhine

And you could cut me up just like a pizza,°
and everyone would get a slice of it!

Calonice

And I would climb the highest Spartan mountain:°
from there I see where they have hidden peace!

---

115 In Greek 'flatfish' (turbot), which resembles only half a fish. Plato apparently borrowed this joke for a memorable philosophical metaphor in Aristophanes' speech in *Symposium*.

117 Mount Taygetos, the highest mountain in the Spartan territory (Laconia).

Lysistrata

All right, I'll tell you. No need keeping secrets.
Well, women, if we're really serious
and want to make our husbands end the war,
we must swear off—

Calonice

Off what?

Lysistrata

You'll do it, then?

Calonice

We'll do it, even if it means our death!

Lysistrata

All right, here goes: we've got to swear off fucking.
Hey, where are you going? What's this backing off?
You shake your heads, you make a pickle-face.
How come you're all so pale? How come you're crying?
Are you with me or not? What do you want to do?

Calonice

I'm out. I guess I'll let the war drag on.

Myrrhine

Me too. I guess I'll let the war drag on.

Lysistrata

This from you, Ms. Pizza? You just said
you wanted us to slice you up in pieces.

Calonice

If there's anything else at all, that's fine. Through fire
I would even walk. But as for fucking, no.
There's nothing like it, dear Lysistrata.

Lysistrata

And you?

Wife

I guess I'll walk through fire too.

Lysistrata

Oh, what a low and shameless race are we!
No wonder men write tragedies about us.
We're nothing but a diaper and a bed.
But Lampito, comrade, surely you'll be willing.
If you alone would join me, we could do it!
What do you say?

Lampito
Is definitely hard
for women to sleep alone without the penis.
But nevertheless we must. We need the peace.

Lysistrata
Oh, dearest comrade, manliest of women!

Calonice
Look, *if* we really swear off...what you say,
which God forbid, would that be really likely
to bring peace?

Lysistrata
I am absolutely positive.
If we go home, and get ourselves made up,
and slip on one of our imported gowns
with nothing underneath, and show some crotch,
our husbands will get hard and want to screw;
but if we keep away and don't go near them,
they'll soon enough make peace, you have my word.

Lampito
Remember Helen of Troy, whose warrior husband°
looked at her naked tits and dropped his sword!

Calonice
But what if our husbands pay us no attention?

Lysistrata
As the saying goes, you've got to use your head.

Calonice
But that's no good, I wouldn't stoop to that.
And they might resort to violence, and drag us off
to the bedroom.

Lysistrata
Then you'll have to grab the door-jamb.

Calonice
And if they beat us up?

---

155 Alluding to a memorable scene in Euripides' play *Andromache*, which followed the story of Helen and Menelaus on their return to Sparta after the Trojan War. The meeting of the betrayed husband and his faithless wife after the fall of Troy, when Menelaus did not have the nerve to kill her, was a favorite scene with painters. With typical daring, Euripides added Helen's breast-baring. This example of Spartan wimpishness must have cheered up the Athenians, and in terms of Lysistrata 's scheme it is a well-chosen 'historical' precedent.

Lysistrata

Then don't cooperate.
Men don't enjoy it when they have to force you.
And make them suffer otherwise as well.
They'll give. There's never been a happy man
who doesn't have a peaceful married life.

Calonice

If you and Lampito want to, so do I.

Lampito

So: I am sure that we persuade our men
for peace with honor, nothing up the sleeve.°
But Athenians are a democratic mob:°
how you propose to get them to agree?

Lysistrata

Don't worry, I'll take care of the Athenians.

Lampito

But the military and industrial complex, °
your capital funds stored on the citadel!

Lysistrata

I tell you, I've anticipated that.
We're seizing the whole citadel today.
The old women took on that assignment.
They'll pretend to have religious business there.
They're at it now, while we conclude our plans.

Lampito

I must admit, your plan sounds quite complete.

Lysistrata

Then, Lampito, let's swear an oath without

---

169 Pro-war Athenians often claimed that Spartans did not negotiate truthfully or keep agreements.

170 Athenian democracy was a radically new form of government in the fifth century and was not universally applauded, even at Athens, where right-wing factions from some aristocratic families (the former ruling elite) hoped that it would be a short-lived experiment. Sparta lived under her traditional dual monarchy and perceived democracy as a dangerous threat to international order and stability. One of the great issues of the war was whether Athens should be allowed to spread democracy throughout Greece: the Athenian imperial policy was, wherever possible, to replace ruling elites with democratic governments. Anti-democractic states considered this 'mob-rule.'

173 The imperial democracy of Athens relied on its superior navy and its wealth during the war. In their disastrous defeat at Syracuse in 413 Athens had lost a lot of both, so that their enemies were now more than an equal match, but Aristophanes maintains the flattering self-image of his Athenian audience. The Athenian Treasuries were kept on the citadel (the Acropolis), under the protection of their city-goddess Athena: for her significance in the play see the Introduction.

delay, and then our plan will be official.

Lampito

Propose the oath, and we all swear to it.

Lysistrata

All right, then. Officeress! Where is she? Wake her up![o]
Put down your shield here. No, the other way.
Now someone get a victim.

Calonice

Say, Lysistrata,
what sort of oath is this?

Lysistrata

What sort of oath?
A slaughter in a shield, like tragic ones,
the fatted calf: you know.

Calonice

We can't do that,
we shouldn't use a shield if we want peace.

Lysistrata

What's *your* suggestion, smarty?

Calonice

I suggest,
we get a full-grown cock and slaughter that.

Lysistrata

You've got a one-track mind.

Calonice

But then what *will*
we swear on?

Lysistrata

Something's hit me. Want to hear?
Let's chuck the shield and get a giant wine-glass,
and slaughter a great big bottle of red bordeaux,
and swear we'll never fill the glass with water!

Lampito

Oh da! One cannot quarrel with that oath.

Lysistrata

So someone get the bottle and the glass.

---

184 The Athenians used slave-archers, mostly from Western Asia, as police and as security guards for officials like the Magistrate who appears later (387 ff.). Lysistrata has a female version.

Myrrhine
Oh God, girls, take a look at all that glassware!
Calonice
And just to touch this bottle makes me come!
Lysistrata
So put it down! Join hands, now, everyone.
O Goddess of Persuasion, Conspiratorial Glass:
receive this offering from the wives. Amen.
Calonice
Behold the color of the gurgling blood.
Lampito
Perceive the sweetness of its fair aroma.
Myrrhine
I'd like to be the first to take the oath.
Calonice
Hey, not so fast, you've got to wait your turn.
Lysistrata
No! *All* hands on the glass. You also, Lampito.
Let one of you repeat the oath I make,
and everybody else swear her allegiance.
I won't allow my lover or my husband—
Calonice
I won't allow my lover or my husband—
Lysistrata
to get near me with a hard-on. I can't hear you!
Calonice
to get near me with a hard-on. Oh my God!
My knees are getting weak, Lysistrata!
Lysistrata
At home my life will be completely chaste.
Calonice
At home my life will be completely chaste.
Lysistrata
I'll wear my sexiest dresses and cosmetics—
Calonice
I'll wear my sexiest dresses and cosmetics—
Lysistrata
to make my man as horny as can be.
Calonice
to make my man as horny as can be.

Lysistrata
But never will I willingly give in.

Calonice
But never will I willingly give in.

Lysistrata
If he should get his way by violence—

Calonice
If he should get his way by violence—

Lysistrata
I'll simply lie there uncooperative.

Calonice
I'll simply lie there uncooperative.

Lysistrata
I will not wrap my legs around his back—

Calonice
I will not wrap my legs around his back—

Lysistrata
nor will I crouch down like a lioness.

Calonice
nor will I crouch down like a lioness.

Lysistrata
As I drink this wine, so will I keep this oath—

Calonice
As I drink this wine, so will I keep this oath—

Lysistrata
but if I break it, may the wine be water.

Calonice
but if I break it, may the wine be water.

Lysistrata
So say you one and all?

All
So say we all!

Lysistrata
All right, I'll do the honors.

Calonice
Just make sure
you take one share: we must have solidarity.

Lampito
What's that?

Lysistrata

The signal: as I said before,
the ladies who would seize the citadel.
They've done it already! Listen, Lampito:
return to Sparta now, and start the strike.
And leave these women here as hostages.
The rest of us will enter the citadel
and lock the gates and barricade ourselves.

Calonice

But don't you think the men will try to stop us?
And pretty quickly?

Lysistrata

They don't worry me.
They'll come with torches, shouting and making threats,
but they can't make us open up these gates
until they promise to honor our demands.

Calonice

By Sex and Love they can't!° For otherwise,
we're nothing but a weak and gutless gender.

Men's Chorus

Leader

Come on, sergeant, get a move on,
even if your shoulder's raw
Hefting all this heavy wood and
dragging all of it uphill.

Chorus (1^1)°

Incredible and shocking too
for wives to act like this!
We fed and clothed them: now we find
they're dirty terrorists!

They seized the City Treasury
and Offices of State.
They occupy our holy ground
and won't unlock the gate!

Leader

Butts in gear, men, double-time it,

---

252 She swears by Aphrodite, the goddess of sexual enjoyment.

256 Greek dramatic choruses (the songs and dances performed in the orchestra by the chorus) were normally strophic, that is, composed in two or more strophes (stanzas) that had the same rhythmical structure. In this translation, each chorus is numbered (there are eight) and each strophe comprising a chorus is numbered by superscript: this is the first strophe of the first chorus.

stack them right against the gate;
then we'll pile them all around it,
sealing in the enemy troops:
every single female traitor
party to this coup d' etat.
Then we'll make a giant bonfire:
toss your flares at my command.
Death by burning is our verdict,
starting with the bitch in charge.°

Chorus (1^2)

While we're alive they'll never have
the laugh on this old geezer!
Remember when the Spartans first °
attempted such a seizure?

They came on big but went out small,
their reputation shot.
We didn't even let them keep
a rag to wipe their snot!

Leader

Ranks in order, siege positions,
just the way we did it then.
Let these women beat us now and
all our reputation's gone.°

---

270 They mention the wife of the wealthy Lykon. She was apparently known for her scandalous living: the comic poets frequently joke about her extravagance and adulteries. Her name was probably Rhodia, but this also means 'woman from Rhodes' (implying non-Athenian ancestry) and so might have been a nickname whose significance is now lost.

274 In 508 a Spartan force under King Cleomenes I came to Athens and seized the Acropolis in support of Isagoras in his power-struggle with Cleisthenes, a founding hero of the democracy, who accepted the Spartans' surrender after a two-day siege. During the play the old men boast of having taken part in battles that would make them well over 100 years old: too old for realism but not too old for their characterization as men who had struggled to establish the democracy, which was popularly thought to have begun with the fall of the last Athenian tyrant in 510 (1150 n.).

285 They allude to the battle of Marathon in 490, when a Persian expeditionary force under Darius and guided by the ousted Athenian tyrant Hippias (1150 n.) landed at the Bay of Marathon and marched toward Athens, 26 miles SW. At the town of Marathon they were met and defeated by an Athenian-Plataiean army. This victory, considered by Athenians to be their most glorious, ended Darius' European ambitions, and the Persians did not invade again for ten years, when they returned under Xerxes. Later legend told how one Phidippides (or Philippides) ran back to Athens to announce the good news. Although he reportedly dropped dead of fatigue as soon as he had done so, the marathon race still commemorates his run.

Chorus (2^1)

The goal of our journey's around the bend.
but the steepest part's at the very end.
Our shoulders are aching, we're out of fuel.
It would have been smarter to bring a mule.

But keep it moving all the same,
and don't forget to fan the flame.
There's little point in climbing higher,
then finding out we've lost our fire.
God, the smoke!

Chorus (2^2)

The smoke's rushing out like a raving bitch
and biting our eyes with an awful itch.
Can't see where we're going: it seems to us
we're climbing the slopes of Vesuvius.

But hurry onward anyhow:
We've got to save the goddess now!
Our Purple Hearts aren't worth a dime
unless we help her out this time.
God, the smoke!

Leader

Now the fire's burning lively,
  now the gods are on our side.
Stack the logs and set your torches,
  then we'll charge the gate like rams,
Open up, you wives, or else we'll
  burn the gates and smoke you out.
Place the logs in orderly fashion.
  Ah, this smoke is terrible!
Can't the generals hear us? Won't they
  lift some logs? Our arms are dead.
Pot of Coals, it's up to you now:
  furnish fire; I'll lead the charge.
Victory Goddess,° lend assistance,
  help us beat these mutinous wives!

---

317 The Victory Goddess (Nike) had a shrine on the Acropolis that was part of the massive building program undertaken by the democracy under Pericles and whose construction had been competed some ten years earlier. The shrine still stands today. The cult of Nike, decreed in the 440's, was democratically organized (its priestess being elected or allotted from among all citizen women). By contrast, Lysistrata and her women align themselves with the citadel-goddess Athena Polias, whose cult was older than the democracy and was run by women from high-born families.

Women's Chorus

Women's Leader
I think I see the smoke and rising flames!
The siege is underway. We've got to hurry!

Chorus (3[1])
Faster, faster, we've got to fly,
or else our friends will surely die!
Some nasty elders have got a view
to hold a female barbecue!

We started early but might be late:
we had to fill our pitchers.
The well was jammed, we got delayed
by slaves and pushy bitches,

shouting, shoving, smashing pots,
banging heads and raising knots.
Now we're here with pitchers filled
to keep our friends from being grilled.

Chorus (3[2])
There they are, the demented bums!
They're stacking logs to burn our chums,
shouting threats of an awful kind,
to leave but ash and smoke behind.

O Goddess,° spare the women's life!
They occupied your temple
to save the Greeks from war and strife
and madness pure and simple.

Be our ally, help defend
women fighting evil men.
Help us with our pitchers filled
to keep our friends from getting grilled.

Women's Leader
Hold it, girls! What's this I see here?
Men, and evil bastards too.

Men's Leader
What the hell is going on here?
Where's this swarm of women from?

Women
Scared of us? We're not so many.
Still, there's more where we came from.

341 They pray to Athena Polias (317 n.).

Men

Boys, do you hear all this babble?
  Someone bash her with a log.

Women

Put your pitchers on the ground, girls:
  looks as if they want a fight.

Men

How'd you like to have your mouth shut?
  Two or three punches ought to do.

Women

Come on, hit me: I'm not moving.
  I would love to chew your balls.

Men

Quiet, or I'll bust your wrinkles!

Women

  Go ahead, just lift your hand.

Men

What about my knuckles? What then?

Women

  Want to have your guts pulled out?

Men

Tragic poets have a saying:
  nothing's wilder than a woman!

Women

Come on, girls, let's lift our pitchers.

Men

  What's this water for, you bitch?

Women

What's this fire, you mausoleum?

Men

  Just a pyre for your friends.

Women

I'm about to douse your pyre.

Men

  Douse it?

Women

          That's exactly right.

Men

How'd you like your hair on fire?

Women

Get some soap: I've got your bath.

Men

Bath, you crone?

Women

You really need one.

Men

Listen to her!

Women

I've a right.

Men

Quiet!

Women

You're not judge and jury now.°

Men

Burn her hair!

Women

And now the bath!

Men

Goddamn!

Women

I hope we didn't scald you.

Men

Scald us? Stop! We've had enough!

Women

Maybe now you'll start to blossom.

---

380 'You're not judge and jury now.' In democratic Athens, full popular sovereignty was rooted in the court system, where individuals brought lawsuits or prosecutions personally (there were no official prosecutors or advocates). Cases were heard by large juries that represented the whole people and whose verdict was final. At the age of thirty any males citizen could be a juror, but at this time most jurors were poor and/or old men. One reason was that the young men were away at war. Another was that under Pericles the democracy had begun to pay jurors for service. This made jury-service attractive to men unfit for more remunerative occupations, so that it became in effect a welfare payment for the urban poor and a pension for the old. This arrangement created friction between the generations and social classes (many litigants were wealthy and powerful men who resented being at the mercy of a 'mob'), and it was open to political abuses: all these are explored by Aristophanes in his play *Wasps.* Later in our play the men complain that the women's seizure of the citadel has cut off their pay (625), and the women reply by calling them freeloaders (646 ff.). Since the jurors were essentially the same people who supported the war-policy, Aristophanes attempts to arouse the audience's resentment by calling attention to their low social status and their selfish interests.

Men

No, we'll wither up instead.

Women

You brought the fire: warm yourselves.

SCENE II

Magistrate°

I hear our spoiled wives are out of hand.
Another phony festival for their wine-god,°
a noisy rooftop party for Adonis,°
just like the one that spoiled our assembly.
That ill-starred, foolish politician moved
we sail to Sicily,° while his wife was dancing
and yelling for Adonis. When he said,
let's muster allied troops for this armada,
his wife was on the rooftop getting drunk
and yelling 'Oh doomed youth!' But he persisted,
the goddamned stubborn hotheaded son of a bitch!
That's just the kind of mischief wives can make!

Men's Leader

And wait till I tell you what they did to *us.*
They treated us like slaves and dumped their pitchers
all over us and soaked our clothes through,
so anyone would say we pissed our pants!

Magistrate

It serves your right, I swear by the salty sea-god.
We men have only got ourselves to blame.
We virtually teach our wives to misbehave,
and so they're always nurturing their plots.
What do we say when we visit the marketplace?
'Oh, goldsmith, about that locket I bought from you.
My wife was having a ball the other night
and it seems this bolt here slipped right out of its hole.

---

387 Magistrate: see Introduction.

388 This wine (or beer) god, Sabazius, was a foreign import not recognized by the city and popular with 'outsiders', like women, slaves and the poor.

389 Adonis was another foreign import not recognized by the city. His cult was celebrated by women in spring or summer on rooftops: the women planted quickly flowering and quickly withering gardens and lamented the death of the youth Adonis, favorite of Aphrodite.

392 For the doomed Sicilian Expedition, see Introduction. Since the assembly was deciding to send the flower of Athenian youth into a great battle, the lamentations for Adonis were remembered after the disaster as a bad omen.

I've got to leave, I'm travelling up to Bangor.°
I'd be grateful if you'd visit her some night
with the proper tool and fix the hole that needs it.'
Another husband visits his local shoemaker,
a half-grown boy with a very full-grown cock.
'Say, shoemaker, about this pair of slippers:
my wife complains the orifice grips too tight;
her skin is very soft. While I'm at work,
please loosen up her orifice a bit.'
It's this complacency that leads to trouble,
so here I am, a supplier for the army,
in need of public funds,° and now I find
the women have shut me out of the treasury!
I'm wasting time. You slaves, bring on the crowbars!
I'll put a stop to all this female foolery.
You bozo, look alive! And you as well!
Stop wondering if they're any bars around.°
Pick up those crowbars, take them to the gate,
and pry it open. Here, I'll show you how,
I'll help you pry.

Lysistrata

No need for any prying.
I'm coming out myself. No need for crowbars.
We don't need force, but rather brains and sense.

Magistrate

That so, you bitch? I'm calling a policeman.°
Arrest this woman, put the handcuffs on.

Lysistrata

By the goddess, if he lays a hand on me,
policeman or no policeman, he'll regret it.

Magistrate

Can you be scared of her? Go on and grab her.
And you there, help him out. Hogtie the woman!

Old Woman A

By the goddess, if you even raise your hand
to her, I'll beat you till you shit your pants!

---

411 'To Salamis,' an Attic island which for Athenians had sexual associations, apparently because the Salaminians' oarsmanship on small boats reminded them of women on top in sexual intercourse.

423 Aristophanes implies that public officials steal the city's money, a charge made explicit at 490-1.

427 Comic slaves are conventionally fond of drinking.

433 For the policemen see 184 n.

Magistrate
What, shit my pants? Another policeman here!
Grab this one first, the one with the dirty mouth.

Old Woman B
By the goddess, if you lay a fingertip
on her, you'll need an icebag for both eyes.

Magistrate
Where'd *she* come from? Police! Arrest this woman!
Whoever's on this outing I'll arrest.

Old Woman C
By the goddess, if you make a move toward her,
I'll pull your hair out until you're bloody bald.

Magistrate
My god, I'm out of cops! I'm in a fix.
I *cannot* let myself be screwed by women!
We need a full-scale charge. Attention, Huns!°
Prepare to charge!

Lysistrata
As you will quickly see,
we too have troops, four companies of women:
they're fully armed and on alert inside.

Magistrate
Go forward, Huns, and twist their arms behind them!

Lysistrata
Come forward, allied women, on the double!
You market-women,° meter-maids, bag-ladies!
You check-out girls, mud-wrestlers, waitresses!
Attack them, stomp them, chew them, beat them up!
Cease fire! Stand at ease, don't chase them down!

Magistrate
Alas, my Huns are utterly defeated.

Lysistrata
But what did you expect? Did you imagine
that we were slaves, or did you think that women
can't show courage?

---

451 These archer-police are from Scythia (the modern Ukraine).

456 'Market-women,' who were conventionally older women, had stalls in the marketplace and were poor citizens, resident aliens or slaves. Those singled out here are sellers of wild herbs, porridge, garlic, bread, rooms at inns (which included prostitutes): the social equivalents of the types listed in the translation. They were stereotyped in comedy as bold, loud and abusive, so that they make perfect 'soldiers' for Lysistrata .

Magistrate

Courage, yes indeed,
provided there's a lot of booze inside 'em.

Men's Leader

Why waste your breath, my Magistrate,
why argue with these bitches?
You know the kind of bath we took
without that kind of soft soap.

Women's Leader

Dear sir, it's impolite to raise
your hand against your neighbors.
Try that again, we'll punch you out,
though we prefer decorum.
We promise to be meek as girls,
so don't stir up a mare's nest.

Men's Chorus (4^{1})

King of the gods, these women are beasts!
We need a plan, to say the least!
Let's try to find out
what they're angry about,
why they're raising hell
on our sacred citadel.

Men's Leader

Now question her and test her answers,
and don't be buffaloed.
It's bad enough they've gone this far;
we mustn't let it go!

Magistrate

First I'd like to know the reason
why you took the citadel.

Lysistrata

Confiscation of the money:
thus we put a stop to war.

Magistrate

Money's causing war?

Lysistrata

Exactly:
also the political mess.
Generals and politicians°

---

490 She singles out Pisander, the only named politician abused in the play. For his topical importance see Introduction.

argue war so they can steal.
Go ahead and fight, but henceforth
no more money leaves this place.

Magistrate

You will keep it.

Lysistrata

No, we'll save it.

Magistrate

Save it?

Lysistrata

What's so strange in that?
Don't we manage household money?°

Magistrate

Not the same.

Lysistrata

How so?

Magistrate

It's war!

Lysistrata

Stop the war.

Magistrate

Then who will save us?

Lysistrata

We will.

Magistrate

You?

Lysistrata

That's right.

Magistrate

My god!

Lysistrata

What's your choice?

Magistrate

You're mad!

Lysistrata

Be angry.
Nonetheless we must.

---

495 For wives as domestic managers see Introduction.

Magistrate

No way!

Lysistrata

Must.

Magistrate

If I refuse?

Lysistrata

I'd like that!

Magistrate

Dare you speak of war and peace?

Lysistrata

Yes.

Magistrate

So make it fast.

Lysistrata

I'll do that.
Calm yourself.

Magistrate

It's difficult:
itchy fists.

Old Woman A.

You risk a beating.

Magistrate

Shut up, bag. *You* talk.

Lysistrata

I will.°
All along we kept our silence,
acquiesced as nice wives should—
or else!—although we didn't like it.
You would escalate the war;
we would ask you so politely,
even though it hurt inside,
'Darling, what's the latest war-news?
What did all you men decree?
Anything about a treaty?'
Then you'd say, 'What's that to you?
Shut up!' And I'd shut up.

---

507 Lysistrata's account of dispute between wives and husbands over the war is inspired by the famous conversation between Hector and Andromache in the sixth book of Homer's *Iliad*.

Old Woman B

Not me!

Magistrate

Then I'd smack you!

Lysistrata

There you are.
Then we'd hear some even worse news,
so we'd say, 'How stupid, dear!'
Then you'd give us dirty looks and
say, 'Go mend my cloak or else!°
War is strictly for the menfolk.'

Magistrate

Right we were.

Lysistrata

You stupid fool!
We were quite prepared to warn you;
you refused to hear advice.
Then disaster. Throughout the city
'All our boys are gone!' you cried.
That's when all the wives decided
we must act to save the Greeks.
Thus we're here: no point in waiting.
Want to hear some good advice?
Shut your mouth the way *we* used to,
let us save you from yourselves.

Magistrate

You save *us*? That's madness!

Lysistrata

Shut up!

Magistrate

Me shut up for you? You skirt!
Let me die before that happens!

Lysistrata

It's my skirt that bothers you?
Give the man a skirt and bonnet:
Maybe that will shut him up.

---

520 Proper gender roles were conventionally expressed by the antithesis weaving/fighting. Lysistrata will presently reverse these roles by dressing the Magistrate like a wife and teaching him to weave. The women claim that their domestic work is a better model for running the city than male fighting skills.

Old Woman C

Here's a sewing basket also!

Lysistrata

Now he needs some chewing gum.
Put a little lipstick on him,
stuff your hankies down his shirt.
War is strictly for the women!

Women's Leader

Women arise, let go your jars.
It's time to help these friends of ours.

Women's Chorus (4[2])

I'm dancing forever, I'll never retreat,
never be tired or get cold feet!
I'm ready to strive
for the cause of the wives,
who are decent, smart,
patriotic, bold of heart!

Women's Leader

Most valiant child of bold fore-mothers,
no slow-down or retreat!
You've got him where you want him now:
you're in the driver's seat!

Lysistrata

Goddess of sex and sweet desire,°
breathe upon our breasts and flanks,
give our husbands lasting hard-ons,
help us make them leave the ranks.

Magistrate

What's your plan?

Lysistrata

My first requirement:
soldiers leave the marketplace.

Old Woman A

Hear, hear!

Lysistrata

They strut about in armor,
pushing shoppers, smashing goods.

Magistrate

Manly men!

---

551 For Aphrodite see 252 n.

Lysistrata

But pretty comic,
stacking burgers on their shields.

Old Woman B

God, I've seen those grand lieutenants
use their helmets for a bowl.
Mercenaries slap the salesgirls,
never even pay their bill!

Magistrate

You can stop these wartime hardships,
I'm to gather?

Lysistrata

Sure!

Magistrate

And how?

Lysistrata

Open up your sewing basket:
see the skein of tangled wool?
Put it to the spindle this way,
wind it here, now wind it there.
Thus the war can be unravelled,
making truces here, and there.

Magistrate

Skiens and spindles? I don't get it.

Lysistrata

Sense and skill is all you need.

Magistrate

Show me.

Lysistrata

Gladly. First you wash the
city as we wash the wool,
cleaning out the bullshit.° Then we
pluck away the parasites;
break up strands that clump together,
forming special interest groups;
Here's a bozo: squeeze his head off.
Now you're set to card the wool:

575 Comic poets like to portray social and political problems as being the fault of a small number of selfish and disruptive people—including current political leaders—and suggest that, if these people could be eliminated, all would be well and ordinary people (like most spectators) could live their lives in peace.

use your basket for the carding,
  the basket of solidarity.
There we put our migrant workers,
  foreign friends, minorities,
immigrants and wage-slaves, every
  person useful to the state.
Don't forget our allies, either,
  languishing like separate strands.
Bring it all together now, and
  make one giant ball of yarn.
Now you're ready: weave a brand new
  suit for all the citizens.

Magistrate

War is not the same as wool-balls!
  What do women know of war?

Lysistrata

Even more than you do, asshole.
  First of all we make the children,
Then we send them off to war, then—

Magistrate

  That's enough! I take your point.

Lysistrata

What about young wives? They waste their
  prime of life in solitude.
What about the girls who'll grow old
  long before they find a man?

Magistrate

Men get old too.

Lysistrata

That's quite different.
  Men can always get a girl,
even greybeards. Girls don't have that
  luxury. Their time is short.
Men won't marry older girls: they
  pine away in spinsterhood.

Magistrate

Lucky men! For us it's easy:
  all we need is in our pants!

Lysistrata

Time for you to die, old geezer.
Fetch your coffin. Here's a grave-site.

We'll arrange the funeral.
Put a lily in his hand.

Old Woman C
Here's a wreath.

Old Woman A
And here's a bible.

Lysistrata
What are you waiting for? You're dead!
Off to the big bureaucracy in the sky.
You're holding up St. Peter.°

Magistrate
You haven't heard the last of this. Outrageous!
By god, I'll show the other magistrates
exactly what you've done to me. So there!

Lysistrata
I hope you won't complain about your funeral.
We did our best. I tell you what: we'll hold
a proper service at your grave: a dance!

Men's Chorus

Men's Leader
Wake up men, defend our manhood!
  Strip for action! Dance away!

Chorus (5[1])
There's more to this outbreak
  than you might guess:
we're sure that these women
  are terrorists!°

The Spartans have managed
  to infiltrate
our houses and women:
  and next the state!

The citadel-seizure
  we understand:

---

607 'St. Peter': Charon, who ferried the souls of the dead across the underworld River Styx to Hades where the dead were popularly thought to dwell as shades.

619 They accuse the women of the actionable offense of plotting tyranny (1150 n.), that is, of conspiring to change the democratic constitution in order to limit power to certain individuals or groups. Popular politicians frequently implied that their opponents (especially upper-class ones) were potential 'tyrants' in order to distract attention from substantive issues, just as their modern counterparts imply that an opponent is unpatriotic. Aristophanes regularly pokes fun at these techniques in trying to alert the audience to their shallowness and political divisiveness.

They're putting an end to
our pension plan!°

Leader

Outrageous that these women dare to prate
of war and peace and governing the state!
And then they tell us we should make a deal
with Spartans, who are slipperier than an eel!
It's nothing but a plan for tyranny.
While I'm alive they won't do that to me.
I'll fight these women with my dying breath.
For I say, Give me liberty or give me death!°
I'm standing tall, a loyal patriot:
if you don't like it I'll kick you in the butt!

Women's Chorus

Women's Leader

You'll soon be running home to mommy.
Strip for action, girls, and dance!

Chorus (5^2)

A debt to our country
we must repay:
so we've good advice for
you all today.

we're healthy and happy
and well-to-do,
and all our successes
we owe to you.

Our schools and our temples,°
our social lives:

---

625 See 380 n.

633 They quote from a patriotic drinking-song recalling Harmodius and his friend Aristogiton, who assassinated Hipparchus, the brother of the tyrant Hippias (1150 n.) in 514. These two were popularly revered as founding fathers of democracy, but among the educated upper-classes it was said that they were in reality not freedom-fighters but a pair of lovers avenging a personal insult (Thucydides 6.53 ff.).

641 The women claim the right to offer advice because they have managed their households better than the men have managed the city and because they bore the sons who have been sent to war. Here they list city cults connected with the preparation of young girls for domestic management and for child-rearing. These were the old and elite cults of Athena Polias (317 n.) and Artemis of Brauron, which predated the democracy and were run by aristocratic families. The girls who took part, though they represented all Athenian girls, were chosen only from such families. Aristophanes maintains the contrast between the high-born, educated women and the poor, ignorant men.

they all helped to make us
  your perfect wives.

Leader

With good advice we want to pay you back.°
Don't worry that it comes from Jill not Jack.
Consider it on its merits. Anyway,
we bear the children and deserve our say.
What contribution do these old men make?
They never seem to give, but only take.
We pay for all their laws, their wars, their theft.
And they'll keep taking till there's nothing left.
Old men, I warn you: better hold your peace.
You make a sound, we'll kick you in the teeth!

Men's Chorus (6[1])

I've seen a lot of arrogance,
  but this outdoes it all.
We've got to beat them down to size
  if we've still got the balls.

Leader

Take your shirts off, you're not tacos!
  Let them whiff your manly smell!

Chorus

We once were Athenian raiders,°
we dealt mercilessly with traitors.
  Let's do it again,
  pretend we're young men,
not washed-up old alligators!

Leader

We can't afford to let them get the jump,°
for women are a match for any hump.
They might build submarines and strike below:
we wouldn't know just when to expect the blow.
We'd hate to face equestrian encounters,
for women are indomitable mounters.
You'll never shake them off once they get on:

646 For the old men as freeloaders, see 380 n.

666 They continue their recollection of the struggle against tyranny (1150 n.), alluding to the battle of Leipsydrion, where in the period after the murder of Hipparchus (633 n.) the tyrant Hippias besieged his opponents. After a hard fight Hippias defeated them, but their exploit was later celebrated in a patriotic song. The old men here seem to have got their history wrong, speaking as if they had been the victors, as in the action against Cleomenes (274 n.).

672 Sailing and horsemanship were very commonly used for sexual metaphors and jokes.

just look at pictures of the Amazons!°
We must move now to make their plot a wreck,
so let's move out and grab them by the neck!

Women's Chorus (6^2)

Go on and get our fire going,
  and pull the bitch's tail!
Then all your buddies get to hear
  how loud you weep and wail.

Leader

Take your skirts off, don't be modest!
  Let them whiff an angry sow!

Chorus

We wait for the note of your clarion,
you nattering octogenarian!
  Just give us a chance
  to pull down your pants
and deliver your balls by caesarean.°

Leader

And anyway your efforts are for naught:
the wives are carrying out a foolproof plot.
Pass all the laws you want and call for war:
the decent folks will only hate you more.
Just yesterday I had a picnic planned
for a lovely visitor from a foreign land,
in fact a pot of Theban caviar!°
But nothing doing: that's against your law.
You'll keep on regulating us, no doubt,
till someone picks you up and throws you out.

SCENE III

Hail, leader of our common enterprise!
But why emerge? How come you look so sad?

Lysistrata

The wives reveal their baseness and grow weak.
It's got me down, I don't know what to do.

---

679 The Amazons were mythical women who fought like men and long ago, in the time of the legendary Athenian King Theseus, had invaded Athens and occupied the citadel. This incident was the subject of a well-known public mural by the painter Micon.

695 The old women allude to midwifery, a usual occupation of their age-group, and to a fable in which the lowly beetle avenges the loss of its young by breaking the eagle's eggs (here metaphorical for testicles).

702 They had invited 'a lovely well-bred girl—an eel from Thebes' (36 n.).

Leader

What's that you say?

Lysistrata

It's true, it's true.

Leader

Let's hear it all: we're friends that you can trust.

Lysistrata

A shame to speak but risky to keep quiet.

Leader

Don't hide a crisis that affects us all!

Lysistrata

I'll make it short: they're dying to get laid.

Leader

Oh gods!

Lysistrata

I doubt the gods can get us out of this.
I certainly can't keep on withholding wives
from husbands: they're determined to escape.
I caught one by that grotto with a shovel,
scraping away and widening her hole.
Another one was climbing on that pulley,
pulling herself off. And another one
got on a giant bird, said 'take me to
a whorehouse!'° Luckily I grabbed her hair.
And every excuse for going home there is,
they make. I think that's one of them right now.
Hey you, where to?

Wife A

I've got to run back home.
My bolts of woolen cloth, the finest kind,
are very much in need of moth-balls.

Lysistrata

Moth-balls?
Get back in there!

Wife

I swear I'll come right back.
Just let me spread my wool out on the bed.

---

725 'To Orsilochus' house': he was apparently a pimp, and the name (which suggests erection) may be his trade-name: another pimp, whose real name was Philostratus, is referred to in 957 as 'Dogfox'.

Lysistrata
You won't be spreading anything, nor be leaving.

Wife
But then my wool will go to waste!

Lysistrata
So be it.

Wife B
Oh stupid me, forgetting to tenderize
the meat. I've got to go and beat it.

Lysistrata
Here's
another who forgot to beat her meat.
Get back inside!

Wife
I swear I'll be right back.
Just let me roll it in my hands a bit.

Lysistrata
No! Keep your hands to yourself. If you do this,
then all the wives will want to do the same.

Wife C
O Goddess of Labor, hold my pains a while,
till I can get to a proper birthing place!°

Lysistrata
What's all this yelling?

Wife
I'm having a baby now!

Lysistrata
But yesterday you were skinny.

Wife
Not today.
I've got to see the doctor, dear Lysistrata:
please send me home.

Lysistrata
Let's have a look at you.
What's this? It sounds like metal.

Wife
It's a boy!

---

743 Childbirth in sanctuaries (like the Acropolis) was ritually forbidden.

Lysistrata

I'd swear you've got some hollow metal thing
beneath your dress. Let's pull it up and see.
You card! You've got Athena's helmet there!°
Are you still pregnant?

Wife

Yes indeed I am.

Lysistrata

Then what's the helmet for?

Wife

In case the baby
comes while I'm still here. Then I'd deliver it
into the helmet, like a nesting bird.

Lysistrata

Preposterous, an obvious excuse.
You'll have to exercise the nesting option.

Wife C

I can't get any sleep here on the citadel,
not since I saw the Goddess' sacred snake!

Wife D

I can't sleep either. I toss and turn all night,
what with the hooting of the sacred owls.

Lysistrata

Enough! I won't hear any more excuses!
You miss your husbands, fine. But don't you know
they miss you too? I'm sure the nights they spend
are miserably lonely. Please hold out,
please bear with me a little while longer.
I've got a prophecy here predicting victory,°
provided we stay together. Want to hear it?

Wife A

Let's hear the prophecy.

---

751 The helmet on the great chryselephantine statue of Athena Promachos in the Parthenon, another part of the Periclean building program (317 n.) and therefore associated with the democracy and its war-policy.

767 Oracles and prophecies, written in archaic language and verse, were very popular (especially during the war) and were often used by politicians to enhance their platforms, much as polls and other statistical 'predictors' are today. Educated people like Aristophanes scoffed at prophecies and considered those who used them to be demogogues and those who trusted them to be gullible. Thus Lysistrata is not consistently above using demagogic tactics. The dumb wives are an appropriate audience: Aristophanes implies that any spectators who believe such appeals are as gullible as these wives.

Lysistrata

Be quiet then.
Yea, when the birds shall hole up in a single place,
fleeing the eagles and keeping themselves quite chaste,
then shall their problems be solved, they'll be on top,
so says the King of the Gods—

Wife B

We'll be on top?

Lysistrata

But: if the birds start to argue and fly away
down from the citadel holy, all will say:
no bird more disgusting and shameless lives today!

Wife

A pretty explicit prophecy. My god!

Lysistrata

So let's hear no more talk of backing out.
We'll all go back inside, for what a shame,
dear friends, if we betray the prophecy.

Men's Chorus (7[1])

I want to tell you all a tale.
  I heard it as a lad.
Once there was a man called Black,°
  who lived as a nomad.
A faithful dog his company,
  he hunted and he roamed,
he made his nets and set his traps
  but never would go home.

Because he hated women so,
  and that's where he was wise.
We follow Black's example in
  that women we despise!

Men's Leader

How about a kiss, old ghoul?

Women's Leader

Wash your mouth out first, you fool!

Men's Leader

I've got something for you here.

---

784 Melanion was a mythological figure who resembled Hippolytus (the hero of Euripides' play), being a lone hunter devoted to a virgin goddess (Atalanta who in another tradition was his bride).

Women's Leader

All I see is pubic hair.

Men's Leader

That's right, I'm bushy down below.
But manly men are always so!°
Whenever I display my buns,
the enemy drops his spear and runs!

Women's Chorus (7^2)

Our hero answers all your tales
  about that other dope.
His name was Timon° and he was
  a total misanthrope.

He wandered in the mountains too,
  and acted very mean.
If anybody crossed his path
  he'd pick their carcass clean.

He couldn't stand men's evil ways,
  but women he enjoyed.°
We too stand up for principles,
  of which you are devoid.

Women's Leader

You want me to re-do your nose?

Men's Leader

No way, it doesn't need your blows.

Women's Leader

So what about a stomping, then?

Men's Leader

Your bush resembles a pig-pen.

Women's Leader

You liar! That's a blatant slander!
Just go ahead and take a gander:

---

801 He mentions two dead generals, Myronides and Phormion, who were heroes of the democracy and were remembered as tough commanders.

807 Timon of Athens, probably legendary, was the archetypal misanthrope (a man who becomes fed up with society and deserts it) and inspired a long-lived literary and dramatic type. In recent years the fantasy of simply 'dropping out' (encouraged by the long war) had inspired several plays on this theme, including Aristophanes' *Birds*. A new example that has come to light in recent times is the fourth-century play *Dyskolos* ('The Grouch') by Menander.

816 The women embroider their version of Timon's story, for he is elsewhere portrayed as hating women as well as men.

my hair may be as white as snow,
but I keep myself well-groomed below.

SCENE IV

Lysistrata

Hey, women, women, come and take a look!
Come quick!

Wife

What's happening? What's the fuss about?

Lysistrata

A man is coming. By the look of him
he's suffering from satyriasis.
O Goddess of Love and Pangs of Sweet Desire,
make this man's journey straight and very upright!

Wife

Where is he, whoever it is?

Lysistrata

He's by that cave.

Wife

I see him now! Who is he?

Lysistrata

Anyone know?

Myrrhine

Oh god, I do! That's my own husband, Rod!°

Lysistrata

You've got to light his fire, get him hot,
do everything that turns him on, except
the thing you're under oath not to. OK?

Myrrhine

Don't worry, I can do it.

Lysistrata

Very well.
While you get ready I'll try to get *him* ready
and warm him up a bit. Now out of sight!

Rod

O woe is me! I've got a terrible cramp!
It's like I'm being broken on the rack!

Lysistrata

Who enters our defense perimeter?

---

838 In Greek the name is Kinesias of Paionidai, punning on *kinein* ('screw') and *paiein* ('bang').

Rod

Me.

Lysistrata

A man?

Rod

Just look!

Lysistrata

In that case please depart.

Rod

Who's telling me to leave?

Lysistrata

The daytime guard.

Rod

I've come for Myrrhine. Tell her that I'm here!

Lysistrata

You give me orders? Who do you think you are?

Rod

Her husband, Rodney Balling, from Bangtown.

Lysistrata

A lovely name! You know, we consider it
our very favorite topic of conversation.
Your wife has little else upon her lips.
She'll eat bananas, or a peanut, sighing,
'If only this were really Balling!'

Rod

God!

Lysistrata

Yes sir! And any time the conversation turns
to men, your wife speaks up forthwith and says,
'Compared to Balling, nothing else exists!'

Rod

Please, call her out!

Lysistrata

Got anything for me?

Rod

Indeed I do. You're very welcome, too.
What's mine is yours. How's this? It's what I've got.

Lysistrata

I think I'll call your wife. Hold on.

Rod

Be quick!
I have no joy or pleasure in my life
since my Myrrhine up and left the house.
I open up the door and start to cry,
it looks so empty! Then I try to eat,
but I can hardly taste the food. I'm horny!

Myrrhine

I love him dearly, but he doesn't want
to love me back! Don't make me see him! Please!

Rod

Oh Pussikins, my darling, what's the matter?
Come down here!

Myrrhine

I'm not coming anywhere!

Rod

You won't obey me when I say to come?

Myrrhine

I fail to see a reason for your summons.

Rod

A reason? Don't you see what shape I'm in?

Myrrhine

Goodbye.

Rod

No, wait! Perhaps you'll want to hear
from Junior. Come on, yell for mommy, kid.

Baby

Mommy! Mommy! Mommy!

Rod

Well, what's the matter? Don't you pity him?
You know he's been six days without your breasts!

Myrrhine

I feel for Junior, but it's very clear
you don't.

Rod

Get down here, woman, and see your child!

Myrrhine

O motherhood, what a drag! I'll be right down.

Rod
She seems much sexier and even younger
than I remember. Very tasty looking!
She acted tough, and very haughty too,
but that just makes me want her even more!

Myrrhine
Poor sweetie pie! With such a lousy father.
I'll kiss and cuddle you, my darling child.

Rod
The hell you think you're doing, listening to
those women? You only piss me off and hurt
yourself as well.

Myrrhine
Don't lay your hands on me!

Rod
You know our home's an utter mess. You just
let everything go.

Myrrhine
It doesn't bother me.

Rod
It doesn't bother you that all your clothes
were dragged away by chickens?

Myrrhine
Not at all.

Rod
And worse, your sacred duty as my mate
has been neglected! Thus you must return.

Myrrhine
I'm going nowhere till you swear on oath
to vote to end the war.

Rod
I'll maybe do that,
if it's appropriate.

Myrrhine
Then maybe I'll go home,
if it's appropriate. But now I'm sworn to stay.

Rod
OK, at least lie down with me awhile.

Myrrhine
I won't. But I don't say I wouldn't like to.

Rod
You would? Then why not do it, pussy mine?

Myrrhine
Oh really, Rod, in front of Junior here?

Rod
Of course not. Nurse, take Junior home at once.
All right, the kid's no longer in our way.
Let's do it!

Myrrhine
Do it where, you silly man?
It's public here!

Rod
You're right. Hey, there's a cave.

Myrrhine
I must be pure to re-enter the citadel.°

Rod
Then purify yourself in the sacred spring there.

Myrrhine
But what about my oath? I won't be perjured.

Rod
A women's oath means nothing. I'm not worried.

Myrrhine
Well, let me get a bed.

Rod
But I don't need one:
the ground's OK by me.

Myrrhine
I wouldn't dream
of making you lie there (though you deserve it).

Rod
She really loves me, that's quite obvious.

Myrrhine
Your bed, sir. Lie right down, I'll tuck you in.
But I forgot, what is it, yes, a mattress.

---

912 Sexual intercourse, like childbirth (742 n.), was forbidden in sanctuaries, and even wives who had not douched in running water after intercourse might pollute a sanctuary.

Rod

A mattress? None for me, thanks.

Myrrhine

I'm uncomfortable
on box-springs.

Rod

Give me just a little kiss?

Myrrhine

OK.

Rod

Oh lordy! Get the mattress quick!

Myrrhine

And here it is. Stay down while I undress.
But I forget, what is it, yes, a pillow.

Rod

But I'm all set, I need no pillow.

Myrrhine

I do.

Rod

It's like a restaurant where they serve no food.°

Myrrhine

Lift up, now, up. Well, now I think I'm set.

Rod

I know I am! Come here to papa, darling!

Myrrhine

I'm taking off my bra. But don't forget,
don't lie to me about your vote for peace.

Rod

May lightning strike me!

Myrrhine

You don't have a blanket.

Rod

It's not a blanket I want! I want to get fucked!

Myrrhine

That's just what's going to happen. Back in a flash.

---

928 'This cock of mine is like Heracles cheated of his supper.' The he-man hero Heracles was portrayed in myths as having a giant appetite for food and sex and getting into many embarrassing situations as a result.

Rod
That woman drives me nuts with all her bedding.

Myrrhine
Get up now.

Rod
But I've already got it up!

Myrrhine
You want some perfume?

Rod
Thank you, no, I don't.

Myrrhine
But I do, if it's all the same to you.

Rod
Then get the goddamned perfume. Holy Zeus!

Myrrhine
Hold out your hand. And save a bit for me.

Rod
I don't like perfume as a general rule,
unless it smells like love is in the air.

Myrrhine
Oh silly me, I must have brought Brand X.°

Rod
No, wait, I like it!

Myrrhine
You're just being polite.

Rod
God damn the guy who first invented perfume!

Myrrhine
I found some good stuff. Here's the tube.

Rod
Here's mine!
Come on now, let's lie down, there's nothing more
to fetch.

Myrrhine
You're right, I will, I'll be right there.
I'm taking off my shoes. Remember, dear,
your promise to vote for peace.

944 'Brand X': perfume from Rhodes, one of the allies that had defected after the Sicilian disaster and whose perfume may have been an inferior product.

Rod

I surely will.
Where are you? Hey Myrrhine! Where's my pussikins?
She pumped me up and dropped me flat. I'm ruined!

Duet

What'll I do? No one to screw![o]
I've lost the sexiest girl I knew.
My cock is an orphan,
it couldn't be worse.
I'll just have to get him[o]
a practical nurse.

Men's Leader

Frightful deceit! Pity on you!
We cannot imagine what to do.
What balls can endure
being treated this way,
without any chance of
an actual lay?

Rod

Oh god, the cramps attack anew!

Leader

A dirty bitch did this to you!

Rod

Oh no, she's really sweet and kind.

Leader

That bitch? You must have lost your mind!

Rod

You're right, a bitch
is what she is!
I'll put a curse
upon that miz!

I pray for a tornado,
with lightning bolts and all,
to lift her into heaven
and then to let her fall.

Way down and down she's falling,
above a giant rock.

---

954 This duet parodies the high pathos of tragic laments in its rhythm and music, but the obscene language and the ludicrous predicament lamented are purely comic.

957 See 725 n.

And when she's almost on it,
  I pray she hits my cock!

Spartan Herald
Direct me, please, to party headquarters.
Where are your commissars? You please will speak.

Rod
The hell are you? A man or a Freudian nightmare?°

Spartan Herald
I'm Herald from Sparta, you very cute young man.°
I come with orders to propose a treaty.

Rod
Then why have you got that tommy-gun in there?

Spartan Herald
Is not a weapon.

Rod
Turn around, let's see.
What's pushing out your trousers? What's in there,
your lunch-box?

Spartan Herald
This young man is obviously
intoxicated.

Rod
That's a hard-on, rogue!

Spartan Herald
Do not be silly, please: is no such thing.

Rod
Then what do you call that?

Spartan Herald
Is my attache case.°

Rod
If that's the case, then I've got one just like it.
But let's come clean, OK? I know what's up.
How fare you all in happy Sparta, sir?

Spartan Herald
Not well. The comrades rise, also the allies.

---

982 'or a Konisalos,' a phallic demon worshipped in Spartan territories.

982 According to Athenian humorists, Spartans were fond of anal intercourse with women and with adult men, both of which were distasteful to Athenians. Aristophanes keeps up this motif throughout the following scenes with Spartans.

991 'attache case': the Spartan 'dispatch-stick' (skytale), which was wrapped with leather strips containing coded messages and thus resembled the comic phallos.

We all have hard-on. Have a pussy shortage.

Rod

What's wrong? Some difficulty with your five
year plan?

Spartan Herald

Oh no, was dissidents. Was Lampito.
She lead the women comrades in a plot.
They take an oath of solidarity,
keep men away from warm and furry place.

Rod

What happened?

Spartan Herald

Now we suffer! Walk around
like men with hernia problem,° all bent over.
The women won't permit to touch the pussy,
till each and every party member swear
to make bilateral disarmament.

Rod

So this is global, a vast conspiracy
devised by women! Now I see it all!
Go quickly back to Sparta for the truce.
Arrange to send ambassadors with full powers.
And I will so instruct our leaders here,
to name ambassadors. I'll show them this!°

Spartan Herald

I fly away. You offer good advice.

Choral Dialogue

Men's Leader

No animal exists more stubborn than a woman.
Not even fire, nor any panther, is quite as shameless.

Women's Leader

You seem to understand this, but still you keep on fighting.
It's possible, bad man, to have our lasting friendship.

Men's Leader

I'll never cease to loathe the female sex!

Women's Leader

That's up to you, I guess. But meanwhile I don't like
the sight of you undressed. Just look at you, how silly!
I simply must come over and put your shirt back on.

1003 'like lampbearers,' who had to bend over to keep the wind from extinguishing the flame.
1012 'this': he flourishes his phallos.

Men's Leader

By god, I'd have to say that's no bad thing you did.
And now I'm sorry I took it off before, in anger.

Women's Leader

And now you look like a man again, and not so comic.
And if you hadn't been so hostile, I'd have removed
that bug in your eye, which I can see is still in there.

Men's Leader

So that's what's been rubbing me the wrong way. Here's my ring.
Please dig it out of my eye, and then I want to see it.
By god, that thing's been biting at my eye a long time.

Women's Leader

You're very welcome. Stand still! What a grumpy man!
Great gods, it's huge, a genuinely king-sized gnat.
And there it comes. Look at it. Isn't it Brobdingnagian?°

Men's Leader

You've helped me out a lot. That thing's been digging wells.
And now that it's removed, my eyes are streaming tears.

Women's Leader

There, there, you naughty man, I'll wipe your tears away,
and kiss you.

Men's Leader

I don't want a kiss!

Women's Leader

I'll kiss you anyway!

Men's Leader

You got me, damn you. Women know how to get what they want.
That ancient adage puts it well and sums it up:
women are bad, you can't live with 'em, you can't live without 'em.
But now let's have a truce. We promise never again
to flout you; and you promise never again to hit us.
So now let's get together and sing a happy song!

Chorus (8^{1})

No citizen need fear from us°
the slightest castigation.

1032 'Trikorysian,' characteristic of a swampy region near Marathon (285 n.) where insects must have been large and numerous.

1045 At this point in a comedy the chorus, which has dropped the special identity it had during its active involvement in the plot, often sings free-form abusive songs about individual spectators. Here, in line with the play's theme of reconciliation, the chorus eschews such abuse. An additional reason may well have been Aristophanes' fear of ruffling too many feathers at an unusually tense time.

In recent times we've had our fill
  of trial and tribulation.

Instead , if any man and wife
  should need some extra dough,
we'll gladly let you have what's in
  our piggy banks at home.

And when the war is over with,
  don't bother to repay,
for what we have to loan you now
  is nothing anyway.

Chorus (8^2)

Tomorrow night we'll have a feast,
  a real celebrity ball.
We'll roast a pig and make some soup:
  we'll have enough for all.
So get up early, bathe the kids,
  and bathe yourselves as well.
Then come on over, walk right in:
  you needn't ring the bell.

Then straight on to the dining room,
  as if it were your own.
We'll treat you just as you'd treat us:
  there'll be nobody home.

SCENE V

Chorus Leader

Here they come, ambassadors from
  Sparta. Look, I see their beards.
What's around their waists? They might be
  wearing pig-pens under there.

Ambassadors from Sparta, first: our greetings.
Then tell us, please, what seems to be the matter?

Spartan Ambassador

No use to waste a lot of time describing.
Is best to show condition we are in.

Leader

Oh my! Your problem's big and very hard.
It looks to me like runaway inflation.

Spartan Ambassador

Unspeakable. What can one say? We wish

to talk of peace on any reasonable terms.

Leader

And now I see our own ambassadors.
They look like wrestlers hunkered down like that.
Their pants appear to walk ahead of them.
They suffer from a dislocated boner.

Athenian Ambassador

Can anyone direct me to Lysistrata?
It's obvious we need to find her fast.

Leader

Their syndrome seems to be the same as *theirs.*
These spasms: are they worse in the wee hours?

Athenian Ambassador

They're always bad and getting even badder!
Unless we get a treaty pretty quick,
we'll have to start resorting to each other!°

Leader

You'll cover up, if you've got any sense.
Some fundamentalist° might chop it off.

Athenian Ambassador

God, yes, good thinking.

Spartan Ambassador

Da, is very straight
advice. Come on, let's pull the trousers up.

Athenian Ambassador

So: greetings, Spartans. Shameful situation!

1092 'resort to Cleisthenes,' who for some reason was perennially mocked by comic poets for submitting to anal penetration. Such a charge, if it could be established in the eyes of a jury, could result in the accused losing his citizen rights. Apparently no one had so accused Cleisthenes or been able to convince a jury, but there must have been gossip and comic poets evidently felt safe in exploiting it for this kind of off-hand mockery.

1094 'fundamentalist': 'one of the hermocopidae (Hermes-choppers), an allusion to a notorious incident that occurred just before the Sicilian Expedition sailed in 415. One morning, Athenians discovered that during the previous night the streetside statues of Hermes (patron god of travellers), a common sight all over Athens, had been vandalized by defacement. Some of the statues had phalloi and these had been knocked off. The authorities rounded up the 'usual suspects' (men known to have anti-democratic or anti-war sympathies), but the Athenians were never satisfied that all those responsible had been identified, and the whole incident remained a mystery. The bearded and ithyphallic men in our scene reminded Aristophanes of Hermes, and he insinuates that some of the 'choppers' may be among the spectators.

Spartan Ambassador

Da, comrade, terrible, but would be worse,
if decadent religious ones had seen us.

Athenian Ambassador

All right then, Spartans, time to play our cards.
The reason for your visit?

Spartan Ambassador

Negotiation
for peace.

Athenian Ambassador

That's very good. We want the same.
So now we've got to call Lysistrata,
for she alone can be our arbitrator.

Spartan Ambassador

Lysistratos, Lysistrata, whoever.

Athenian Ambassador

It doesn't look as if we need to call her.
She must have heard us: here she comes herself.

Leader

Hail the bravest of all women!
  Now you must be more besides:
Firm but soft, high-class but low-brow,
  Strict but lenient, versatile.

Delegates from every city,
  captured by your potent charms,
Come before you and request your
  arbitration of their cause.

Lysistrata

My task will not be difficult, since they're all
aroused and not at one another's throats.
How ripe are they? Where's Reconciliation?°
Take hold of the Spartans first, and bring them here.
Be gentle with your hand and don't pull hard,
don't grab and yank the way men handle women,
but use a woman's touch, like home sweet home.
They won't extend a hand? Go farther down.

1114 Reconciliation is personified by a naked girl (that is, a male actor so costumed). She provides comic relief, in the form of lewd asides, during Lysistrata's earnest speeches and creates opportunity for by-play, being used as a map of Greece during the negotiations. Aristophanes typically portrays peace in terms of sensory enjoyments (food, drink, sex and festivals).

Now do the same for our Athenians.
Whatever they extend, take hold of that.
Now, men of Sparta, stand here on my left,
and you stand on my right. Both parties listen.
I'm female, yes, but still I've got a brain.
I'm not so badly off for judgment, either.
My father and some other elders, too,
have given me a first-rate education.
In no uncertain terms I must reproach you,°
both sides, and rightly. Don't you share a cup
at common altars, for common gods, like brothers,
at the Olympic games, Thermophylai and Delphi?
I needn't list the many, many others.
The world is full of foreigners you could fight,
but it's Greek men and cities you destroy!
And that's the first reproach I have for you.

Spartan Ambassador

My hard-on's absolutely killing me!

Lysistrata

Now, Spartans, my next reproach is aimed at you.
You must remember, not so long ago,°

1128 Lysistrata's arguments in the following speeches are, after we allow for comic exaggeration, essentially the ones that anti-war groups in fact advanced: let Greeks fight not Greeks but Asian foreigners, our traditional enemies; let us return to the pre-war arrangement, when Athens and Sparta enjoyed peaceful relations and joint hegemony in Greece, and when both gloriously resisted foreign interference in Europe; remember the mutual good deeds of the past. Comic poets, in the context of festive good feeling and nostalgia, could advance such appeals more easily than could politicians or generals.
Reference to 'foreigners' has an implication that would have made the Athenians feel self-righteous. The Spartans had, since the Sicilian disaster, been getting financial assistance from Persia. The Athenians, on the other hand, had for at least three years been supporting rebels against the Persian King. Aristophanes does not stress this potential slur against the Spartans because his main concern is to make an effective case for renewed peace with them. Only after this play was performed did Aristophanes and his audience learn that some of their own leaders had been negotiating secretly with the Persians for financial assistance.

1138 The great earthquake that devastated Sparta in 464 was followed by a revolt of Sparta's subject populations: helots (public slaves) and Messenians. The rebels fortified themselves on Mount Ithome, and the Spartans appealed for help from their allies, including Athens. The Athenians were divided: the radical democrats (the young Pericles among them) wanted to refuse the request, the conservative democrats wanted to honor it. The latter finally prevailed, sending their leader Cimon with a large army to Sparta. As a result of political infighting on both sides, the Spartans soon sent Cimon home in disgrace, and he was expelled from Athens the following year. This incident was a milestone in Athenian-Spartan enmity and strengthened anti-Spartan feeling at Athens. Here Lysistrata , with a good deal of rhetorical exaggeration, blames the 'Spartans' for starting the feud, but at the same time urges that the damage be put right by returning to the policy of Cimon.

you sent a man to Athens begging us,
on bended knee and whiter than a ghost,
to send an army? All your slaves were up
in arms when that big earthquake hit you.
We sent you help, four thousand infantry,
a force that saved your entire country for you.
And now you pay the Athenians back by ravaging
their country, after all they did for yours?

Athenian Ambassador

That's right, Lysistrata, they're in the wrong!

Spartan Ambassador

We're wrong: but take a look at that sweet ass!

Lysistrata

Do you Athenians think I'll let you off?
You must remember, not so long ago,°
when you wore rags, oppressed by tyranny,
and Spartans routed the army of occupation,
destroying the tyrant's men and all his allies,
and drove them out on a single glorious day,
and set you free, and then replaced your rags
with clothes befitting democratic people?

Spartan Ambassador

I never saw so well-endowed a woman!

Athenian Ambassador

I never saw a better-looking pussy!

1150 With parallel exaggeration (1138 n.), Lysistrata portrays the Athenian tyranny (concentration of power in one family through its alliances with other families) as a monstrously oppressive regime whose end was the beginning of the democracy: in this she caters to popular belief (274 n.). In reality, the period of tyranny in Athens was productive and prosperous and had proto-democratic features. Real democracy was not established upon the fall of the tyranny but only gradually in the course of the following half-century. The last Athenian tyrant was Hippias. After the assassination of his brother in 514 (633 n.), Hippias' rule became oppressive, and he had to exile many rivals for power, among them the Alcmaeonidae clan (maternal family of Pericles and Alcibiades, powerful advocates of the present war). The first attempt of the exiles to overthrow Hippias, at Leipsydrion (666 n.), was a failure, but by 510 the Spartans had come in on their side. In that year a Spartan land force under Cleomenes (see 274 n.) routed the Thessalian supporters of Hippias and besieged the tyrant's men on the Acropolis . After a two-day siege they escaped, never to return. A century later, opinions differed about who had had the most to do with liberation from Hippias' rule. Those who supported the war argued that it was the Alcmaeonidai; those who urged peace stressed the Spartan assistance.

Lysistrata

Considering all these mutual benefactions,
why prosecute the war and make more trouble?
Why not make peace? What keeps you still apart?

Spartan Ambassador

We must demand this promontory here°
return to us.

Lysistrata

Which one?

Spartan Ambassador

This one in back:
we count on having, we can almost feel it.

Athenian Ambassador

By the God of Earthquakes, that you'll never get!

Lysistrata

You'll give it up, sir.

Athenian Ambassador

What do *we* get, then?

Lysistrata

You'll ask for something that's of equal value.

Athenian Ambassador

Let's see now, I know, give us first of all
the furry triangle here, the gulf that runs
behind it, also the two connecting legs.

Spartan Ambassador

My dear ambassador, you want it all!

Lysistrata

You'll give it. Don't be squabbling over legs.

Athenian Ambassador

I'm set to strip and do a little ploughing!

Spartan Ambassador

Me first: before one ploughs one spreads manure!

Lysistrata

When peace is made you'll both do all you want.

1162 The places mentioned during the negotiations had actually been captured during the war and might have been mentioned were real negotiations held. But they were chosen primarily as having sexual double meanings that could be illustrated by reference to Reconciliation's naked body (1114 n.): Pylos ('gate' = anus); Echinous ('sea-urchin' = pubic hair); the Melian Gulf (vagina); the Megarian Walls (legs). According to stereotype, the Spartans like the rear end (982 n.) and the Athenians the other, so that the settlement is satisfactory.

For now, are each of these items to your liking?
If so you'd best confer with all your allies.

Athenian Ambassador

Confer with allies? Too hard up for that.
They'll go along with us. I'm sure they're just
as anxious to start fucking.

Spartan Ambassador

Also ours,
is certain.

Athenian Ambassador

Every Greek is fond of fucking.

Lysistrata

You argue well. And now for ratification.
The women on the citadel will host
the banquet, for we brought our picnic boxes.
You'll swear your oaths and make your pledges there.
And then let everybody take his wife
and go on home.°

Athenian Ambassador

What are we waiting for?

Spartan Ambassador

Please, lead the way.

Athenian Ambassador

You'd best start running them!

Chorus (8^{3})

Fine gowns, embroidered shawls, kid gloves,
and lots of golden rings:
if you've a debutante at home,
you needn't buy these things.

We've got a closet in the house,
we've got a jewelry box.
They're neither of them sealed so tight
we couldn't pick the locks.

1186 Apparently Lysistrata's last words in the play: her plan has been a success and all that remains of the plot is the celebration, which typically ends an Old Comedy, and the men's promise to be better in the future. For these Lysistrata is not needed. In *Assemblywomen*, Aristophanes similarly abandons a heroine when the plot no longer needs her. An early disappearance of the main character, however, would violate a modern audience's sense of theatrical symmetry. For possible solutions to this problem see 1273 n.

So come around, feel free to take
whatever you can find.
But you won't find much unless you have
a sharper eye than mine.

Chorus (8^4)

All those with many mouths to feed
but nothing to provide:
we bought a peck of wheat and made
some bread to put aside.

So anyone who's poor can bring
a basket or a tray.
We've told our slaves to fetch the bread
and give it all away.

One thing we should have told you first:
you can't get near the door.
We've got a giant doberman
who doesn't like the poor.

SCENE VI

Athenian Ambassador

Open up the gate you!° Should have got out of my way!
You slaves, quit loafing. How'd you like your hair
burned off? Slave-beating: what a stale routine!
Director, I won't do it. Ask the audience?
All right, to please you I'll go through with it.

Athenian

We're right behind you, glad to help you out.
Get lost, you slaves! Your hair's in serious danger!

Athenian Ambassador

Get lost: we'd like the Spartans to depart
from their banquet without stumbling over you.

Athenian

I've never seen a banquet quite like this.
The Spartans were delightful company.
And we were pretty clever over drinks.

Athenian Ambassador

That's right. You can't be clever when you're sober.
I'm going to propose new legislation,

1216 A comic reversal of the previous action, when men tried to break into, not out of, the Acropolis .

that diplomats conduct their business drunk.
As things now stand, we go to Sparta sober,
then look for ways to stir up lots of trouble.
And so whatever they say we never hear it,
but hunt for hidden meaning in what they don't say,
and then make contradictory reports.
But now we're straightened out. If someone made
a toast to workers rather than to profits,°
we cheered him anyway and raised our glasses.
What's this? Those slaves are coming back again.
We told you: bugger off, you whipping posts!

Athenian

That's right: the Spartans are emerging now.

Spartan Ambassador

Comrade musician, ready the Spartan bagpipes.
For now I dance and sing a happy song
to honor jointly both our superpowers.

Athenian Ambassador

A splendid treat: some genuine Spartan music!
I love to see you Spartans sing and dance.

Spartan Ambassador

Holy Memory, reveal°
  the glory days of yore:
how Spartans and Athenians
  won the Persian war.

Athens met them on the sea,
  and Sparta held the land,
although the Persian forces were
  more numerous than sand.

All the gods that helped us then,°
  we bid you visit us again,
to help us celebrate our peace
  and see that it will never cease.

Now let mutual friendship reign,
  let's never fight a war again.

1237 Choosing and singing the appropriate song at a banquet was an important social grace. At a diplomatic banquet the songs might have political significance: here the mood was so jovial that even provocative choices were not considered offensive.

1248 The Spartan Ambassador recollects two great battles of 480: the Athenian naval victory at Artemisium and the heroic stand of 300 Spartans under Leonidas against superior Persian forces at Thermopylae.

Put a stop to competition,
  end all mutual suspicion.

Hear our prayer, gods, loud and clear.
  Witness what we promise here.

Athenian Ambassador

Well, now that everything has turned out well,°
reclaim your wives here, Spartans. These are yours,
Athenians. Every husband join his wife,
and wife her husband. Then let's have a dance
and ask the gods to bless us, promising
never again to make the same mistakes.

Form up the dance, the Graces call,
summon Apollo, who heals us all,
Artemis his twin sister too,
Bacchos with his maenad crew,
Father Zeus with lightning crowned,
Hera, Zeus' wife renowned.
Summon every force above,
join us in our dance of love,
peace and freedom are at hand,
thanks to Aphrodite's plan!

Chorus

What can we say?
horray, horray!
We also pray
you liked the play!

Athenian Ambassador

Hey Spartan, what about another song?

Spartan Ambassador

To Sparta, Muse, my song will roam,
where Apollo has his southern home,
where Athena's house has brazen portals,
where Zeus' twin sons, knights immortal,
gallop by Eurotas River,
setting Spartan hearts aquiver,

1262 He invokes Artemis Agrotera, worshiped both at Sparta and at Athens, where her birthday had come to commemorate the victory at Marathon (285 n.).

1273 In the original performance, the Athenian Ambassador made this speech and sang the following song (to match his Spartan counterpart); meanwhile Lysistrata escorted the wives from the citadel and stood Athena-like in the gateway, above and behind the action. A modern director, however, may prefer to have Lysistrata take this part in order to involve the heroine more prominently in the finale.

where heavenly dancers leap and shout,
like colts the maidens frisk about,
raising dust, tossing their manes,
possessed by Bacchus, all insane,
led by Zeus' holy child,
Helen, women's nonpareil.

Hold your hair up with your hand,
beat your feet throughout the land,
help the dancers make some noise,
sing a song of joyous praise
for Athena of Athens, for Spartan Athena
of the House of Bronze!

Aristophanes' Clouds

The Play

Clouds is a comedy about the revolutionary social, intellectual and educational changes that characterized the Athenian enlightenment of the late fifth century and that would profoundly shape the subsequent course of Western history. At its center is the immortal philosopher, Socrates (469-399), 46 years old at the time of *Clouds* and 24 years away from the trial in which he would be condemned to death by his fellow citizens for corrupting the young, failure to believe in the national gods, introducing new gods, and investigating 'the things above and below the earth.' In *Clouds* Socrates is portrayed as the quintessential sophist, or expert in arcane knowledge and techniques, who runs an educational cult (the 'Thinkery') for young men wishing to learn the latest scientific lore and rhetorical skills in order to achieve fame, power and wealth. In the Thinkery are two Arguments: the Better, an old gentleman who represents traditional customs, beliefs and virtues, and the Worse, a young dandy who advocates the techniques of unscrupulous self-promotion and the desirability of selfish hedonism. In the play, Socrates, the Worse Argument and their patron goddesses, the Clouds, join forces to destroy a father and his son, who had unwisely sought dishonest wisdom.

Clouds is both a hilarious comedy of generational conflict and a profound exploration of some of the most fundamental conflicts in Western culture: belief versus reason, nature versus culture, religion versus science, the community versus the individual, the proper content and purpose of education. It also contains a priceless portrait of one of the most gifted and influential men in history, a man otherwise known only from the adulatory writings of such pupils as Plato and Xenophon. Aristophanes' portrait, written from the perspective of a popular humorist of traditional bent, is often in fascinating disagreement with that of the philosophers. But in default of any surviving 'objective' evidence or any writings by Socrates himself, we must treat both the comic and the philosophical portraits as valid reactions, each in its own way. After all, Aristophanes' portrait proved trenchant enough that Plato, in his *Apology*, called it the most important single factor in the people's readiness to condemn Socrates 24 years later.

Clouds was originally produced at the Greater Dionysia in 423 BC, but placed third and last (Cratinus, whom Aristophanes had ridiculed as a washed-up old drunk, won the first prize). This defeat—Aristophanes' first after an initial string of victories—hurt and angered Aristophanes, for in the following year he called *Clouds* his best play and abused the spectators for rejecting it (in *Wasps* 1037-47). At some point he began to revise the play with a re-staging in mind, but for some reason he abandoned the revision before it was completed (internal evidence suggests a date between 419 and 416); perhaps he lost interest, and perhaps he was discouraged by friends or officials. Somehow the revised text got into circulation, perhaps by Aristophanes' friends or literary executors after his death. Although ancient editors had both the original festival version and the incomplete revision at their disposal, it is only the revised version that has survived.

Lack of evidence about the first version of *Clouds* makes it impossible to tell just how much Aristophanes altered in the process of his revision. Obviously new is the parabasis-speech (518-62) discussing the defeat of the original play and hoping for success with the new version. In other respects we must rely mainly on the testimony of an anonymous ancient scholar who wrote,

> 'this play is the same as the first, but has been revised in details, as though the poet wanted to produce it again but for whatever reason did not after all do so. To take the play as a whole, correction, which has occurred in almost every part <...>. Some parts have been removed, while others have been woven in and altered both in the arrangement and in the alternation of speaking parts. Some parts as they stand belong entirely to the revised version: thus the chorus' parabasis has been replaced, and where Better Argument speaks to Worse, and finally where Socrates' school is burned.' (*Hypothesis* I)

Clouds, Aristophanes and the Athenian Enlightenment

Clouds is above all a satire and a critique of the Athenian sophistic movement and its impact on ethics and education, as exemplified by the experience of a father and his son. In the play, Socrates typifies the sophistic movement, even though in reality (as we will see) he differed in important respects from other sophists. In *Clouds*, Socrates is portrayed as an impoverished guru who spends his contemplative hours suspended in a basket, the better to let his mind fly free. He is the master of a school called the Thinkery (in Greek, *Phrontisterion*), where he closets himself with his young pupils, a flock of pale, unathletic eggheads who spend their time doing strange experiments and collecting what is portrayed as useless knowledge (even though such knowledge is today the basis for all advanced education). The Thinkery is supported by tuition fees and petty theft. Outside the Thinkery is a ceramic image of Vertigo (Dinos), whom the inhabitants revere instead of Zeus, along with other novel deities like Emptiness, Tongue, Air and Trickery. Prospective pupils must renounce Zeus and the traditional gods, vow to lead a life of asceticism and undergo a mystical initiation, as if they were joining a religious cult. Indeed, the initiation ceremony bears an unmistakable resemblance to such august religious cults as the Eleusinian Mysteries, and thus was sure to suggest to the audience a kind of black mass.

Drawn to this strange company is the old and wealthy country-villager, Strepsiades, who has run up mountainous debts as a result of his son Pheidippides' preoccupation with chariot-racing and the traditional aristocratic lifestyle that goes with it. He has heard that Socrates can teach anyone the ability to win any case, however unjust, and hopes that Socrates will teach his own son how to evade his debts. When Pheidippides refuses, Strepsiades enrolls himself. But he is unable to learn the new techniques, and finally begs and bullies Pheidippides into reconsidering his refusal. In order to entice Pheidippides, Socrates stages a debate between two Arguments that he keeps in the Thinkery: the Better (a cranky old man.who defends the traditional education) and the Worse (a suave young man who defends the new). Better Argument, who urges obedience and modesty, is utterly defeated by Worse Argument, who promises success and gratification. Better Argument deserts to the side of his opponent, so that Pheidippides must enroll in the Thinkery.

Meanwhile, Strepsiades confronts two of his creditors (one his own age, the other a friend of his son's) and refuses to repay them, (mis)using the lessons he had learned from Socrates. But it is clear that by doing this he has made himself a pariah in his village and will ultimately have to justify his behavior in court. Pheidippides then emerges from the Thinkery and assures Strepsiades that the debts will be no problem. Elated at the success of his son's education, Strepsiades invites him to a graduation feast. But things go terribly wrong. Pheidippides has renounced all the cultural bonds that had tied him to his father and has embraced the newest fashions; when Strepsiades objects to Pheidippides' new attitudes and behavior, Pheidippides beats him up. Worse, he forces Strepsiades to agree that father-beating is justified. But when he offers to do the same for his own mother, Strepsiades finally sees the error of his ways and sets off to burn the Thinkery to the ground.

Among Aristophanes' plays *Clouds* is in many respects unusual, not least in its having no really sympathetic character. The role usually reserved for the sympathetic hero, who finds a way to right an unjust situation and to discredit those responsible, is occupied by an amusing but fundamentally unsympathetic character, Strepsiades. Instead of struggling against impossible odds to do what is right, Strepsiades struggles to do wrong; and instead of standing up against an evil authority (Socrates), Strepsiades joins forces with him in order to further his own nefarious scheme. In addition, he compels his normal and wholesome (if spoiled) son Pheidippides to submit to Socrates' teachings as well. As a result, both Strepsiades' family life and his standing in his village are destroyed, and so is Pheidippides' character. Strepsiades' sudden attack on Socrates' Thinkery at the very end of the play seems to be an essentially incoherent act of violence that in any case does nothing to undo the harm that Strepsiades has brought on himself and his family.

Clouds is also unusual in having no obvious moral center of gravity. The point of the play is to satirize, and to expose the fraudulence of, sophistic teaching by showing its ruinous effect on traditional values as they are exemplified by one family. But at the same time, by framing his satire in an antiheroic plot, in which victim and victimizer join forces, and by caricaturing Better Argument—the only systematic defender of traditional values in the play—as vehemently as he does Worse Argument, Aristophanes seems to be emphasizing both the weakness of traditional values and their ready vulnerability to the corrupting influence of sophism. If Strepsiades, Pheidippides and Better Argument are typical representatives of traditional values, we are left with the impression that these values were pretty shallow to begin with. And when Better Argument is quite unable to make an adequate defence of his values when the chips are down and Pheidippides' soul is at stake, in what sense can we be expected to side with him anyway? Thus neither side in the great debate is given an admirable champion. When Socrates is burned out at play's end it is not because his ideas have been formally discredited but because they have triumphed. Is the kind of incoherent and unprincipled violence that Strepsiades unleashes at the end the only possible response to the sophistic threat? This ambiguous outcome suggests that in *Clouds* Aristophanes created a true comedy of ideas that captured the perhaps ineluctable essence of a cultural dilemma that worried thinking Athenians and even in our own day has yet to be resolved. This dilemma can be stated rather simply: when a society suddenly generates serious intellectual challenges to the norms and beliefs that over long periods of time have given it cohesion and stability, how should people react?

This dilemma in its fifth-century form was precipitated by the influx of foreign intellectuals, scientists, technicians and teachers into Athens. Such men were attracted to Athens because she had become a prosperous imperial city as a result of her expansionist policies following the Persian invasions (which ended in 479) and a fertile ground for progressive thought, individual ambition and freedom of expression as a result of her adoption (in the 460s) of a fully democratic polity. The long political ascendancy of the aristocratic populist and intellectual Pericles (*c.* 490-429) did much to attract and encourage the avant garde of Greek intellectuals, who have come collectively to be known as 'sophists' (a word describing those possessing systematic technical, intellectual and social skills). Although this term covers a wide range of pursuits (natural and social sciences, philosophy and logic, linguistics and philology, musicology and literary criticism, theology and history, law and rhetoric) and a wide range of styles (from formal teaching and writing to mere hobbyism), a public stereotype of the typical sophist seems to have developed by Aristophanes' time: a sophist was a man, usually a foreigner, who possessed arcane knowledge and had untraditional, often counter-intuitive ideas, and who offered to teach these to anyone who could afford the high tuition-fees.

A sophist's typical pupil was a well-to-do young man seeking an alternative to the traditional Athenian education, which combined athletic and military training with indoctrination in traditional values (such as honesty, modesty and deference to the gods and to the older generation), and in the music and poetry by which these were largely transmitted. Although some of these pupils were interested in the new education for its own sake, out of intellectual curiosity, many (perhaps the majority) had a more practical motivation. A young man aiming for power and public distinction in democratic Athens had to be a capable orator and debater, able to persuade the Assembly and to win in the law-courts. Many of the sophists claimed that they could teach these very skills and that the traditional education no longer could; as proof of their claim they could point to the meteoric success of a good many pupils, among them not only the great Pericles but also some of the most promising leaders of the next generation, like Alcibiades.

Aristophanes, reflecting the fear and resentment of the man in the street, portrays the sophists and their pupils in the most unfavorable light. Their intellectual concerns are useless and absurd. Worse, they are amoral, caring not about the justice of an argument but only how to win it, and atheistic, denying the existence of Zeus and the other traditional gods and substituting new deities of their own—deities reflecting their own selfish and dishonest ambitions. Because of their contempt for traditional community values, they teach the young to pursue wealth, power and pleasure at the expense of others and in whatever way they please, however shameless; to despise the laws; and to ignore the well-being of the state. As a result, many members of the younger generation have become either a reclusive rabble of pale eggheads or an amoral, disobedient cadre of greedy hedonists. As a result, the younger generation not only cannot be relied on to help safeguard the state but also invite the vengeance of the gods.

The plot required that someone represent the typical sophist, and Socrates was an obvious choice. Unlike most sophists, who were wealthy foreigners teaching in private for high fees and who were often away from Athens, Socrates was a native Athenian of average means who never left Athens and who spent his time in the marketplace and the wrestling-schools, relentlessly questioning and arguing about anything and everything with whomever he could engage. He had a loyal following of restless and ambitious young men, including such celebrities as Alcibiades, who imitated him and who keenly enjoyed his ability to debunk the most formidable men of their fathers' generation. He was notoriously critical of unexamined beliefs (particularly religious ones) and of the (inevitably messy) processes of democratic polity. And he was charismatic: ugly in a compelling way, brilliant, courageous, visionary.

Most of Aristophanes' audience seem to have credited his portrayal, to have felt that, despite its exaggerated and humorous features, the poet had voiced essentially their own views: in 399 they condemned Socrates to death on charges of having corrupted the young and undermined the traditional religion. Socrates was lucky in having in his adoring pupils, Plato and Xenophon, two great defenders, so that he has been triumphantly acquitted by posterity of the charges that seemed justified in the eyes of his fellow-citizens. But if we set Plato and Xenophon to one side and try to imagine ourselves as ordinary contemporaries of Socrates, the Aristophanic caricature does not seem wholly unfair. Many of Socrates' followers did in fact do great harm to Athens, either by actively undermining or even (like Alcibiades) betraying the democracy, or (almost as bad) by refusing to participate in it (like Plato). If Socrates seems not to have had an actual 'school' or to have taken money for tuition, he nevertheless did keep company with the other sophists who did run schools and charge fees, and he was a frequent guest in the sumptuous houses of their pupils. And if Socrates did not pursue 'wisdom' (*sophia*) in the same (largely technical) fashion as most sophists, he took a serious interest in the same pursuits, was in his own way the same kind of sceptic about traditional values and beliefs, and attracted the same young men to be his followers. Thus the later Platonic distinction between Socrates as *philosopher* (good) and the teachers of practical knowledge as *sophists* (bad) is a distinction that few of Socrates' contemporaries would have cared to draw.

The contemporary conflict of generations and educational ideologies is well captured by the debate between the Arguments. Although it would have been easy simply to portray Better Argument (like Strepsiades' creditors) as being unfairly cheated of a rightful victory, Aristophanes instead chose to expose the strengths and weaknesses of both sides. Better Argument embodies the sort of attitudes that Strepsiades' generation held and hoped to pass on to their sons; these attitudes, he claims, made possible the astounding prosperity that Athens had achieved in his own time. But Better Argument cannot have appealed very strongly to the young men in the audience, with his ludicrously rosy version of the good old days and his tired harping on the virtues of obedience, modesty, deference, self-effacement and toil; his whole harangue amounts to a series of negatives. In addition, he seems obsessed with boys' genitals and unhealthily repressed emotionally. Worse Argument, by contrast, is a cheerful young hedonist who voices the positive injunctions that young men are always so eager to hear: find your own path, have fun, do as you like, be successful and wealthy, don't bother about your parents' wishes and advice. After all, he asks, who ever became successful by being modest? Even though Worse Argument's argument is specious at best, it is quite adequate to the task of refuting and silencing his opponent, whose only argument is blind obedience to tradition. Better Argument, Aristophanes seems to be suggesting, had better do better if young men like Pheidippides are to be recalled to the traditional education. That Aristophanes portrays Better Argument so lamely may reflect his personal experience. After all, Aristophanes was himself a member of the younger generation and therefore not immune to the effects of its enlightenment; no doubt he, like Pheidippides, had been torn between the pull of the old and the lure of the new.

Above the action of the characters in our drama float the ever-changing (Chorus of) Clouds. Their whimsicality and apparent uselessness made the clouds unsuitable to be god(desse)s in the traditional Greek pantheon. But for the natural scientists among the sophists they were important physical entities who (not Zeus!) were responsible for thunder and lightning, and for Aristophanes their protean vaporousness suggested the shifting and amoral thought that he wanted to associate with the sophistic movement. At the beginning of the play they are accordingly invoked by Socrates as members of his new menagerie of scientific deities, embodying the airy fancies and daydreams of the new contemplative man and mirroring the unstable structure of his ethical universe. The Clouds participate in luring Strepsiades into the Thinkery and encourage his scheme. But as the action develops, we gradually come to realize that the Clouds are in reality great powers aligned with Zeus and the traditional gods; like the gods, they have the power to reward good and punish bad. Like a wishing-mirror for people in love with evil, they lure misguided men like Strepsiades to disaster as an object lesson to all who would follow a similar path. This ambiguous nature of the Clouds, for whom the play is named, aptly reflects the complex and ambiguous nature of the play as a whole.

Suggestions for Further Reading

Readers interested in the Greek text are referred to the editions with commentary by K.J. Dover (Oxford 1968) and A.H. Sommerstein (Warminster 1982), which has an excellent literal translation.

Readers interested in the philosophical portrayal of Socrates are referred to the works of Plato (especially the *Apology* and the dialogues *Crito, Phaedo, Phaedrus, Republic* and *Symposium*) and Xenophon (especially the *Apology* and the *Memorabilia*).

Worth reading among the very numerous studies bearing on *Clouds* are:

Adkins, A.H.W. 'Clouds, Mysteries, Socrates and Plato', *Antichthon* 4 (1970) 13-24

Fisher, R.K. *Aristophanes' Clouds. Purpose and Technique* (Amsterdam 1984)

Guthrie, W.K.C. *A History of Greek Philosophy* vol. III (Cambridge 1969) 3-319

Havelock, E.A. 'The Socratic Self as it is Parodied in Aristophanes' *Clouds*', *Yale Classical Studies* 22 (1972) 1-18.

Hubbard, T.K. 'Parabatic Self-Criticism and the Two Versions of Aristophanes' *Clouds*', *Classical Antiquity* 5(1986) 182-97.

Kerferd, G.B. *The Sophistic Movement* (Cambridge 1981).

Nussbaum, M. 'Aristophanes and Socrates on Learning Practical Wisdom', *Yale Classical Studies* 26 (1980) 43-97

Ostwald, M. 'The Polarizations of the 420s', Ch. 5 in *From Popular Sovereignty to the Sovereignty of Law* (California 1986) 199-290.

Segal, C.P. 'Aristophanes' Cloud-Chorus', *Arethusa* 2 (1969) 143-61.

Silk, M. 'Aristophanes as a Lyric Poet', *Yale Classical Studies* 26 (1980) 99-151.

Strauss, L. *Socrates and Aristophanes* (Chicago 1966).

Vlastos, G. 'Socratic Irony', *Classical Quarterly* 37 (1987) 79-96.

Aristophanes' Clouds

CHARACTERS

SPEAKING CHARACTERS

Strepsiades, an old Athenian
Pheidippides, Strepsiades' young son
Slave of Strepsiades
Pupils of Socrates (two)
Socrates the philosopher
Chorus of Clouds
The Better Argument
The Worse Argument
First Creditor, Strepsiades' fellow-villager
Second Creditor

MUTE CHARACTERS

Pupils of Socrates
Witness summoned by First Creditor
Xanthias, slave of Strepsiades
Slaves of Strepsiades

SCENE I

(Strepsiades, Pheidippides, Slave)

Strepsiades°

Aargh!
Good God almighty, what a monstrous night!
It's endless. Will the daylight never come?
I heard the cock crow quite a while ago,
but the slaves are snoring. They wouldn't in the old days.
Damn the war, it's messed up lots of things,

Strepsiades. Though the name Strepsiades is attested of real people, Aristophanes probably chose it because it expresses this character's anxious 'tossing and turning' (*strephei*, 36) over his debts and his subsequent attempts to 'reverse' (*ekstrepson*) his son's life and to 'twist lawsuits' (*strepsodikesai*, 434) to avoid repaying his debts.

when I can't even whip my own slaves anymore.°
But this fine young man here isn't any better;
he won't get up 'fore daylight, just keeps farting away,
wrapped up in five thick woolly coverlets.
Oh, I give up! Let's *all* cover up and snore.
Tarnation! How can I sleep a wink, tormented
by all my bills and stable-fees and debts,
because of my son here, who never gets a haircut,
who's totally into horses and chariot-racing.
He even *dreams* about horses! But *I'm* the goner,
always watching the moon phase out the month,
and my credit-rating with it. Boy! Light a lamp,°
bring me my ledgers, so I can calculate
how many I owe to, and what the interest is.
OK, the bottom line. Twelve grand to Pasias.
Twelve grand to Pasias? Why did I borrow that?
When I bought the horse with the K-brand. What a fool!
I should have had my eye knocked out with a stone.

Pheidippides

Yo Philon! Don't be cheating! Ride in your own lane!

Strepsiades

That's it! That's just the kind of crap that's done me in.
He's riding horses even in his sleep!

Pheidippides

How many laps are the war-chariots down to drive?

Strepsiades

It's me, your father, you're driving round the bend!
Well, after Pasias, what's the next IOU?
Amynias, three grand for a seat and a set of wheels.

Pheidippides

Groom, roll the horse in the dust, then stable him.

Strepsiades

It's *you*, dear lad, who's been rolling—in *my money*.
And now I've been served papers, and other creditors
are threatening to sue me.

---

6 During the Peloponnesian war, neighboring Megara and Boeotia were hostile powers and Peloponnesian armies periodically invaded the Attic countryside, so that ill-treated slaves might be tempted to run away from their masters and seek refuge in another land. This would be much harder to do in peacetime, when international agreements discouraged the harboring of runaway slaves.

18 'Boy' was the conventional way to address a male slave.

Pheidippides

Really, father!
Why are you tossing and turning all night long?

Strepsiades

There's a bailiff in the bedclothes biting me.

Pheidippides

What a crazy guy! Please let me catch some sleep.

Strepsiades

Excuse me! Sleep away! But I'm warning you,
one day these debts will all be on *your* back.
Gawd.
That matchmaker ought to die a horrible death
for getting me to marry that mother of yours.
I had a mighty good life there, down on the farm,
unwashed, unswept, lying around as I pleased,
brimming with honey-bees, sheep and olive-trees.
And then I married the niece of Megacles,°
Megacles' son. Farmer weds urbanite,
a snobby, spoiled clothes-horse kind of girl.
When we hitched, I climbed up to the wedding bed
smelling of new wine, figs, fleeces and good produce;
while *she* smelled of perfume, saffron, tongue-kisses, expense,
of overeating and Aphrodite's shrines.°
I don't say she was lazy; she did her weaving.
I'd show her these pants of mine as evidence
and say, 'Wife, you needn't pack the threads so close.'°

Slave

The oil in the lamp's run out on us.

Strepsiades

Oh dammit, why'd you light the thirsty lamp?
Come here and take your beating!

Slave

Why *should* I?

Strepsiades

Because you put in one of the fattest wicks!

---

46 Although a contemporary Megacles, son of Megacles is known, there is no apparent reason why we should think particularly of him here; such names were not uncommon and they connote wealth and aristocratic pedigree.

52 'Kolias and Genetyllis', divinites associated with Aphrodite, goddess of sexual enjoyment, and (according to comic poets) a popular gathering-place for housewives up to no good.

55 I.e., use so much (expensive) thread in simple mending.

And then, when this here boy was born to us,
to me and to my high-class wife, that is,
we started yelling at each other about his name.
She wanted a name with *hippus*, meaning *horse*,
Xanthippus or Chaerippus or Callipides,
while I liked Pheidonides, his granddad's name.°
We compromised and called him Pheidippides.
She used to pick him up and coo at him,
'When you grow up you'll drive a chariot to town,
like Megacles, and wear fine robes'. And I'd say,
'No, when you drive the goats home to the barnyard,
like your very own dad, you'll wear a leather jacket'.
But he didn't listen to anything I said,
but gave my wallet a case of the galloping trots.
That's why I've spent the whole night searching for
one little path of escape, an excellent miracle-cure.
If I can convince my son, I shall be saved!
But first I've got to get him out of bed.
Now what's the gentlest way for me to wake him?
Pheidippides. Pheidippidoodle.

Pheidippides

What, dad?

Strepsiades

Gimme a kiss and show me your right hand.

Pheidippides

OK. What's up?

Strepsiades

So tell me: do you love me?

Pheidippides

By this Poseidon, Lord of Horses, I do.°

Strepsiades

Don't give me any of that Poseidon stuff!
That god's the very source of all my troubles!
But, if you really love me with all your heart,
please do what I say, my son.

Pheidippides

And what is that?

---

65 'Pheidonides' means 'Thrifty'.

83 Evidently Pheidippides has a picture or a statue of the horse-god Poseidon by his bed.

Strepsiades
I'd like you, as soon as possible, to reverse your life,
and go to learn the things I want you to.

Pheidippides
So tell me, what are these 'things'?

Strepsiades
You'll do it?

Pheidippides
Sure,
by Dionysus, I will.

Strepsiades
Look over there, then.
You see that little door, that little house?

Pheidippides
I see it. So tell me, dad, just what *is* it?

Strepsiades
That house is a Thinkery for clever souls.
Some gentlemen live there who argue that the sky
is a casserole-cover—and make us all believe it—
and that it covers us all, and we're charcoal briquets.°
These people train you, if you pay them money,
to win any argument, whether it's right or wrong.

Pheidippides
Who *are* these people?

Strepsiades
I can't exactly *name* them.
Reflective cogitators, upstanding gentlemen.

Pheidippides
Yuk! That scum! I know who you mean. The charlatans,
the pasty-faces, the ones who don't wear shoes,
like that miserable Socrates, and Chaerephon!°

Strepsiades
Hey now, be quiet! Don't speak childishly.
And have a care about your father's daily bread.
Lay off the racing and join their company.

---

97 No such theory is attributed to any philosopher outside of comedy; if anything it is a popular misunderstanding of some cosmogonic theory.

104 Chaerephon was the long-time friend of Socrates who (according to Plato's *Apology*) asked the Delphic oracle if any man was wiser than Socrates. He was nicknamed 'The Bat' because of his thin, pale countenance, and comic poets ridiculed him as a thief, an informer and a parasite.

Pheidippides

No way, no, by Dionysus! Not even if you gave me
those fancy pheasants that Leogoras breeds!°

Strepsiades

Come on, I implore you, dearest of all to me,
matriculate.

Pheidippides

And what do you want me to study?

Strepsiades

I'm told they have both kinds of argument:
the Better, whatever that is, and the Worse.
And one of these Arguments, the Worse, I'm told,
can argue even an unjust case and win!
So if you could learn this Worse Argument for *me*,
then all these debts I owe on your account
I wouldn't have to pay, not even a penny!°

Pheidippides

I just can't. How could I even dare to *look*
at the Knights with all the tan scraped off my face?

Strepsiades

Then, by Demeter, you've had your last meal here,
and so's your yoke-horse and your thoroughbred.
I'm throwing you out of the house, and go to hell!

Pheidippides

My godlike uncle Megacles won't leave me
horseless. I'll go to him and pay *you* no mind.°

SCENE II

(Strepsiades, Pupil, other Pupils)

Strepsiades

And I won't take this setback lying down.
I'll say a little prayer and go myself
to the Thinkery to get an education.
But how's an old man like me, forgetful and dense,

---

109 Leogoras, father of the orator Andocides, was a wealthy aristocrat related to the family of Pericles.

118 The philosopher Protagoras seems to have been the first to claim that there are always two arguments about any issue and that it is possible for a skilled pleader to make a convincing case for either side, however weak the case may seem to be to the unskilled person. In Plato's *Apology* Socrates complains of his reputation for 'making the worse argument the better' and says that philosophers are always easy targets for such an accusation, just as lawyers are today.

125 Pheidippides marches off to Megacles' house.

to learn precise, hair-splitting arguments?
I've just *got* to go. What use is procrastination?
Just knock on the door. Hello? Boy! Little boy!

Pupil
Buzz off to blazes! Who's pounding on the door?

Strepsiades
Strepsiades, son of Pheidon, from Cicynna.°

Pupil
An ignoramus, I'd say, the way you furiously
stomp on the door so inconsiderately,
aborting a cogitation just conceived.°

Strepsiades
Forgive me, please, I live way out in the country.
But tell me about the thing that was aborted.

Pupil
It's sacrilege to tell anyone but the pupils.

Strepsiades
Go on, don't worry; the man you see before you
has come to the Thinkery to be a pupil too.

Pupil
I'll tell you, then. But these are holy secrets.°
This morning Socrates asked Chaerephon
how many of its own feet a flea can jump.
A flea had bitten Chaerephon on the eyebrow
and then jumped off and landed on Socrates' head.

Strepsiades
And how did he measure the jump?

Pupil
Most cleverly.
He melted wax, then picking up the flea,
he dipped both its little feet into the wax,
which, when it cooled, made little Persian slippers.
He took these off and was measuring the distance.

Strepsiades
Good God almighty, what subtlety of mind!

---

134 The full version of an Athenian name; Cicynna was a small, rural and relatively insignificant deme (local community) and was probably chosen by Aristophanes for that reason.

137 Strepsiades had probably knocked very timidly.

143 Aristophanes portrays the Thinkery as a kind of mystery-cult, with Socrates as its guru.

Pupil
That's nothing! Just wait till you hear another idea
of Socrates'. Wanna?

Strepsiades
What? Please tell me!

Pupil
Our Chaerephon was asking his opinion
on whether gnats produce their humming sound
by blowing through the mouth or through the rump.

Strepsiades
So what did Socrates say about the gnat?

Pupil
He said the gnat has a very narrow gut,
and, since the gut's so tiny, the air comes through
quite violently on its way to the little rump;
then, being an orifice attached to a narrow tube,
the asshole makes a blast from the force of the air.°

Strepsiades
So a gnat's asshole turns out to be a bugle!
Thrice-blessed man, what enterology!

Pupil
But the other day he lost a great idea
because of a lizard.

Strepsiades
Really? Please tell me how.

Pupil
He was studying the tracks of the lunar orbit
and its revolutions, and as he skyward gaped,
from the roof in darkness a lizard shat on him.

Strepsiades
Ha ha ha ha. A lizard shitting on Socrates!

Pupil
Then last night we hadn't a thing to eat for dinner.

Strepsiades
Aha. So how did he contrive to get your food?

Pupil
Over the table he spread a thin coat of ashes,
and bent a skewer,° then picking up a queer

164 Caricaturing contemporary scientific models that sought to explain the mechanics of hearing.
178 As if to perform a scientific or magical procedure.

over at the gymnasium, he stole his clothes.

Strepsiades
And why do people still admire Thales?°
Open up the Thinkery, and make it quick;
I want to see Socrates as soon as possible.
I yearn to learn. Come on now, open up!°
Good God, what kind of creatures have we here?

Pupil
What's the matter? Do they look strange to you?

Strepsiades
They look like prisoners of war, the ones from Sparta.
But why are they peering at the ground like that?

Pupil
Investigating subterranean phenomena.

Strepsiades
I see,
they're after truffles. But you needn't bother with that:
I know where you can find big, tasty ones.
But why are these pupils here bent over so?

Pupil
They're scrutinizing the gloomy realms below.

Strepsiades
Then why are their assholes pointing toward the sky?

Pupil
Their assholes are learning astronomy on their own.
But all of you, go in; he mustn't catch you here.

Strepsiades
Not yet, not yet! Please let them stay awhile.
I want to tell them a small problem of my own.

Pupil
I'm sorry, they're not allowed to be outside
in the open air for any great length of time.

Strepsiades
Pray tell me what these are, these instruments?

Pupil
This here's astronomy.

---

180 Thales, the sixth-century founder of Milesian philosophy, had a reputation for genius and wisdom comparable to Einstein's today.

183 Stage-hands roll out the *ekkyklema*, a wheeled platform kept inside the stage-building that was used to reveal what was supposed to be going on inside. On the *ekkyklema* are a number of pupils and a pegboard on which various instruments and objects are hung.

Strepsiades

And what are these?

Pupil

Geometry.

Strepsiades

And what's the use of that?

Pupil

For measuring land.

Strepsiades

Like land for settlers?

Pupil

All *kinds* of land.

Strepsiades

A very urbane device,
both useful and entirely democratic.°

Pupil

And here we have a map of the whole world. See?
Here's Athens.

Strepsiades

What do you mean? I don't believe you.
I don't see any jurors hearing cases.°

Pupil

Take it from me, this really is Attica.

Strepsiades

Then where's Cicynna and my fellow villagers?

Pupil

They're over here. And here, you see, is Euboea,
this area laid out all along the mainland.

Strepsiades

I know: we laid it out ourselves with Pericles.°
But where is Sparta?°

Pupil

Here it is. Over here.

---

205 Strepsiades seems to think that geometry is a device for distributing all the world's land to Athenians like himself.

208 The courts, with their large paid juries of ordinary citizens, were Athens' principal means of making and enforcing the laws that governed not only the Athenians but all members of their empire as well. Because of the prominence of the courts in Athenian public life, the Athenians had a reputation for being litigious and meddlesome. Aristophanes satirizes Athenian juries in his play *Wasps*.

213 Twenty-three years earlier Pericles had led an Athenian force to Euboea to suppress a revolt.

214 Sparta and her allies were at this time Athens' great enemy in the Peloponnesian War.

Strepsiades
So close? You'd better think about *that* some more,
and move them a whole lot farther away from *us*.

Pupil
Impossible.

Strepsiades
Just move it, or, by God, I'll—
Hey, who's that man there hanging in the air?°

Pupil
The master.

Strepsiades
Master?

Pupil
Socrates.

Strepsiades
Socrates!
OK you, introduce me, good and loud!

Pupil
You call him yourself; I haven't got the time.

SCENE III

(Strepsiades, Socrates)

Strepsiades
Oh Socrates!
Socratikins!

Soc rates
Why callest thou, mere mortal?

Strepsiades
First tell me, pray, just what you're doing up there.

Socrates
I tread the air and contemplate the sun.

Strepsiades
You're spying on the gods from a wicker basket?
Why can't you do that, if you must, down here?

Socrates
Never

218 Socrates is swung into view on the *mechane* ('machine'), a crane attached to the stage-building, usually used to bring on heroes or gods (hence the phrase *deus ex machina*). The Socrates of Plato's *Apology* complains of his airborne portrayal in our play, saying that people long remembered it and that it contributed to his bad reputation as one who despised ordinary people and their conventions.

could I make correct celestial discoveries
except by thus suspending my mind, and mixing
my subtle head with the air it's kindred with.
If down below I contemplate what's up,
I'd never find aught; for the earth by natural force
draws unto itself the quickening moisture of thought.
The very same process is observable in lettuce.°

Socrates

How's that?
It's thought that draws the moisture into lettuce?
Come down, Socratikins, come down here to me,
so you can teach me what I've come to learn.

Socrates

And what might that be?

Strepsiades

I want to learn oratory.
By debts and interest payments and rapacious creditors
I'm assailed and assaulted and stand to lose my property.

Socrates

So how did you manage to slip into this condition?

Strepsiades

It's an equine ailment that's eating me up alive.
No matter. Teach me one of your Arguments,
the one that pays no debts. Whatever your fee,
I'll pay it, I swear by all the gods, in cash.

Socrates

What do you mean, 'the gods'? In the first place, gods
aren't legal tender here.

Strepsiades

Then how do you swear?
With iron coins, as in Byzantium?

Socrates

You want to know the truth about the gods,
what they really are?

Strepsiades

By God I do, if it's possible.

---

234 Caricaturing (and muddling) the ideas of the physicist Diogenes, who studied the role of the wet and the dry in nature. Among Diogenes' theories was that animals are less intelligent than human beings because the air they breathe, coming from near the ground, is moister and so produces an intellect less 'pure and dry' than ours.

Socrates

And to enter into communion with the Clouds,
who are our deities?°

Strepsiades

I'd like to very much.

Socrates

Then sit yourself upon the sacred sofa.

Strepsiades

I'm ready.

Socrates

Very well. Now take hold of this,
the wreath.

Strepsiades

A wreath? Good heavens, Socrates,
you're not going to sacrifice me, like Athamas?°

Socrates

Oh no. We perform this ceremony for everyone
we initiate.

Strepsiades

But what do *I* get out of it?

Socrates

You'll be a spieler, a gong, the flower of orators!
Hold still now.°

Strepsiades

Oh my god, I see you weren't joking:
the way you're dredging me I *will* be flour!

Socrates

Let the oldster speak with reverence,
let him hear our pious prayer.
Mighty Master, Air unbounded,
thou who hold the floating earth;°

---

253 No Greek would think of worshipping the clouds; they are 'goddesses' suitable only for the comic Thinkery of Socrates, who teaches men how to obscure reality by making it as changeable and evanescent as the clouds.

257 Recollecting the scene in Sophocles' play *Athamas* (not extant) in which the hero sits, wreathed, on the altar of Zeus, about to be sacrificed for a wrong he had done to his wife, Nephele (whose name means 'cloud').

261 Socrates sprinkles him with flour, like a sacrificial beast.

263 Ionian philosophers as early as Anaximenes held that the earth was a disc supported by air (one of the four 'elements', along with earth, water and fire); for Aristophanes air (empty and insubstantial) symbolizes the emptiness and insubstantiality of Socratic theories and values.

Ether bright,° and Clouds so awesome,
goddesses of thunder loud!
Rise on high, o mistresses,
appear to him who thinks on you!

Strepsiades

Wait until I get my raincoat;
I don't want a drenching here!
What a fool I was to come with
nothing, even a simple hat!

Socrates

Come then, Clouds most glorious, and
show yourselves to this man here.
Whether on the holy snowy
peak of Olympus ye now sit,
or nymphs to a holy dance you're calling
in father Ocean's garden, or
whether again in the Nile delta
you're drawing water in golden bowls,°
or hanging out at Lake Maeotis
or up on Mimas' snowy crag:
hearken to my call; accept my
sacrifice;° enjoy our rites!

SCENE IV (PARODOS)

(Chorus, Socrates, Strepsiades)

Chorus (I^1)°

Clouds everlasting,
rise and appear in your radiance dewy,
rise from your deep-crashing father, the Ocean,
rise to the towering peaks of the forested mountains!

---

264 The 'ether' was thought to lie between the air and the sky; though it was popularly considered to be divine because of its proximity to the gods, the philosophers speculated about its relationship (if any) to the four elements of the biosphere.

272 In Diogenes' theory explaining the Nile's summer flooding, it was the sun (a traditional god) and not the clouds that drew up moisture.

274 Perhaps Socrates is thinking of Strepsiades as a sort of sacrifice; perhaps he had burned some incense as part of the rigamarole in 260 ff.

Chorus The songs and dances performed in the orchestra by a Greek dramatic chorus were normally strophic, i.e. composed in two or more strophes (stanzas) that had the same rhythmical structure. In this translation each chorus is numbered and each strophe comprising a chorus is numbered by superscript; thus the song beginning in line 275 is the first strophe of the first chorus; the second strophe begins in line 299.

This entry-song of the chorus (technically called the *parodos*) is unique in Aristophanes in that it is sung offstage: the Clouds do not actually enter the orchestra until 323. This staging is a novel surprise, creates suspense and establishes our feeling for the impermanence, the whimsicality and the untrustworthiness of the Clouds.

Let us look down on the hill-tops majestic,
down on the holy earth's crops that we rain on,
rivers resounding in spate divine,
oceans resounding in thunderous booms!
Heaven's untiring eye is ablaze
with sparkling rays.
Shake from our deathless shapes the mist of rain;
look on the earth with telescopic eye!

Socrates

Clouds that we revere so greatly,
show that you have heard my cry!
You: you heard their voice, their thunder,
bellowing with force divine?

Strepsiades

Honored Clouds, I do revere you;
let me answer with a fart
all their thunder: that's how scared they've
made me, that's how terrified!
Now, if its allowed, or even
if it's not, I need to crap!

Socrates

Don't be joking, don't behave like
one of these comedians!
Reverence, please! A swarm of gods are
stirring and prepared to sing.

Chorus (I²)

Rain-bearing maidens,
come to the glistening land of Athena,
Cecrops' soil with its crop of fine he-men;°
here is the home of the sanctified rites none may speak of,°

301 Cecrops was a legendary king of Athens.

302 The Mysteries of Demeter and Kore, located at Eleusis (about 12 miles from Athens), was an internationally renowned cult that initiated thousands of people annually. The cult's central myth (recounted in the *Homeric Hymn to Demeter*) told of the rape of the daughter (Kore) of Demeter (goddess of crops, especially grain) by Hades (lord of the underworld and brother of Zeus); Demeter's search for Kore, during which no crops were permitted to grow; Demeter's arrival in Attica; the compromise by which Kore is restored to Demeter for part of the year (when crops grow) but spends the remainder (winter) with her husband in the underworld; and the foundation of the Mysteries to commemorate these events. It was considered sacrilegious (and very bad luck) to defame the Mysteries or to reveal their central acts. The Clouds' emphasis on Athenian reverence for the Mysteries contrasts strikingly with Socrates' contempt for the traditional gods and with his own private 'mysteries', and it prepares us for the revelation in 1452 ff. that the Clouds have come not to support but to punish the impiety of Socrates and the dishonesty of Strepsiades.

the temple in festival open for worship,
gifts for the heavenly gods in abundance,
temples on high, sacred statues and
holy processions and sacrifice,
ubiquitous garlands, festivities here
  throughout the year.
The onset of spring brings Dionysian joy,
maddening dance, the music of the pipes.

Strepsiades

Tell me, Socrates, I beg you,
  who these ladies are that sang
such a reverent song as this? They
  aren't some kind of heroines?

Socrates

Not at all. They're clouds from heaven,
  goddesses for idle men.
They're the ones who give us judgment,
  dialectic, intelligence,
fantasy and double-talking,
  eloquence and forceful talk.

Strepsiades

Just to hear their voices makes my
  very soul take wing and fly,
makes me long to chop some logic,
  blow some elocutive smoke,
bust big maxims with little maxims,
  counterpoint an argument!
Time to see the ladies close up;
  I'm ready now, if now's the time!

Socrates

Look this way, then, toward Mt. Parnes;
  now I see them coming down
peacefully.

Strepsiades

Where? Show them to me.

Socrates

Quite a bunch are coming on
through the hollow vales and forests,
  to your side.

Strepsiades

What's going on?

I can't see them.

Socrates

Look offstage there.

Strepsiades

Now I think I'm seeing them!

Socrates

Now you've simply *got* to see them,
unless you've got pumpkins in your eyes!

Strepsiades

There they are! O reverend ladies!
They're settling over everything.

Socrates

So, you didn't think that they were
goddesses, and disbelieved?

Strepsiades

Right. I thought that they were only
lots of dew and steam and gas.

Socrates

Didn't know that they sustain and
feed a host of specialists,
sayers of sooth, quack doctors, hairy
idlers with onyx signet-rings,
writers of chorus-bending screeches,
phony meteorologists,
doing nothing useful, living
only to sing about the Clouds?

Strepsiades

That's why they write 'O dire downdraft
drumming rainclouds radiant',°
'Locks of hundred-headed Typho',
'blasting squalls of mighty blow',
'airy scudders crook'd of talon,
birds breast-stroking up on high',
'rain of waters down from dew-clouds.'
Then, for poems like that, they get
fine fillets of choicest mullet,
avian breast of thrush supreme!

---

335 Parodies 'writers of chorus-bending screeches', i.e. the new style of dithyramb (a choral song for Dionysus), which explored complex rhythms and orchestration and featured coloratura singing of florid poetic texts.

Socrates
Thanks to the Clouds; don't they deserve it?

Strepsiades
Tell me, if they're really clouds,
what's the reason why they look so
much like mortal women do?
Sky-clouds don't resemble *these* clouds.

Socrates
What do *they* look like to you?

Strepsiades
Can't exactly say. They *look* like
balls of wool spread out up there,
not at all like women, no sir;
these are wearing noses, too.

Socrates
Answer me a little question.

Strepsiades
Fire away, whatever you like.

Socrates
Ever gazed up and seen a cloud that
looked just like a centaur, or
a wolf, or bull, perhaps a leopard?

Strepsiades
Sure I have; but what's the point?

Socrates
Clouds take any shape they fancy.
Say they see a shaggy tough,
one of those hairy guys we all know,
e.g. Xenophantus' son:°
they'll make fun of his affectations,
making centaurs of themselves.

Strepsiades
Say they spot a man who steals from
public funds, as Simon does?

Socrates
They'll expose his character by
turning into hungry wolves.

Strepsiades
That's why, when yesterday they saw

348 The tragic and dithyrambic poet, Hieronymus.

Cleonymus who lost his shield,
showing up his cowardice they
took the shape of running deer!°

Socrates

Now it's Cleisthenes° they've spotted:
see him? Thus the Clouds are women.

Strepsiades

Hail then, sovereign Ladies! If you've
ever so favored another man,
break for me too, Queens almighty,
a sound that spans the heavens wide!

Chorus Leader

Greetings, superannuated
codger, seeking artful words;
you too, priest of subtlest hogwash,
tell us what your heart desires.
You alone we listen to, of
all the scientists today,
Prodicus° excepted, for his
cleverness and judgment fine.
You we like because you swagger
all over town, and roll your eyes,
barefoot, suffering every kind of
woe, and proud on our account.

Strepsiades

Mother Earth, the sound they make! How
holy, august, wonderful!

Socrates

These are the only gods, my man; and
all the rest are fantasies.

Strepsiades

Come now, don't you all consider
Zeus on high to be a god?°

---

353 Cleonymus was a minor politician often ridiculed in comedy for obesity and gluttony; in *Clouds* and in subsequent comedies he was teased for having thrown away his shield in battle, probably in the Athenian retreat after the battle of Delium in 424.

354 A man who was beardless, or unable to grow a proper beard, and so was often satirized as effeminate; here the actor playing Socrates points him out in the audience.

361 A Cean philosopher with interests ranging from natural science to semantics and religion.

366 Zeus, traditionally the king of the Olympian gods, was popularly conceived as the principal weather-god: compeller of clouds, maker of rain and storms, and wielder of the thunderbolt, with which he controlled divine enemies and punished human malefactors. Socrates' following explanations of storms, lightning and thunder as natural

Socrates
Zeus, you say? Don't kid me! There's no
Zeus at all.

Strepsiades
What's that you say?
Who makes rain, then? That's what I would
like to know right off the bat.

Socrates
Clouds, of course! I'll prove it so by
arguments irrefutable.
Tell me, have you ever seen it
raining when there were no clouds?
Why can't Zeus produce a rainstorm
while the clouds are out of town?

Strepsiades
By Apollo, what you say jibes
well with what you said before.
When it rained I used to think that
Zeus was pissing through a sieve!
Tell me, though, who makes the thunder:
that's what makes me shake and quake.

Socrates
Clouds do, when they roll around.

Strepsiades
You'll
stop at nothing! But tell me, how?

Socrates
Clouds fill up with lots of water,
then they're forced to move about,
sagging soddenly with rain, then
getting heavier perforce,
collide with one another, breaking
up and making crashing sounds.

Strepsiades
Who is it, though, that starts them moving?
Isn't that the work of Zeus?

Socrates
Hardly. It's cosmic Vertigo.°

---

phenomena connected with the clouds are humorous versions of scientific theories then in circulation, whether or not the historical Socrates involved himself in their study.

379 *Dinos*, 'rotation' or 'whirling', was an important feature of Democritus' atomic theory of the universe; but in everyday usage *dinos* meant a kind of cup. Possibly (see 1473)

Strepsiades

What?
Vertigo? I never realized
Zeus is gone and in his place this
Vertigo's become the king.
Still you've not explained what makes the
crashing of a thunder-clap.

Socrates

Weren't you listening? I said that when the
clouds fill up with water, then
collide with one another, they make a
crash because of their density.

Strepsiades

Who would fall for that? Come on now.

Socrates

I'll use your body to prove my case.
Ever gorged yourself with soup at a
festival, then got a pain
there in your belly, and suddenly it
starts to make a rumbling noise?

Strepsiades

By Apollo, yes I have! It
starts to make an awful fuss;
just a bit of soup starts rumbling,
making awful thunder-sounds,
gently at first—bap bap bap bap—then
harder—boomba boomba boom—
then I shit and really thunder—
whamba wham—just like the clouds!

Socrates

Just consider what a fart your
little belly can produce;
don't you think the boundless air
produces mighty thunder-claps?
That's in fact the reason why we
say a fart is breaking wind.

Strepsiades

Tell me this, though: where does lightning
come from, with its blaze of fire,

---

such a cup stood outside the Thinkery. Strepsiades misunderstands Socrates' reference to a cosmic principle and thinks that the Socratics worship *Dinos* in the way he worships Zeus; the presence of a *dinos* (cup) would thus suggest a divine image.

making us a heap of ash, or
  sometimes merely singeing us?
Plainly that's the weapon used by
  Zeus to punish perjurers.

Socrates

What a moron! You're a throwback,
  truly a neanderthal.
Punish perjurers? Then how come
  Simon isn't lightning-struck?
Or Cleonymus, or Theorus?
  They're as perjured as can be!
No, instead he usually zaps his
  very own temple at Sunion,
his own great oak-trees too. What for? The
  oak-trees can't be perjurers!°

Strepsiades

I can't say. You've got a point, though.
  So, what *is* a thunderbolt?

Socrates

When a dry wind lifts aloft and
  gets locked up inside these clouds,
inflating them like big balloons, it
  causes them by natural force
to burst; the wind's borne out in a whoosh by
  dint of compressive density,
burning itself entirely up by
  friction and velocity.

Strepsiades

I had the same experience
  myself at Zeus' festival,
roasting a sausage for my kinsmen:
  I forgot to make a slit;
suddenly it bloated up and
  bam! went off just like a bomb,
singeing both my eyebrows off and
  covering my face with guts!

Chorus Leader

Creature who desires from us
  magnitudes of cleverness,
blessed shall you be in Athens,

402 Oak-trees were considered sacred to Zeus.

blessed too in all of Greece:
if you have a memory, *if* you
like to think, and have a hardy
soul, and don't get tired standing
still or when you walk about,
don't mind freezing cold too much, or
doing without between-meal snacks,
or staying away from wine and stupid
things like manly exercise,
thinking that it's best to have what's
fitting for a clever man:
success as a doer and a counselor
and a warrior of the tongue!°

Strepsiades

Never fear: my soul is hard, I'm
used to brooding through sleepless nights,
my belly's thrifty and lined with iron,
used to eating terrible grub.
These are my credentials, and I'm
ready for hammering into shape.

Socrates

Promise that you'll recognize no
god but those *we* recognize,
Emptiness and Clouds and Tongue, the
one and only Trinity?

Strepsiades

Even if I met the other
gods I wouldn't speak to them,
or sacrifice or pour libations
or burn the incense on their altars.

Chorus Leader

Tell us what you'd have us do, then.
Speak up, you'll be quite all right,
if you honor and revere us,
if it's cleverness you seek.

Strepsiades

Sovereign Ladies, all I want from
you is something very small:

---

419 These qualities are all attested for the historical Socrates except for abstinence from wine (characteristic of orators in training for a speech) and avoidance of manly exercise (Socrates was an avid wrestler).

to beat the greatest orator in
Greece by at least a hundred miles.

Chorus Leader

That we'll give you: in the future
none will carry more motions than you.

Strepsiades

Not for me, no motions, please! I
don't desire political clout,
just the power of twisting lawsuits,
and giving my creditors the slip.

Chorus Leader

That you'll have if that's your pleasure;
what you want is no big deal.
Now come forth and with confidence
commit yourself to our agents here.

Strepsiades

Here I go, with faith in you. And
anyway I've got no choice:
those thoroughbred horses and spendthrift wife
have put me on the brink of ruin.

Now I'm totally in *their* hands;
I'll do whatever they might command,
suffer beatings, hunger, thirst,
flagellation, freezing, dearth.
Only let me shirk my debts
and gain renown as the very best
pusher, spieler, bastard, wheel,
artful liar, total heel,
shyster, con-man, fount of words,
loophole, fox, plea-copper, turd,
slippery liar, shifty skunk,
loathsome villain, pesty punk,
master-chef of total bunk.

If people think me all of these,
let the Thinkers do as they please;
let them grind me for baloney
to put on the students' macaroni.

Chorus (2)

He's got intestinal fortitude,
a bold, ambitious attitude.

Study hard and play our game,
and you shall win immortal fame.

Strepsiades

Tell me what's in store for me.

Chorus

You'll live with us for eternity,
a paradigm of prosperity.

Strepsiades

Is that what I will really be?

Chorus

Imagine throngs of clients at your door,
imploring your advice and consultation
on cases worth a million bucks or more,
a worthy outlet for your cogitation.

Chorus Leader

Now it's time to test the old man's
  elementary aptitude;
diagnose his mental fitness,
  try his base intelligence.

Socrates

Now, tell me what your disposition is:
I need to know so I can bring to bear
the latest pedagogical artillery.

Strepsiades

How's that? You wanna make war on me? My god!

Socrates

No, no. I only want some basic info,
like, how's your memory?

Strepsiades

Well, I've got two kinds:
if someone owes me money, it's very good;
but if it's me that owes, it's awful bad.

Socrates

Well, are you naturally gifted as a talker?

Strepsiades

A gifted speaker? No. A deadbeat? Yes.

Socrates

Then how do you expect to learn?

Strepsiades

Just fine.

Socrates

All right. I'm going to throw you clever bits
of cosmological lore; you snap them up.

Strepsiades

I have to eat my lessons like a dog, eh?

Socrates

The man's an ignoramus, a barbarian!
Old man, I fear you're going to need a whipping.
Let's see now: someone hits you, what then?

Strepsiades

Hits me?
I play dead, then I summon witnesses,
and after a little while I go to court.

Socrates

OK, remove your shirt.

Strepsiades

Have I been bad?

Socrates

No, candidates must disrobe before they enter.

Strepsiades

But I'm not after stolen goods in there!°

Socrates

Take it off, stop horsing around.

Strepsiades

So tell me,
if I study hard and pay real close attention,
which of your disciples will I be like?

Socrates

You'll be the spitting image of Chaerephon.°

Strepsiades

Good heavens no! I'll look just like a zombie!

Socrates

Stop chattering now, and follow me inside.
And make it snappy!

---

498 Citizens who claimed that their belongings had been stolen could search the suspect's house, but only if they removed any clothing that might enable them to bring in something to plant. Strepsiades' protestation would be insulting to any honest citizen.

503 See line 104.

Strepsiades

Put pennies on my eyes
before I enter: I'm absolutely terrified
of this descent into the underworld!°

Socrates

Get going! Stop this skulking on the threshold!

PARABASIS°

(Chorus)

Chorus

All the best of luck to you:
you've shown us lots of derring-do!
I wish that man felicity,
for, though far gone in senility,
he's taken the plunge into novelty
and set his course for sophistry!

Chorus Leader

You spectators, I will openly speak my mind and tell you
the truth, I swear by Dionysus who nurtured me°
As I hope to win the prize and be deemed a skillful poet,
I took you for an audience of great intelligence
and considered this play to be my most sophisticated,
deeming you most worthy to taste it first,° a play
I worked on extra hard. But then I lost the contest,
defeated undeservedly by vulgar men.° Your fault,

---

508 In the Greek, 'put a honey cake into my hands...into the cave of Trophonius.' The hero Trophonius had a subterranean oracular shrine at Lebadeia (in Boeotia) in which there were sacred snakes; those who entered the cave to experience prophetic visions took along a honey-cake to placate the snakes.

510 The *parabasis* (self-revelation) of the chorus is a standard feature of Old Comedy that allowed the poet, through speeches by the Chorus Leader, to address, and also to admonish, the spectators about any issues he cared to raise, whether or not they were directly relevant to the issues raised in the rest of the play. Our parabasis was written for a new version of the play some five years after its first performance (see Introduction); what had been in the parabasis-speech of the original version we do not know. There is a second, more rudimentary, parabasis later in the play (1115 ff).
The Chorus Leader (speaking for Aristophanes) first defends the virtues of the original play and blames its failure on the spectators' lack of artistic refinement and on their preference for the less sophisticated work of his rivals. Then, resuming his identity as the Leader of the Cloud-chorus, he delivers two *epirrhemes* (responding speeches of 20 lines each) introduced by two responding songs by the Chorus, in which he upbraids the spectators as the Clouds or the Moon might do if they could express political grievances. This structure—*ode*, *epirrheme* followed by their responsional *antode* and *antepirrheme*—is technically known as an epirrhematic syzygy (*epirrhemes* 'yoked together' by songs).

519 Dionysus was the patron-god of the theater and therefore of dramatic poets.

you clever ones, whom I took the extra trouble to please!
But even so I'll never willingly desert you.
Because here my Good Boy and my Punk° were recommended
by certain gentlemen whom it's an honor even to speak of.°
I was still a maiden, not yet allowed to have a child,
so I exposed my child, and another maiden picked it up for me,
and you made sure that it was reared and educated generously.°
Since then I've been able to count on your favorable verdict.°
So now, like the famous Electra of old, this new comedy
has come in quest of some similarly intelligent spectators:
she'll recognize, if she sees it, the lock of her brother's hair.°
Just see how modest is her nature! First of all,
she hasn't come all fitted out with a dangling phallus,
red at the end and thick, a joke for little boys;°
she doesn't ridicule bald men, or dance lewd dances,
or feature an aged protagonist with a walking-stick
that he bashes on whomever's around, thus hiding his terrible jokes;
she doesn't run on with torches, or yell 'ow ow ow ow'.
Not she! This comedy trusts in herself and in her script.
And I'm the same kind of poet myself: don't act like a bigwig,°
don't try to fool you by using the same jokes two or three times.
I'm skilled at introducing new ideas every time out,

---

523 He might have produced it at another Athenian festival, or even abroad (though there is no hard evidence that comedies in this period were produced outside Athens, as tragedies could be).

525 In the contest of 423, *Clouds* came in third (and last) behind Cratinus' *Wine-Flask* and Ameipsias' *Konnos.*

528 The main characters in Aristophanes' first play, *Banqueters*, which was produced in 427 and won the second prize. In that play, a traditionally-minded landowner has two sons, the Good Boy (who has had a traditional athletic-musical education) and the Punk (who has dropped out of school to learn the new sophistic methods); their contrasting styles of life provided an opportunity, as in *Clouds*, to criticize the 'new education'.

529 I.e. influential patrons had helped the neophyte poet win a place in the comic contest.

532 I.e. Aristophanes was then too young to be entrusted with a comic production on his own; an experienced producer (Callistratus or possibly Philonides, both of whom were later to produce other plays by Aristophanes) took on the job; and the people of Athens sponsored the training of the play's performers.

533 *Clouds* was Aristophanes' first failure to win either the first or the second prize.

536 Alluding to the recognition-scene in Aeschylus' *Libation-Bearers*, where Electra comes to the tomb of her father Agamemnon and recognizes there a lock of Orestes', her long-lost brother's, hair.

539 Aristophanes is not denying that the male characters in *Clouds* wore the phallus (a standard accoutrement in comedy), only that none wore the grotesquely large, circumcised phallus characteristic of barbarians. Young boys were a prominent element of the theater audience.

545 The Greek *komo* means both 'wear my hair long' and 'be stuck up'; Aristophanes was prematurely bald.

each one different from the other and all of them good.
I'm the one who hit almighty Cleon with an uppercut,
but I wasn't so brazen as to hit him again when he was down.°
Not so my rivals: once they got a hold of Hyperbolus,
they've never stopped stomping the poor man, and his mother too.°
First there was Eupolis, dragging his *Maricas* onto the stage,
a cheap and incompetent rehash of my own play, *Knights*,°
adding to it only the drunken crone dancing lewdly,
Phrynichus' old joke, when the sea-monster tried to eat her.°
Then Hermippus entered the parade against Hyperbolus,°
and now all the others are launching into Hyperbolus too,°
all of them copying my own similes about the eels.°
Think *they're* funny? You better not enjoy *my* plays then!
But if you like me and the material I think up,
posterity will consider you to have had good taste!

Chorus (3[1])

Zeus, who rule the gods on high,
you're the first celebrity

---

550 Cleon was the most influential politician in Athens after the death of Pericles in 429. In 426 Aristophanes had attacked him in his play, *Babylonians*, and again in 424 in his play, *Knights*; both times Cleon had subsequently tried to prosecute him. It is not true that Aristophanes spared Cleon after his death in 422: he attacked him in *Peace* (produced in 421) and attacks him again later in this very *parabasis* (a holdover from the first version of the play).

552 The popular politician Hyperbolus, said to have made his fortune in the lamp-making business, assumed Cleon's political position after Cleon's death. In Athenian politics, attacks on an opponent's wife or mother were an accepted competitive technique. Aristophanes himself would later insult Hyperbolus' mother, in *Women at the Thesmophoria* (produced in 411).

554 Eupolis and Aristophanes were contemporaries and the leading comic poets of their generation. In Eupolis' play (produced in 421) the title character, Maricas, was a barbarian slave representing Hyperbolus, just as the barbarian slave, Paphlagon, had represented Cleon in Aristophanes' *Knights*. No evidence contradicts Aristophanes' frequent claim to have invented this type of 'demagogue-comedy', and Eupolis could counter it only by claiming to have contributed ideas to *Knights*.

556 In *Maricas* the old crone represented Hyperbolus' mother. Phrynichus the comic poet was a contemporary of Aristophanes and Eupolis. He had apparently used the crone in a parody of the myth of Andromeda, the beautiful princess whom Perseus rescued from a sea-monster. Later, in *Women at the Thesmophoria* (produced in 411), Aristophanes would parody the same myth, but he substituted an old man for Andromeda.

557 An older contemporary of Aristophanes who attacked Hyperbolus and his mother in the play, *Breadsellers*, produced in 420 or 419.

558 The comic dramatist Plato wrote a play entitled *Hyperbolus*, and probably there were (as Aristophanes claims) others as well, though we have no record of them.

559 Referring to *Knights* 864-67, where Paphlagon (Cleon) is compared to a sniggler who likes to fish in troubled waters (i.e. as dishonest politicians flourish in a climate of war and political instability).

invited to our dance.

Next Poseidon, mighty keeper
of the trident, savage shaker
of the earth and the briny sea.

Then our famous father, Sky,
nourisher of every life;
then our charioteer, the Sun,
illuminating everyone,

for the gods above a mighty force,
for mortals, too, upon the earth.

Chorus Leader

Spectators and critics, give an ear to what I say.
We've a gripe against you, and we'll lodge it openly.
Of all the gods we do the most good for this city,
but we're the only gods that get no sacrifices,
no libations, though we look out for you. Whenever
you marshal a stupid expedition, we rain and thunder.°
When you went to vote for the god-hated tanner Paphlagon,°
in the election for generals, we knitted our brows together
and made a lot of noise with lightning and thunderbolts,
and the Moon eclipsed herself from orbit,° and the Sun
pulled his blazing wick right back into his lamp
and refused to shine on you if you elected Cleon.°
But you went ahead and elected him. They say your city
is always making bad decisions, but the gods will always
see that all is well, whatever mistakes you make.
We'll easily show you how to fix this blunder too:
convict that vulture Cleon for theft and bribery,
then grab his neck and lock it in the wooden stocks.
Then everything will be as it was before you made
your error, and the city will be on course again.°

---

580 I.e. as a bad omen; rain and thunder were in fact reasons to suspend deliberations in the popular Assembly and could sometimes be taken into account when deciding military actions.

581 I.e. Cleon, whom Aristophanes had portrayed in *Knights* as a Paphlagonian slave and whose wealth at least in part derived from a leather-works. A few weeks after the performance of *Knights* (in February 424) the Athenians elected Cleon as one of the ten generals to hold office the following year.

584 On 9 October 425, about four months before the election.

586 Referring to the solar eclipse of 21 March 424, a few weeks after the election. Aristophanes might have added that there was an earthquake a few days after the eclipse, but earthquakes (associated with the sea and earth god Poseidon) were not in the Clouds' power to initiate.

Chorus (3[2])

Lord of Delos, join us also,
Phoebus Apollo, high on Cynthus'
escarpment of sheer rock.

Blessed Artemis too, who hold in
Ephesus a house all golden,
whom the Lydian girls revere.

Goddess of our native land,
Athena, city-guardian,
aegis-wielder, please draw nigh,
and you who haunt Parnassus high,

where torches blaze and maenads stir,
Lord Dionysus, reveller!

Chorus Leader

As we prepared to set off on our journey here,
the Moon by chance ran into us and said she wanted
to say hello to all the Athenians and their allies,
but she's most annoyed at your treating her so shamefully
despite her many evident and actual benefactions.
First off, she saves you at least ten bucks a month in torches:
that's why you all can say, when you go out in the evening,
No need to buy a torch, my boy, the moonlight's fine!
She says she helps in other ways too. But you don't keep
your calendar correct; it's totally out of sync.
As a result, the gods are always getting mad at her,
whenever they miss a dinner and hungrily go home
because you're celebrating their festival on the wrong day,
or hearing cases or torturing slaves instead of sacrificing.°
And often, when we gods are mourning Memnon or Sarpedon,°
you're pouring wine and laughing. That's why Hyperbolus,
this year's sacred ambassador, had his wreath of office
blown off his head by us gods, so that he'll remember well

---

594 Since Cleon died in 422, before Aristophanes revised *Clouds*, this *epirrheme*, which speaks of him as still holding office, must be a relic of the original version of 423.

620 The archon, a public magistrate, was in charge of the official calendar, whose months were often out of strict synchronization with the moon. Sometimes the archon inserted intercalary days into a given month to achieve synchronization or to postpone such events as a periodic festival in honor of a god or gods. In our passage, the gods plan their calendar by the Moon and so blame her when an expected festival (and sacrifice) is not held on the appointed day; but, as the Moon maintains, that is rather the fault of the Athenians' manipulation of the calendar.

621 Two sons of Zeus (by mortal women) who were killed in the Trojan War.

that the days of your lives should be reckoned by the Moon.°

SCENE V

(Socrates, Strepsiades)

Socrates

By Respiration, by Emptiness, by Air,
I've never seen a man so rustic anywhere,
such a clueless, brain-dead case of Alzheimer's!
I give him a teeny table-scrap of knowledge,
but he can't remember it long enough to learn it!
I'll call him out of doors here, into the light.
Where are you, Strepsiades? Come out here. Bring your bed.

Strepsiades

I can't; the bugs refuse to let me move it.

Socrates

Right now! And pay attention.

Strepsiades

There you are.

Socrates

All right then, what's the first thing you would learn,
of all the things you never learned? Come now,
will it be measures, or diction, or rhythms perhaps?

Strepsiades

Oh, measures for me, 'cause just the other day
a grocer shortchanged me two whole liters of flour.

Socrates

Not *that* sort of measure! But what *poetic* measure
do you favor, the three-measure or the four-measure lines?

Strepsiades

For me, the gallon measure can't be beat.

Socrates

You're talking rubbish!

Strepsiades

You wanna bet
the gallon isn't made of four quart-measures?

Socrates

To hell with you, you cloddish ignoramus!

---

626 Hyperbolus had probably called for a vote authorizing an intercalation resulting in the postponement of a regularly scheduled sacrifice; apparently his official wreath of office (as sacred emissary to the Amphictyonic Council, a panhellenic religious body that controlled temples at Thermopylae and Delphi) was blown off by the wind on some public occasion.

Perhaps you have an aptitude for rhythms.

Strepsiades
But how will rhythms help me make a living?

Socrates
First of all, it's socially sophisticated
to be able to discriminate between
parade-ground rhythms, say, or the fingered kind.

Strepsiades
The fingered kind? That one I know.

Socrates
So show me.

Strepsiades
Let's see, it's got to be this finger. Yes,
when I was a little boy it went like this.°

Socrates
You stupid lout!

Strepsiades
Look here, you silly goose,
I don't want to learn that stuff.

Socrates
What *would* you learn?

Strepsiades
That thing you teach, you know, that Worsest Argument.

Socrates
But first you need preliminary studies,
like which quadrupeds are in the masculine gender.

Strepsiades
I know which ones are masculine, all right:
the ram, the billygoat, the bull, the dog, the duck.

[**Socrates**
And the feminine?

Strepsiades
Ewe, she-goat, cow, bitch, and duck]°

Socrates
You see what you've done? You call the female duck
a 'duck', and you call the male duck 'duck' as well.

---

654 Strepsiades gives Socrates the finger.
662 After line 661 a line has been lost which, as Socrates' response in 662-63 shows, must have contained what the supplement (in brackets) supplies.

Strepsiades
So what?

Socrates
I mean, you call them both a duck.

Strepsiades
I do, by god. And what should I say instead?

Socrates
The male's a 'duck', while the female is a 'duchess'.

Strepsiades
A duchess! That's a good one, by the Air!
For that one little lesson alone I swear
I'll fill your thermos up with duchess soup!

Socrates
But there you go again. You give the thermos
the masculine gender; it's feminine.

Strepsiades
How do you mean,
I call a thermos masculine?

Socrates
Just the way
you say Cleonymus.°

Strepsiades
And how is that?

Socrates
You confuse the endings of thermos and Cleonymus.°

Strepsiades
Dear fellow, Cleonymus doesn't have a thermos;
to fill him up you simply use his can!
But how should I say thermos properly?

Socrates
How?
You say 'therme', like the woman's name 'Sostrate'.

Strepsiades
So, therme feminine?

Socrates
That is quite correct.

673 For Cleonymus see 353 n. For the Greeks, cowardice in battle suggested effeminacy or slavishness, the basis for the following jokes about Cleonymus' 'gender'.

Strepsiades
And I should say 'Cleonyme has no therme'?

Socrates
Now let's go on to the following lesson: names,
which ones are masculine, which are feminine.

Strepsiades
I know which ones are feminine.

Socrates
Tell me then.

Strepsiades
Lysilla, Philinna, Clitagora, Demetria.

Socrates
And which are masculine?

Strepsiades
Millions of them are:
Philoxenus, Melesias, Amynias.

Socrates
You rascal, those aren't masculine names at all!

Strepsiades
You say they're not?

Socrates
Not masculine at all.
Look, how would you greet Amynias if you saw him?

Strepsiades
I'd use the vocative, 'Hi there, Amynia'.

Socrates
You see? You used the feminine ending there.

Strepsiades
But isn't that appropriate for a draft-dodger?
But why learn things that everybody knows?

Socrates
Oh, never mind. Get into bed.

Strepsiades
Why bed?

Socrates
To contemplate a problem of your own.

Strepsiades
Oh please, I beg you, not in that bed! I'd rather
lie on the ground to think, if that's OK.

Socrates

There's no alternative.

Strepsiades

Now I'm really done for!
The bugs are gonna take it out on my hide today!

SCENE VI

(Duet: Strepsiades and Chorus)

Chorus (4[1])

Cerebrate and contemplate,
oscillate and agitate,
in hyperkinetic ratiocination!

No mental snag
should be a drag;
you simply move
to another groove.

Sleep is good for relaxation,
but terrible for speculation!

Strepsiades

Ow! Ouch!

Chorus

How dost thou suffer? Wherefore this yelling?

Strepsiades

I'm perishing wretchedly! In this little bed
some Brobdingnagian bugs are biting me,
chomping my flank,
draining my gut,
pulling my crank,
poking my butt,
and altogether killing me!

Chorus

Yet be thou in thy grief not overzealous.

Strepsiades

Easy for you to say, when I'm the one
who's lost his dough,
his suntan too,
who's lost his soul,
can't find his shoes!

Thus suffering
in a darkened room,

I lie and sing,
but pretty soon
I fear I'll lose *myself*!

SCENE VII

(Socrates, Strepsiades, Chorus Leader, Chorus)

Socrates
Hey, what are you doing? Aren't you thinking?

Strepsiades
Me?
I am, by god.

Socrates
And what have you come up with?

Strepsiades
Wondering how much of me these bugs will eat.

Socrates
Oh, go to hell!

Strepsiades
I'm already there, dear sir!

Chorus Leader
Don't soften on us! Cover up your head
and think of something thoroughly fraudulent
and scammish.

Strepsiades
Damn, I wish someone would give me
a crooked idea instead of this coverlet!

Socrates
All right, let's see what the fellow's doing now.
Hey you! Are you asleep?

Strepsiades
Good heavens no!

Socrates
Got hold of something?

Strepsiades
Nothing.

Socrates
Nothing at all?

Strepsiades
Nope. All I've got ahold of is my dick.

Socrates
Then cover your head and think of something quick!

Strepsiades
But what? You tell me something, Socrates.

Socrates
Tell me what you'd most like to discover.

Strepsiades
You've heard what I want at least a thousand times!
My debts! I want to get out of paying them!

Socrates
All right then, cover up, and slice your mind
into slivers; examine the problem piece by piece,
sorting it systematically.

Strepsiades
Ow! Ouch!

Socrates
Be quiet! If one idea doesn't work,
then toss it aside and move along, then later
try putting that idea in play again.

Strepsiades
Socratikins, my darling!

Socrates
What, old man?

Strepsiades
I've found a crooked scheme for evading debts!

Socrates
I'm all ears.

Strepsiades
Here we go.

Socrates
Let's hear it then!

Strepsiades
I buy a voodoo woman from Thessaly,
and get her to pull the moon down from the sky,
and hide it in a hatbox, like a mirror,
and then make sure that nobody can find it—

Socrates
And how would that be any use?

Strepsiades

It's easy!
The moon doesn't rise, the month would never end,
and bills would never come due!

Socrates

Why wouldn't they?

Strepsiades

Because you pay your bills on the first of the month!

Socrates

Not bad! But here's another problem for you.
Let's say somebody sues you for a million:
how do you make that lawsuit go away?

Strepsiades

Hmm. Hmm. You've got me there. I need some time.

Socrates

Don't wind your thoughts up like a ball of string,
but reel them out a little at a time,
as if you had a cockroach on a leash.

Strepsiades

I've found a brilliant way to bury that lawsuit!
Even you will have to admit it!

Socrates

Well?

Strepsiades

Have you ever seen that stone at the sorcerer's shop,
the beautiful stone that you can see right through,
the one that starts a fire?

Socrates

You must mean glass.

Strepsiades

That's it! So look: if I got some of that stuff,
and watched for the clerk to file my case at court,
just standing around, like this, with my back to the sun,
I could zap my case clean off the record books!

Socrates

Very good, by the Graces!

Strepsiades

Gosh, I'm feeling good!
I've erased a lawsuit for a million bucks!

Socrates

All right then, snap up this one.

Strepsiades

Fire away!

Socrates

Now: tell how you'd defend yourself against
a case you were losing for lack of witnesses.

Strepsiades

That's nothing; very simple.

Socrates

Yes?

Strepsiades

I'll tell you:
when just one case was pending ahead of mine,
before they called me I'd run off and hang myself.

Socrates

What rubbish!

Strepsiades

On the contrary, by god:
no one would take me to court if I were dead!

Socrates

Absurd. Get out! I'm resigning as your teacher.

Strepsiades

But why? By all the gods, dear Socrates!

Socrates

But everything you learn you quite forget.
Like, what was your first lesson? Can you tell me?

Strepsiades

All right then, lesson one. What was it now?
The feminine thing we use to carry soup?
Oh damn, what was it?

Socrates

Go to blazes, you,
you sieve-brained idiotic little old man!

Strepsiades

Oh dear! *Now* what will happen to poor old me?
If I can't learn tongue-twisting I'm a goner.
You Clouds, please help me with some good advice.

Chorus Leader

Old man, we're ready to give you some advice.
If you've got a son who's fully raised and grown,
send *him* to school to learn instead of you.

Strepsiades

I have a son, a fine young gentleman, too,
but he refuses to learn, so what am I to do?

Chorus Leader

And you give in?

Strepsiades

He's healthy and well-built,
the scion of high-flown women, Coesyra's clan.°
But I'll go fetch him, and if he still says no,
I'll absolutely throw him out of the house.
So wait for me here a little while, please.°

Chorus (4^2)

Great rewards are on their way
from us to you this very day,
for Socrates wants to do whatever you ask him.

Ho, Socrates:
he's on his knees;
you can hear him cluck
like a sitting duck.

Better pluck him while you're able:
schemes like yours are quite unstable.

SCENE VIII

(Strepsiades, Pheidippides, Socrates)

Strepsiades

Get out! By Fog, you're welcome here no more!
Go eat the columns of Megacles' mansion!

Pheidippides

Good heavens, father, what's the matter with you?
By Zeus on Olympus, your mind has come unhinged.

Strepsiades

Just listen to him! Zeus on Olympus! Stupid!
Believing in Zeus, a boy as old as you!

---

800 Coesyra of Eretria (who claimed descent from Zeus) was the wealthy grandmother of Strepsiades' wife (see line 46).

803 Probably addressed to Socrates.

Pheidippides
And what's so funny about that?

Strepsiades
I'm only thinking
how babyish you are and how old-fashioned.
But anyway, come here, if you're interested:
I'll tell you a secret that'll make a man of you.
But promise not to share it with anyone.

Pheidippides
All right. What secret?

Strepsiades
You just swore by Zeus?

Pheidippides
I did.

Strepsiades
Now look what education does:
there is, Pheidippides, no Zeus.

Pheidippides
No Zeus?

Strepsiades
No! Zeus has been dethroned by Vertigo.

Pheidippides
Psh! Now you're raving.

Strepsiades
That's the way it is.

Pheidippides
Who told you that?

Strepsiades
The Melian, Socrates,°
and Chaerephon, the flea-footologist.

Pheidippides
You've gone so absolutely bonkers that
you trust those bilious quacks?

Strepsiades
You watch your mouth!
And don't make light of gentlemen so ingenious

830 Socrates was a native Athenian; by having Strepsiades refer to him as 'the Melian' Aristophanes alludes to Diagoras of Melos, author of a sophistic proof of the nonexistence of the gods. Around the time Aristophanes was revising *Clouds* Diagoras was accused in the Athenian Assembly of having defamed the Eleusinian Mysteries and was declared an outlaw, with a large bounty being put on his head.

and sensible, so frugal that not one
of them has ever had a haircut, ever oiled
himself, or even had a bath. While *you've*
been taking me to the cleaners like a wastrel.
So get a move on and take my place at school!

Pheidippides
But what could I learn from them that's any use?

Strepsiades
Oh really? The sum and total of human wisdom!
Find out how thick and ignorant you really are!
Just wait right here a minute; don't go away.

Pheidippides
Good lord, what now? My father's off his rocker.
I could take him to court and have him judged insane,
or report his madness to the coffin-makers.

Strepsiades
OK now: tell me, what's the word for this?

Pheidippides
A duck.

Strepsiades
All right. And what's the word for this?

Pheidippides
A duck.

Strepsiades
The same for both? You *are* a joke!
You better stop doing that! This one here is called
a duck, while this one here is called a duchess!

Pheidippides
A duchess? Is that the cleverness you learned
in your recent sojourn with that scum of the earth?

Strepsiades
All that and more! But every lesson I learned
I right away forgot. I'm just too old.

Pheidippides
I guess that's also how you lost your shirt.

Strepsiades
I didn't lose it, I invested it in knowledge.

Pheidippides
And what about your shoes, you simpleton?

Strepsiades

As Pericles said, you spend what you have to spend.°
Come on, let's go. Get moving. Humor your father,
even if it's wrong. I've done the same for you—
remember?—you were a whining six-year-old,
and the very first buck I made for jury-service
you made me spend on a toy car at the festival.

Pheidippides

You'll live to regret this, dad, just mark my words!

Strepsiades

You'll do it? Good for you! Oh, Socrates!
Come out! I've brought this son of mine to you,
though he's reluctant.

Socrates

This one's still a baby!
How could he learn the ropes in a place like this?

Pheidippides

You learn the ropes: go off and hang yourself!

Strepsiades

God damn you, boy! How dare you curse your teacher?

Socrates

You hear how he said 'wopes'? How babyishly,
with his wittle wet wips all slack and pouty?
And he's supposed to learn courtroom defence
and summonsing and how to bullshit juries?
But still, Hyperbolus learned—for a hundred grand.°

Strepsiades

Money's no object; teach him, he's a natural.
Why, when he was just a little tyke this high,
he could build sand-castles, carve a little boat,
he'd put together cars from balsawood
and frogs from lemonpeels, as pretty as you please!
Just see that he learns that pair of Arguments,
the Better, whatever that is, and the Worse,
the one that makes the weaker case the stronger.
Or, if not both, at the very least the Worse.

---

859 When the Spartans invaded Attica in 445 Pericles was said to have bribed their King, Pleistoanax, to withdraw and to have used this phrase when accounting for that expenditure of public funds.

876 The only place in comedy where Socrates is portrayed as a teacher of a politician, as he was accused at his trial of having been the teacher of political figures who had harmed the democracy.

Socrates

He'll learn all that from the Arguments themselves;
I've other things to do.°

Strepsiades

But just remember:
he's got to learn how all just claims are countered!

SCENE IX

(Better Argument, Worse Argument, Chorus Leader)

Better Argument

Come on out here, be a star,
exhibitionist that you are!

Worse Argument

At your service: the bigger the crowd,
the faster I shall have you cowed.

Better Argument

Cow me? Who do you think you are?

Worse Argument

An Argument.

Better Argument

But inferior!

Worse Argument

I'll refute you anyway.

Better Argument

What could you possibly do or say?

Worse Argument

Deploy some fancy principles.

Better Argument

They're all the rage with these imbeciles!°

Worse Argument

Geniuses!

Better Argument

I'll lay you flat!

Worse Argument

Tell me how you'll accomplish *that*.

---

887 The actor who plays Socrates must now play one of the Arguments. A choral song would be structurally normal after line 888 and would have allowed the actor time to change his costume, but Aristophanes apparently stopped work on his revision of the play before he had written one.

897 Pointing to the audience.

Better Argument
By speaking what is just and fair.

Worse Argument
And I'll refute it with hot air!
I say that Justice doesn't exist.

Better Argument
Oh no?

Worse Argument
Then tell me where she is.

Better Argument
Among the gods does Justice dwell.

Worse Argument
Zeus locked his father in a cell
with impunity: how so, pray tell?°

Better Argument
Yuk! This is getting worse and worse;
give me a basin, I'm nauseous!

Worse Argument
Sprung a leak, you poor old fart?

Better Argument
Shameless faggot, little tart!

Worse Argument
Thank you!

Better Argument
You're a clown to boot!

Worse Argument
What compliments!

Better Argument
A parricide too!

Worse Argument
Don't you know those names are gold?

Better Argument
They were lead in days of old.

Better Argument
Nowadays they bring you credit.

Better Argument
You're a swine!

---

906 After overthrowing his father Cronus and the Titans, Zeus imprisoned them in the underworld: behavior contrary to the Greek principle of honoring one's parents.

Worse Argument
And you're decrepit!

Better Argument
You've made the younger generation
uninterested in education.
Just wait until the Athenians
find out what fools you've made of them!

Worse Argument
You're moldy.

Better Argument
While you're well-to-do.
But recently you were destitute,
claiming to be a king in rags,
with brilliant thoughts in a paper bag.°

Worse Argument
How clever—

Better Argument
How bizarre—

Worse Argument
your allusions!

Better Argument
that you are
supported by our nation while
its tender youth you quite defile!

Worse Argument
This boy you'll never teach, old fool.

Better Argument
I will, to keep him safe from you
and your blabbering ineptitude.

Worse Argument
Let him rave; come here, my lad!

Better Argument
Touch him and I'll crack your head!

---

923 Literally, 'claiming to be Mysian Telephus and munching the ideas of Pandeletus out of a little bag'. Telephus, King of Mysia in the mythical Trojan War period, was the subject of a play by Euripides (produced in 438) who disguised himself as a pitiful beggar in order to plead his cause; *Telephus* is extensively parodied in Aristophanes' *Acharnians* of 425. Pandeletus was a popular politician and prosecutor of the 430's; his connection with the character Telephus is unclear but would make sense if Pandeletus' eloquence and (pretentious?) ambition seemed at odds with his relative lack of wealth or family distinction.

Chorus Leader

Stop your fighting and abuse!
You expound just how you used
to educate the men of old;
you, the modern teacher's goal.
After judging the pros and cons,
the boy will choose the school he wants.

Better Argument

Fine by me.

Worse Argument

And fine by me.

Chorus Leader

OK, so who will take the lead?

Worse Argument

He can have it;° whatever his line,
I'll shoot him down with phrases fine,
concepts novel and thought sublime.
Result? If he so much as sighs,
I'll sting his face and both his eyes
with intellectualities
as fatal as a swarm of bees!

AGON°

(Chorus, Chorus Leader, Better Argument, Worse Argument, Strepsiades, Pheidippides)

Chorus (5[1])

Now's your opportunity
to show superiority
in intellectuality
and verbal ingenuity.
Everything is now at stake
for higher education's sake;

---

942 Worse Argument is so confident as to be indifferent to the order of speaking in the contest; but he is probably aware that the last word tends to be the most effective. In all of Aristophanes' formal debates (except the one in *Wealth*), the first speaker ultimately loses.

948 *Agon*. The *Agon*, or formal debate, is a standard structural feature of Old Comedy consisting of formal arguments in long-verses by two contestants, each argument prefaced by a choral song and a two-line introduction by the Chorus Leader; the Chorus Leader usually presides and may (along with the idle contestant) interject comments or questions to break up or otherwise enliven the long speeches. In this *Agon*, as in the *Agons* of *Knights* and *Frogs*, the arguments are differentiated rhythmically: the Better Argument speaks in anapests, the Worse in iambics (a less dignified rhythm).

for those in our dear coalition°
this is the crucial competition.

Chorus Leader

You who crowned the men of old
with solid traits of character,
lift your voice in joyful speech
and tell us what your nature is.

Better Argument

Very well: I'll now describe
what education used to be,
back when I spoke truth and flourished,
back when decency was in vogue.
First of all, a boy was expected
not to make the smallest noise.
Boys would march along the streets
to school at the music master's house,
orderly squadrons of them, almost
naked, even in the snow.
Then he'd have them memorize
a song—and keep their legs apart!—
'Pallas Dire City-Sacker',
or 'What a Cry Sounds From Afar',
tuning their voices to the mode
their fathers handed down to us.
Any of them played the clown
by jazzing up the melodies—
all the rage today, that awful
dittybopping Phrynis° played—
that one got a good old-fashioned
thrashing for ruining the tune.
When in gym-class, all the boys
would cross their legs when sitting down,
so they'd not expose to the grownups

956 Ambiguous: the spectators will suppose that the Clouds' friends are Socrates and his cohort, but in fact the Clouds will end by punishing the Socratics. Even during this *Agon* the Clouds speak sympathetically to Better Argument but not to his opponent.

969 The standard line-numbering includes an anonymously attested line (970) that is in the proper meter and concerns musical styles but was not transmitted as part of the play; it was inserted by the seventeenth-century scholar L.C. Valckenaer but is not considered genuine by modern editors.

971 Phrynis of Mantineia was a famous cithara-player credited with introducing the sort of rhythmical modulations complained of here; his victory in the Panathenaic musical competition in 456 probably contributed to the adoption of this new style by Athenian players.

anything provocative.
When they rose again, they'd have to
smooth the sand they'd sat upon,
careful not to leave behind
the marks of their manhood for lovers to see.
No boy then would dare anoint
himself below the belly-button:
thus their genitals were dewy
and downy, like a succulent peach.
Nor would he liquify his voice to
simper softly to his lover,
prancing around with goo-goo eyes
as if he were pimping for himself.
Nor when dining could he reach for
even a single radish-head,
no, nor grab for celery
or dill from any grownup's plate,
no hors d'oeuvres, no canapes,
no crossing legs at dinnertime!

Worse Argument

Antiquated rubbish, full of
crickets° and prehistoric rites,
moldy tunes and sacred oxen!°

Better Argument

Isn't that precisely how
my generation's education
bred the men of Marathon?°
You, by contrast, teach our boys
to swaddle up in cloaks from birth,
such a turn-off when they're dancing
at Athena's festival,°
one of them with his shield held low,

---

984 Before the Persian invasions, which ended in 479, well-to-do Athenians had worn golden crickets as brooches in their hair.

985 Referring to the Dipolieia, an ancient agrarian festival for Zeus that featured the elaborate ritual sacrifice of an ox

986 In 490 an expeditionary force under the Persian King Darius landed at the bay of Marathon and marched toward Athens (26 miles SW). At the town of Marathon they were met and defeated by an Athenian-Plataean army. This victory, considered by Athenians to be their most glorious, ended Darius' European ambitions, and the Persians did not invade again for ten years, when they returned under Xerxes. Later legend told how one Pheidippides (or Philippides) ran back to Athens to report the good news. Although he reportedly dropped dead of fatigue as soon as he had done so, the marathon race still commemorates his run.

afraid he'll get his hambone poked!
Thus, my boy, be bold and opt for
me, the Better Argument.
You shall learn to loathe the market,
to shun the public baths as well,°
to feel ashamed of what is shameful,
to burn with rage at any slight,
to offer your seat to any grownup
you may see approaching you;
never to treat your parents rudely,
never to act disgracefully
or any way that might dishonor
the sacred shrine of Modesty;
never to invade a go-go
dancer's house and lose your head,
making the whore get sweet on you,
thus shattering your good repute;
never to contradict your father,
calling him Methuselah,
laughing at how old he is,
forgetting how he reared you!

Worse Argument

Follow *this* advice, my boy,
I swear by Dionysus
people will call you Casper Milquetoast,
just like the sons of Hippocrates.°

Better Argument

No, you'll spend your time in gyms,
your body hale and glistening,
not chattering in the market about some
thorny topic, like modern boys,
not getting dragged to court to settle a
disputatious nuisance case.
No, down to the Academy° you shall go,
and under the sacred olive-trees
crown yourself with reeds and race

---

988 The Panathenaia, held in July, was the principal festival for Athena and (along with the theatrical festivals for Dionysus) the most lavish of the year. One of the events was a martial dance performed by warriors naked except for a shield.

991 Places frequently mentioned as hang-outs for young men.

1001 Hippocrates, a nephew of Pericles, had three sons frequently ridiculed in comedy for having misshapen heads (a family trait) and for being boorish and ill-educated.

with fine upstanding boys your age,
redolent of briar and leisure
and the catkins flung by the poplar trees,
glorying in Spring's return,
when plane-trees whisper to the elms.

Follow up on my suggestions,
give them serious consideration,
then you'll be in proud possession
of a chest that ripples, skin that gleams,
shoulders humongous, tongue petite,
buttocks of iron, prick discreet
But follow the path of modern boys
and *this* is the look you'll soon enjoy:
shoulders narrow, pasty skin,
sunken chest, tongue gigantic,
buttocks tiny, prick titanic,
motions long-winded.° Listen to *him*,
you'll think what's bad is good,
what's good is bad. Moreover,
you'll catch a serious disease:
Antimachus' faggotry!°

Chorus (5^2)

What masterful proficiency
in wisdom fair and towering,
each word with virtue flowering!
Happy the men of old indeed!

You who must reply to *that*,
you with your clever line of chat,
must now find something new to say;
your opponent has spoken splendidly.

Chorus Leader

It seems you'll need some awesome schemes
to bring to bear against him,
if you hope to overtake the man
and not become a big joke.

Worse Argument

My guts have actually been churning
quite a while now, longing

1005 Academeia was a park sacred to the local god Academus, with a stream, wooded paths and sporting fields; later Plato chose it as the site of his school.

1019 Punning on 'motions' presented to a political assembly.

1023 Known only from comic references to his effeminacy.

to demolish everything he said
with considered refutations.
I got the name Worse Argument
among the intellectuals
for just this very reason, that
I pioneered a new technique,
a logical way to contradict
established laws and morals.
And *there's* a skill that guarantees
a million dollar income:
to take the cases that are worse
but nevertheless to win them.
Observe the way I cross-examine
his vaunted pedagogy.
Now, first of all, he won't allow
hot water in your bathtub.
So tell me, please, the principle
on which you scorn hot water.

Better Argument

Because it's utterly base and makes
a warrior a pussy.

Worse Argument

OK now, wait! I've got you in
a hammerlock already.
Just tell me, which of Zeus' sons
you think the greatest he-man,
the one you think most spirited
and performed the greatest labors?

Better Argument

I judge no man superior
to Heracles the mighty!

Worse Argument

In that case, have you ever seen
a Heraclean cold bath?°
And yet, who was manlier than he?

Better Argument

That's just the sort of quibble
the teenaged boys spend all their time
expatiating over,

1051 Natural hot springs were known as Heraclean because they were popularly thought to have been created by Athena or other friendly gods for Heracles to bathe in during the course of his wanderings and labors.

that makes the bath-house popular
and leaves the gym deserted!

Worse Argument

And loitering in the market-place
you forbid, while I commend it
If the market's such a sleazy place,
then why did Homer always
call Nestor 'man of the *agora*',
and every other wise man?°
And now the question of the tongue,
which my opponent flatly
forbids young men to exercise,
while I would strongly urge it.
He also insists on modesty;
another bad idea.
For where has anybody ever
seen a man get famous
and rich by being modest? Well?
Just name him and I'm refuted.

Better Argument

A lot of people. Peleus got
his knife for being modest!°

Worse Argument

A knife you say! A charming piece
of profit! Lucky devil!
Hyperbolus, who manufactures
lamps, has made a million
through sheer dishonesty, but never
got a knife, I grant you°

Better Argument

And Peleus got to marry Thetis,
for being very modest.°

1057 A sophistic argument: in classical Athens the market-place (*agora*) was the commercial 'downtown' area of the city, while in the Homeric epic poems *agora* meant 'gathering-place for deliberation'.

1063 Achilles' father Peleus, during a visit to the hero Acastus' house, refused the amorous advances of Acastus' wife, who then accused him of attempted rape. Acastus had Peleus taken unarmed to the forest to be eaten by wild animals, but the gods pitied him for his honorable character and gave him a knife to defend himself.

1066 For Hyperbolus see 552 n.

1067 Since the sea-nymph Thetis was destined to bear a son mightier than its father, the male gods arranged to have her married off to a mortal man.

Worse Argument

And then she up and left him flat
because he wasn't man enough
to satisfy her in the sack
when the lights went off at nighttime.
For women like their loving rough;
but you're an ancient ruin.
Just look, young man, at all the toil
the virtuous life consists of,
and look at all the fun you stand
to lose, if you pursue it:
young boys, young women, games of chance,
good eating, drink and laughter.
Why live a life at all if you're
deprived of all these pleasures?
OK, then, let's proceed to look
at the necessities of nature.°
Let's say you've messed up, fallen in love,
been taken in adultery.
You're screwed if you can't talk your way
out of trouble. Come with *me*, though,
you'll indulge your instincts, leap and laugh,
consider nothing shameful.
If taken in adultery
you'll tell the angry husband
there's nothing wrong with what you did,
that Zeus himself's the culprit:
for even Zeus falls victim to
a lust for lovely women,°
so how can you, a mortal man,
be stronger than the sky-god?

1069 As in all folktales involving mermaids and mortals, Thetis returned to the sea; the standard story was that Peleus had annoyed her by interrupting a magical ceremony by which she was making Achilles immortal.

1075 Contemporary philosophers drew a sharp distinction between customs and laws (which they saw as social inventions) on the one hand, and nature (which they thought of as a universal imperative) on the other, a distinction that amoralists could use to justify conduct that law or custom would prohibit.

1081 Zeus was indeed one of the great philanderers of mythology; in Euripides' play *Trojan Women*, Helen uses the same argument to justify her adultery with Paris of Troy. The often unethical behavior of the gods in myth had become an embarassment for traditional moral philosophers, some of whom denied the truth of such myths.

1083 Under Attic law a cuckolded husband could do what he liked with an adulterer, including killing him or exacting a monetary compensation. The husband might also make a public example of an offender by pushing a radish into his anus, singeing his genitals with hot ashes and plucking out his pubic hair.

Better Argument
But say he gets his anus reamed,
and his whatsis baked with ashes?°
What kind of argument would he use
to keep his asshole narrow?

Worse Argument
What harm is there in turning out
to have a gaping asshole?°

Better Argument
You mean, what greater harm could be
endured than a gaping asshole?

Worse Argument
And what would you say if I refute
your argument on this point?

Better Argument
I'll close up shop; what else could I do?

Worse Argument
All right, then, here's a question:
What type of person is a lawyer?

Better Argument
A gaping asshole.

Worse Argument
Quite correct.
And what about a tragic poet?

Better Argument
Gaping asshole.

Worse Argument
Right you are.
And what about a politician?

Better Argument
Gaping asshole.

Worse Argument
Now you see,
your argument was total crap!
What about the audience there,

1085 The conventional way of referring to a male who had submitted himself to anal penetration by another male and had thus reduced himself to the condition of women, slaves and prostitutes. For citizen males such behavior was not merely a disgrace but a crime punishable by debarment from the exercise of civic rights. Nevertheless, comic poets routinely assumed that political advancement entailed prostitution, much as humorists today assume that women with celebrity or power must have offered sex to attain it.

the majority?

Better Argument

I see them now.

Worse Argument

And what do you see?

Better Argument

The majority,
by god, are gaping assholes! Him,
at any rate, and that one there,
and that one with the longish hair!

Worse Argument

So, what do you have to say for yourself?

Better Argument

I'm beaten! Here, you dirty fags,
for heaven's sake please take my rags,
I'm deserting to your side!°

Worse Argument

What now? You want to take this son of yours
away, or have me teach him oratory?

Strepsiades

Why, teach him and discipline him, and don't forget
to put sharp edges on his tongue. One edge
for hacking little lawsuits; hone the other
for cutting into meatier affairs.

Worse Argument

Don't worry, he'll come home a seasoned sophist.

Pheidippides

More likely, I think, a wretched pasty-face.

SECOND PARABASIS°

(Chorus, Chorus Leader)

Chorus

Go right ahead. But I imagine
that you'll come to regret this course of action.

1104 Evidently, Better Argument now wants to learn the secrets of oratorical success for himself, and so dashes into Socrates' school (where he will change back into the role of Socrates).

1113 *Second Parabasis.* The ancient commentator Heliodorus noted that five verses from the first version of the play do not appear in their proper place between lines 1114 and 1115; probably Aristophanes removed them in the course of his revision. That this second parabasis has only a rudimentary choral introduction and only one *epirrheme* may be an indication of incomplete revision.

Chorus Leader

Now we'll tell the audience the
goodies the judges stand to get,
if they do this chorus a favor,
as by rights they ought to do.°
First of all, if you want to sow and
plough your fields when the season's right,
we will rain on your fields first, on
others' only after you.
Then we'll act as guardians for
all your crops and all your vines,
making sure they're never harmed
by drought or by a drenching rain.
Any mortal man who would
dishonor our divinity,
let him learn from us the evil
consequences he will face.
From his farmland he will take no
wine or any other crop;
when his olive trees and vineyards
start to bloom with tender shoots,
just as quick we'll shoot them off with
bullets from a stormy sky.
Let him try to dry his bricks, we'll
make it rain torrentially,
then we'll blast the tiles off his
roof with hailstones big and round.
When he's getting married himself,
or any friend or relative,
all night long we'll make it rain,° and
thus he'll start to wish he were
a resident of Egypt rather
than a man who miscast his vote.

1116 The judges are the ten men whose names had been drawn by lot from a list of eligible men submitted by each tribe (there were ten tribes) and who swore to give an impartial verdict in voting on the relative merit of the competing plays. Each judge wrote down his ranking on a tablet and put it into an urn; the presiding official (the *archon*) drew five of the tablets at random to determine the order of prizes. The sort of appeal to the judges that our chorus makes was not uncommon in Old Comedy.

1129 A main event of an Athenian wedding was the evening, torch-lit procession of family, friends and guests that escorted the bride to her new home; hard rain would not only ruin the procession but would also be taken as a bad omen.

SCENE X

(Strepsiades, Socrates, Pheidippides)

Strepsiades

Twenty-sixth, twenty-seventh, twenty-eighth, then twenty-ninth,
and after that the day of days, the day
that makes me tremble, shudder and shit my pants,
because the very next day's the Old and New,°
and every single creditor I owe
has sworn to sue me, ruin me and destroy me.
I've made some fair and reasonable requests—
'Look here, my man, this payment isn't urgent;
please put this off, forgive that'—but they refuse
to deal on any such terms. They call me names,
like chiseler, and promise to drag me into court.
Well, let them drag me now! I couldn't care less,
if Pheidippides has learned his lessons well.
I'll soon find out, if I knock at the Thinkery.
Boy! Boy, I say! Boy!

Socrates

Hello, Strepsiades!

Strepsiades

Hello. But first, a little gift from me;
one's got to butter up the teacher some.
And tell me, has my son been able to learn
that Argument you recently brought on stage?

Socrates

He has.

Strepsiades

Omnipotent Trickery, that's great!

Socrates

So you can beat whatever rap you please.

Strepsiades

Even if witnesses saw me borrow the dough?

Socrates

Even if thousands of witnesses saw you do it.

Strepsiades°

Then I'll shout a fortissimo shout!

1134 The last day of the month, when lawsuits could be lodged, was thought to have a double identity because it stood between the outgoing and the incoming month.

1154 *Strepsiades.* Elements of the following song by Strepsiades and of the lyric dialogue following it parody contemporary tragic (especially Euripidean) style.

Creditors, eat your hearts right out!
And eat your principal and interest too!
No longer am I scared of you!
What a son I'm having reared
within this edifice right here,
with a gleaming switchblade for a tongue
my fortress, my estate's salvation,
my enemies' enemy! Surely he
will rescue his dad from calamity!
Now run inside and summon him here to me.
My child, my boy, come forth from out these halls,
to thy father lend an ear!

Socrates

Here is the man thou seekest.

Strepsiades

Dear, dear boy!

Socrates

Claim him and depart.

Strepsiades

Hurrah, hurrah, my child! Wow,
how great it is to see your pale complexion!
You're obviously ready to take the fifth,
to rebut accusers. You've sprouted that true Athenian
expression, the Who-Me? look of being wronged
when you're guilty, even of serious crimes. I know
that look, and I see it blooming on your face!
So save me, since it was you that ruined me.

Pheidippides

And what are you scared of?

Strepsiades

The day that's Old and New.

Pheidippides

You mean there's a day that's old and also new?

Strepsiades

The day my creditors plan to sue me, yes!

Pheidippides

They'll lose their cases, then. There's just no way
a single day can possibly be two days.

Strepsiades

It can't?

Pheidippides
How *could* it be? Unless you also
maintain that a crone can be a girl as well.

Strepsiades
But that's our custom, anyway.

Pheidippides
I think the law
is improperly understood.

Strepsiades
So what's the point?

Pheidippides
Our venerable Solon was a natural democrat.°

Strepsiades
I've yet to see the connection with Old and New Day.

Pheidippides
Well, Solon established the summons for two days,
for the Old Day first and then for the New Day second,
so that sureties would be scheduled for the new moon.

Strepsiades
What purpose did the Old Day serve?

Pheidippides
Dear sir,
it allowed defendants to come a day in advance
to settle their cases if they chose; and if they didn't,
they'd have a serious problem on new moon day.

Strepsiades
Then why don't magistrates accept the sureties
on new moon day, but only on Old and New Day?

Pheidippides
They're like the officials in charge of sacrifice:
they want the cash deposits a day in advance
to get an early start embezzling tidbits.

Strepsiades
All right! You pitiful fools who sit out there,
you're money in the bank for intellectuals,

1187 Solon, who held the archonship in 594/3, was credited with inventing the traditional Athenian law-code. Although he could hardly have been a democrat (it took democracy another century to establish itself at Athens), fifth-century Athenians tended to believe that the man to whom they credited the laws should also be credited with their form of government.

you're rock-heads, sheep, a bunch of empty jars!
I've got to sing a song for me and my son,
a jubilant paeon to our joint success!

Strepsiades, happy happy man,
whom no one else is smarter than,
who also raised his son to be
a paragon of mentality!

My friends and neighbors will agree,
with envy they will all turn green,
when this son of mine has speechified
and got my lawsuits nullified!

But now, my son, let's take a break,
and have a feast to celebrate.

SCENE XI

(Strepsiades, First Creditor with Witness, Second Creditor)

First Creditor

Am I supposed to kiss my money goodbye?
I won't! I shouldn't have made the loan at all,
a brazen refusal instead of all this hassle.
And now I'm dragging *you* along to serve
as witness to my foolish loan. What's more,
I'm sure to make an enemy of my neighbor.
But I'd rather die than be unpatriotic!°
I hereby serve Strepsiades—

Strepsiades

Who's there?

First Creditor

—to appear on Old and New Day.

Strepsiades

Audience, note
that he's summoned me for different days. What charge?

First Creditor

The twelve thousand that I lent you for the purchase
of the charcoal-colored horse.

Strepsiades

Horse? Listen to that!
Why, everybody knows I can't stand horses!

1220 To equate bringing a lawsuit with patriotism is a joke on Athenian litigiousness.

First Creditor
By Zeus, you swore by the gods you'd pay me back.

Strepsiades
By Zeus, when I swore that oath Pheidippides
had yet to learn the unshakeable Argument.

First Creditor
And that's your reason to deny the debt?

Strepsiades
I'm entitled to *something* for educating him.

First Creditor
You're ready to swear by the gods you owe no debt,
wherever I specify?

Strepsiades
What sort of gods?

First Creditor
Why, Zeus, Poseidon, Hermes.

Strepsiades
Certainly Zeus;
I'd even pay a buck to swear by him!

First Creditor
Then shame on you, and may you roast in hell!

Strepsiades
That belly of yours would make a real nice wineskin.

First Creditor
Oh! Mock me, will you?

Strepsiades
It'd hold five gallons.

First Creditor
Almighty Zeus and all the gods, you won't
get away with this!

Strepsiades
The gods! How funny!
To swear by Zeus is a joke among the learned.

First Creditor
In time you'll get your just deserts for this!
For now, just tell me plainly whether or not
you'll repay your debt.

Strepsiades
Hold on a sec, OK?

I'll come right back with an answer to your question.

First Creditor

What do *you* think he'll do? You think he'll pay?

Strepsiades

Now where's the guy that wants my money? Sir,
do you know what this is?

First Creditor

That? Why, sure. A thermos.

Strepsiades

And *you* want money, being such a fool?
I wouldn't trust you with a single dime,
for saying thermos when you should say therme.°

First Creditor

I take it you won't pay.

Strepsiades

That's *all* you'll take.
Now take a hike, and make it snappy too;
get out of here.

First Creditor

With pleasure. But rest assured,
I'm filing suit, if it's the very last thing I do.

Strepsiades

You lost twelve grand; why lose a lawsuit too?
I wouldn't want you to have to suffer that,
merely because you foolishly said 'a thermos'.

Second Creditor

Oh woe is me!

Strepsiades

What's that?
Who's making lamentation here? It couldn't
be one of Carcinus' gods who made that sound?°

Second Creditor

Why seekest thou to know who I may be?
Let 'man accursed' suffice.

Strepsiades

Then take a hike.

1251 See 669 ff.

1261 Carcinus was a tragic poet; presumably a lamenting god had figured in one or more of his plays. Lines 1264-65 are lines that had been spoken by Alcmene in the tragedy *Licymnius* by Carcinus' son Xenocles.

Second Creditor
O deity cruel, o mischance that unhorsed
my chariot-rail! Athena, my undoing!

Strepsiades
And what's your beef against Tlepolemus?°

Second Creditor
Don't mock me, sir, but tell that son of yours
to pay me back the money that he borrowed,
if only in sympathy for my bad luck.

Strepsiades
What money is that?

Second Creditor
The money that he borrowed.

Strepsiades
You're really badly off, it seems to me.

Second Creditor
God yes! While charioteering I lost my grip.

Strepsiades
The way you're raving I'd say you lost your mind.

Second Creditor
Me rave? Is it raving to want my money back?

Strepsiades
A hopeless case of lunacy.

Second Creditor
How so?

Strepsiades
In my opinion, your brain's completely scrambled.

Second Creditor
In *my* opinion, you're gonna get sued, by Hermes,
unless I get my money.

Strepsiades
So tell me this:
do you think that when Zeus makes it rain, the water
is always different, or do you think the sun
draws up from below the very same water again?

Second Creditor
I haven't got a clue, nor do I care.

1266 In Xenocles' tragedy (see the previous note) Alcmene's half-brother had been killed by her grandson Tlepolemus.

Strepsiades

Then how can you demand your money back,
if you're ignorant of meteorology?

Second Creditor

All right, if you're short of money, pay at least
the interest.

Strepsiades

Interest? Please define that term.

Second Creditor

You know: the property borrowed money has
of growing larger and larger, daily and monthly,
as the stream of time flows on?

Strepsiades

That's very well put.
Now then, the sea: would you say it's larger now
than it used to be?

Second Creditor

God, no; it's just the same.
It's unnatural for the sea to grow.

Strepsiades

Then how,
you wretched fool, though rivers flow to the sea
but the sea does not grow larger, do *you* attempt
to make *your* sum of money grow in size?
So prosecute yourself right off my property!
Boy, fetch my stick!

Second Creditor

I'm taking note of this!

Strepsiades

Get going! Giddyup, you gelded nag!

Second Creditor

Atrocious assault!

Strepsiades

Move out! You want a whipping?
You want me to jam this up your thoroughbred ass?
Just look at him run! I knew I'd get you moving,
for all your chariot-wheels and teams of steeds.

CHORUS

Chorus (6[1])

How dangerous to entertain
a lust for villainy,
like *this* old man, who'd now evade
the debts he ought to pay.

Before the day has run its course
the time will surely come
when our old sophist feels remorse
for all harm he's done.

I think that he will soon obtain
the answer to his prayer:
a son who's able to maintain
what's unjust and unfair.

And though the son wins every case
with wickedness and lies,
perhaps, *perhaps* his dad will pray
his tongue gets paralyzed.

SCENE XII

(Strepsiades, Pheidippides)

Strepsiades

Help! Help!
Oh neighbors, kinsmen, fellow-villagers!
I need your help right now, I'm being beaten!
Oh Lord! My unlucky head! My face! My jaw!
You scum! You'd beat your father?

Pheidippides

That's right, dad.

Strepsiades

You see? He admits he beat me!

Pheidippides

Sure I do.

Strepsiades

You scum! You parricide! You criminal!

Pheidippides

Please call me all those names, and add some more.
You know, I enjoy it when you call me names?

Strepsiades

You giant asshole!

Pheidippides

Flatter me some more!

Strepsiades

You'd beat your father?

Pheidippides

Yes, by God; what's more,
I'll prove it's right to do so.

Strepsiades

What a scumbag!
Just how could it be right to beat a father?

Pheidippides

I'll show you with unbeatable arguments.

Strepsiades

You could beat me in an argument like *that*?

Pheidippides

Quite easily.
Just choose which argument you plan to use.

Strepsiades

Which argument?

Pheidippides

The better or the worse.°

Strepsiades

I guess you've learned your lessons well, my boy,
to argue against what's just, if you can make
this case convincing, that it's just and right
for fathers to be beaten by their sons.

Pheidippides

But all the same I think I can convince you,
and you'll have nary a point to make against me.

Strepsiades

And I can't wait to hear what *you* will say.

SECOND AGON

(Chorus, Chorus Leader, Strepsiades, Pheidippides)

Chorus (7[1])

Your job, old man, is to conceive
  how you'll refute this lad;

1337 Pheidippides is not only ready to defend an outrageous proposition but does not care whether it is true or not, being prepared to argue either side.

for had he nothing up his sleeve
he wouldn't act so bad.

Yes, something makes him confident
in being boldly insolent.

Chorus Leader

How this fight originally
began, the Chorus wants to know.
Tell us what the motive causes
were; you'll tell us anyway.°

Strepsiades

Certainly I'll tell you why we
first began to scream and shout.
You'll recall I held a feast to
celebrate my son's success.
First I asked him quite politely,
Grab your lyre and sing that song,
'Ram Got Shorn and Who's Surprised?',
the song by old Simonides.°
He replied that playing the lyre is
absolutely out of date,
so is singing at a banquet,
like a grandma husking corn!

Pheidippides

You're the one who ought to have been
stomped and beaten then and there,
asking me to sing a song, as
if you're entertaining crickets!

Strepsiades

That's the kind of thing he said the
whole time we were partying.
And on top of that he called
Simonides a total hack!
Nonetheless I held my tongue, as
aggravated as I was.
Then I asked if he at least would
put a garland on his head,

1352 Aristophanes pokes fun at the structural convention of Old Comic *Agons* that required the Chorus to introduce each speaker in the debate; see the note on the first *Agon* (above, 947 ff.).

1356 Simonides of Ceos was an internationally celebrated poet of an older generation (his dates are *c.* 556-468); this song was a victory-ode for a wrestler who had defeated one Crius (whose name means 'ram') at the Nemean Games in the late sixth century.

and read me something by Aeschylus;°
he right away replied (I quote),
'I regard old Aeschylus as
being first among our bards:
first at incoherence, noise and
words as steep as mountaintops'!
You can just imagine how I
almost had a heart-attack!
Still, I held my temper, bit my
tongue and said, OK, my boy,
read me something clever by a
modern poet, if you can.
Right away he tosses off some
discourse by Euripides,
how a brother—holy moly!—used to
screw his own sister!!°
That was it; I'd stand no more, and
started to abuse the boy,
using lots of bad and shameful
words. As you can guess,
he began to match me word for
word, and then he jumps right up,
bashes me and punches me and
chokes me, totally trashes me!

Pheidippides

Had it coming, anyone who
doesn't praise Euripides,
cleverest of poets.

Strepsiades

Clever?
Him? You—what's the word I want?
Better not say, I'll get punched again.

Pheidippides

That's right, and you'd deserve it too!

1365 Aeschylus was the greatest tragic poet of the era that saw the Greek victory over the Persians and the establishment of the Athenian empire (his dates are 525-456), so that men Strepsiades' age tended to regard him as the embodiment of the ethical values that had made such achievements possible. In Aristophanes' play *Frogs* (produced in 405), Aeschylus is pitted against Euripides (whom Aristophanes regarded as embodying the inferior values of his own era) in a contest of poetic and moral power.

1372 Euripides (see previous note) was fond of treating provocative myths in provocative ways; the allusion here is probably to the incestuous relationship of Aeolus' children Macareus and Canace and their concealment of the resulting child, which Euripides dramatized in his play, *Aeolus*.

Strepsiades

How deserve it? I'm the one who
raised you! Do you have no shame?
I'm the one who understood your
baby-talk and what it meant.
You said 'dwik' and I would know to
go get something for you to drink.
You demanded 'bob' and I would
fly away to bring you bread.
Then before you'd even finish
saying 'poopie' I'd be there,
taking you to the yard to do it.
Just now, though, when you began
strangling me, and I yelled and shouted,
I'm about to shit! you balked,
wouldn't take me to the yard—
villain!—but you strangled on,
made me do a poop right there!

Chorus (7^2)

The young men's blood is up to know
their counterpart's reply:
should he be glib enough to show
that what he did was right,
there's nothing that could make me choose
to be in any father's shoes!

Chorus Leader

Now's your chance, you word-mechanic,
shooter of the latest rap:
find a way to talk us into
thinking what you did was right.

Pheidippides

What a joy to hang around with
everything that's new and hip,
being free to disregard all
customary laws and norms!
Just a while ago, when all I
wanted was the cavalry,
I could barely speak three words
before I stumbled over them;
now, since dear old dad here made me
put a stop to all of that,
I'm at home with subtle thoughts, with

words and contemplations,
confident that I can show you
why it's right to beat my pa.

Strepsiades

Back to the cavalry, then, dear God! It's
better for me to spend my dough
keeping up a team of horses than
serving as your punching-bag!

Pheidippides

Let's return to my earlier point, the
one you made me interrupt;
answer me this, to start things off:
did *you* beat *me* when I was small?

Strepsiades

Sure I did; I cared for you, and
did it for *your* own good.

Pheidippides

Then look:
isn't it just as right for *me* to
care for *you* in a similar way,
inasmuch as one's own good
depends on being beaten up?
How's it fair that your own body
stays immune but mine does not?
After all is said and done, I'm
a free-born man, the same as you.
'The children scream; you think the father shouldn't?'°
You'll reply it's customary
that only children suffer this;
I reply with a well-known fact:
old age is a second childhood.
What is more, it makes more sense for
older men to scream than younger:
they're the ones with less excuse to
stray from good behavior.

Strepsiades

Nowhere does the law permit a
father to be so treated.

1415 Adapting a line (691) from Euripides' play *Alcestis* (produced in 438), in which Admetus, who seeks a volunteer to die in his stead, has rebuked his own father Pheres for refusing to do so, and Pheres replies, 'You like the daylight; you think your father doesn't?'

Pheidippides

Wasn't it a man who wrote the
  law originally, a man
just like you or me? And didn't
  he persuade the men of old?°
Why should I not have the right
  to argue for a different law,
valid for tomorrow's sons, that
  henceforth they should beat their dads?
All the beatings that we took
  before the new law took effect
we forgive our fathers, we
  declare an amnesty on those.
Take a look at poultry now, and
  all such other animals:
don't they stand up to their fathers?
  Aren't we animals, more or less,
save that animals don't propose
  decrees the way we humans do?

Strepsiades

Well then, if you want to ape the
  animals in everything,
why not also eat your dung and
  sleep on wooden perches too?

Pheidippides

Not the same, dear fellow, nor would
  Socrates accept that line.

Strepsiades

Then I say, stop beating me, or
  someday you'll regret you did.

Pheidippides

Why is that?

Strepsiades

As things now stand, I
  have the right to punish you;
you will have the right to punish
  your son.

1422 The historicist version of social-contract theory, which considers laws to have been invented at particular times by particular people in order to create civilization out of anarchy, is first attested in the late fifth century in the writings of the oligarch Critias, one of Socrates' most notorious pupils.

Pheidippides

If I have a son.
If I don't, I've screamed in vain, and
you'll be laughing in your grave!

Strepsiades

Age-mates in the audience, I
think that what he says is right:
give the younger generation
credit for making a valid point.
There's no reason why they shouldn't
beat us if we don't behave.

Pheidippides

I've got one more point to make.

Strepsiades

No, it'll be the death of me!

Pheidippides

Not at all. You might be less
annoyed about your suffering.

Strepsiades

How is that? Explain how you can
benefit me in all of this.

Pheidippides

Beating mother as I beat you!

Strepsiades

What's that? What did you say just now?
That's a different and far worse matter!

Pheidippides

What if, with Worse Argument,
I could justify to you
mother-beating as a law?

Strepsiades

My response is, if you do,
I don't give a damn if you
end up being put to death,
right along with Socrates
and Worse Argument as well!

SCENE XIII

(Strepsiades, Chorus Leader, Pheidippides, Pupils, Socrates)

Strepsiades

You Clouds, it's all your fault I suffer this!

I trusted you to handle my affairs.

Chorus Leader
No, you're responsible for doing it to yourself:
you took the twisting road that leads toward evil.

Strepsiades
Why didn't you tell me that at the very start,
instead of leading a poor old clod astray?

Chorus Leader
We do the same thing every time we see
a man who's fallen in love with what is wrong;
we cast him down in sheer calamity
until he learns devotion to the gods.

Strepsiades
Alas, O Clouds, a lesson hard but fair!
I shouldn't have tried to cheat my creditors
of their money. Now, my dearest boy, what say
that bastard Chaerephon° and Socrates
we go and murder for cheating us this way?

Pheidippides
I couldn't lift a finger against my teachers!

Strepsiades
'Yea verily respect Paternal Zeus!'°

Pheidippides
Paternal Zeus! Just listen! How old-fashioned!
Does Zeus exist?

Strepsiades
He does.

Pheidippides
He doesn't either,
'cause Vertigo deposed him and now reigns.

Strepsiades
He hasn't really. I thought he had, myself,
because of that object over there. Poor sap,
to think I took some pottery for a god!

Pheidippides
Well, rant and rave to yourself; I'm going in.

1465 See line 104.
1467 A quotation from an unknown tragedy.

Strepsiades

What lunacy! Damn, I must have been insane,
to drop the gods because of Socrates!
Well, Hermes old boy, don't be annoyed with me
or bring me some disaster, but pity me
for acting crazy because of their idle talk.
You be my lawyer: should I slap them with a suit
and prosecute them? I'll do as you advise.
That's good advice! I shouldn't cook up lawsuits,
but rather, quick as I can, burn down the house
of these con-men. Xanthias, come here! Xanthias!
Go get the ladder and a hatchet, too,
then climb up on the roof of the Thinkery
and break the tiles—do it for your master!—
until the house caves in on top of them!
And someone else go get me a lighted torch.
Today they're going to pay for what they've done,
and I don't care how fast they run their mouths!

Pupil 1

Help! Help!

Strepsiades

All right, my torch, throw up a lot of flame!

Pupil 1

Hey, what are you doing, man?

Strepsiades

What do you think?
I'm engaged in subtle argument with your house!

Pupil 2

Oh no! Who's making a bonfire of the house?

Strepsiades

Remember me? The guy, you stole his coat?

Pupil 2

You'll kill us, kill us all!

Strepsiades

That's my intention!
I only pray the hatchet does its job
before I fall somehow and break my neck!

Socrates

You! You on the roof! The hell you think you're doing?

Strepsiades

I walk aloft and contemplate the sun!

Socrates

I'm done for! Help! I'm going to choke to death!

Pupil 2

I'm done for too! I'm going to burn to death!

Strepsiades

Then what were you up to, laughing at the gods
and peering at the backside of the moon?
Pursue them°, hit them, stone them for many crimes,
but most of all for injustice toward the gods!

Chorus Leader

Lead the dancers on their way;
we've done our dancing for today.